GUIDE TO YOUR
CAT

◆ ◆ ◆

GUIDE TO YOUR
CAT

UNDERSTANDING AND CARING
FOR THE TIGER WITHIN

• • •

FOREWORD BY
ELIZABETH MARSHALL THOMAS

DISCOVERY BOOKS
London

DISCOVERY COMMUNICATIONS

Founder, Chairman, and Chief Executive Officer:
    John S. Hendricks
President and Chief Operating Officer: Judith A. McHale
President, Discovery Enterprises Worldwide: Michela English
Senior Vice President, Discovery Enterprises Worldwide:
    Raymond Cooper

DISCOVERY PUBLISHING

Vice President, Publishing: Natalie Chapman
Editorial Director: Rita Thievon Mullin
Senior Editor: Mary Kalamaras

DISCOVERY CHANNEL RETAIL

Product Development: Tracy Fortini
Naturalist: Steve Manning

Discovery Communications, Inc., produces high-quality
television programming, interactive media, books, films, and
consumer products. Discovery Networks, a division of Discovery
Communications, Inc., operates and manages the Discovery Channel,
TLC, Animal Planet, and Travel Channel.

Wild Discovery Guide to Your Cat was created and produced by
St. Remy Media Inc. for Discovery Publishing.

A CIP catalogue record for this book is available from the British Library

ISBN 0 297 82570 4

Discovery Channel Online website address: www.discovery.com

Printed in the United States of America on acid-free paper.
9 8 7 6 5 4 3 2 1
First Edition

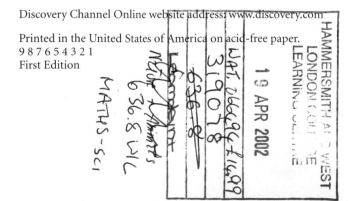

CONSULTANTS

Deborah A. Edwards, D.V.M., *owns a feline veterinary practice, All Cats
Hospital, in Largo, Florida. She is certified by the American Board of
Veterinary Practitioners (Feline Practice) and is a past-president of the
Academy of Feline Medicine.*

Linda Goodloe, Ph.D., *is a certified applied animal behaviorist. Based in
New York City, she has a private clinical and consulting practice for behavior problems of companion animals.*

Jack Grisham, B.S., *is Director of Animal Management at the Oklahoma
City Zoological Park. He is also involved with the American Zoo and
Aquarium Association, Species Survival Plan Management groups, and the
International Union for the Conservation of Nature (I.U.C.N.) Cat
Specialist Group.*

Nigel Gumley, D.V.M., *is a partner in the Alta Vista Animal Hospital in
Ottawa, Ontario. He is a past-president of the Ontario Veterinary Medical
Association, and is currently on the National Issues Committee of the
Canadian Veterinary Medical Association.*

Margaret E. Lewis, Ph.D., *is an Assistant Professor of Biology at The
Richard Stockton College of New Jersey. She specializes in the behavior,
ecology, and evolution of carnivores.*

Carolyn Osier *has been an all-breed judge with the Cat Fanciers'
Association, Inc., since 1984. Her cattery, Wil-o-glen, in California, is
known for Burmese and Abyssinians, but has also been the home of
Persians, American shorthairs, and exotics.*

CONTRIBUTOR

Elizabeth Marshall Thomas, *an anthropologist, is the author of the best-
selling books* The Tribe of Tiger *and* The Hidden Life of Dogs.
*She lives in New Hampshire with her nine cats, three dogs, and four par-
rots. Her long list of publications includes a novel,* Reindeer Moon.

ST. REMY MEDIA

President: Pierre Léveillé
Vice-President, Finance: Natalie Watanabe
Managing Editor: Carolyn Jackson
Managing Art Director: Diane Denoncourt
Production Manager: Michelle Turbide
Director, Business Development: Christopher Jackson

Senior Editor: Heather Mills
Art Director: Odette Sévigny
Assistant Editor: Jim Hynes
Researcher Writers: Ned Meredith, Robert Sonin
Photo Researcher: Linda Castle
Indexer: Linda Cardella Cournoyer
Senior Editor, Production: Brian Parsons
Systems Director: Edward Renaud
Technical Support: Jean Sirois
Scanner Operators: Martin Francoeur, Sara Grynspan

· CONTENTS ·

Top: British shorthair
Left: Snow leopard

·FOREWORD·

Although people have been keeping cats as pets for more than eight thousand years, they still seem mysterious to us even while we take them almost for granted. But perhaps we shouldn't. More than any other kind of animal, they are creatures of the edge. Most of the so-called carnivores eat a variety of foods, but cats in the wild live exclusively by hunting. If they can't catch prey, they starve, hence the elegant design of their bodies, which have changed very little since the original cat, a lynx-like animal, first evolved. Today, some of the modern cat species are much larger than lynxes, others are much smaller; some have acquired stripes and others spots, but the original shape was so successful that it has stayed more or less the same, and even today, the basic differences between the largest cats, the Altai tigers of Siberia, and the smallest cats, the black-footed cats of southern Africa, are mainly those of size and camouflage.

In fact, even the process of domestication has had less effect on the cat than it has upon most other animals. The wolves who became dogs, for instance, underwent profound physical and mental changes, but the African wildcats who became domestic cats changed hardly at all. The first wildcats to hunt mice in the granaries of the Neolithic farmers looked for all the world like the tabby cats in any town or city, some of whom could pass for the little tabby wildcats that still live on the African plains. Why? Because the early farmers, so adept at making sheepdogs out of wolves and milk cows out of wild aurochs, seem to have left the cats alone. Perhaps the farmers were satisfied with the service the cats were already providing, ridding their granaries of pests. Or perhaps even the farmers' considerable skills at dominating pack animals and herd animals were not up to molding animals as self-contained and self-sufficient as cats.

Thus to this day cats live in our homes with their wildness still upon them. If we find them mysterious, it is because we have forgotten much of what our own ancestors knew about the wilderness. A book such as this, with the cat as its subject, is a window on the natural world.

Elizabeth Marshall Thomas
Author of *The Tribe of Tiger*

**"Cats live in our homes
with their wildness still upon them."**

♦

ELIZABETH MARSHALL THOMAS

*Opening photographs:
Page 2: Sand cats
Pages 6-7: Chinchilla Persian
Pages 8-9: Cheetahs
Pages 10-11: Red tabby domestic shorthair
Pages 12-13: Bengal tigers
Opposite: Jaguarundi*

· I ·

CAT
PRIMER

· · ·

**"If a man could be crossed
with the cat, it would improve man
but deteriorate the cat."**

·

MARK TWAIN

CAT
·DESIGN·

The sleek frame hides compact yet powerful muscles. A flexible skeleton allows turns on a dime. A highly attuned nervous system tracks every sound and smell. In the jungles and savannas of the world, lions and tigers and other big cats unleash these attributes to kill in a fur-covered flash, demonstrating yet again why humankind has so long been in awe of the big cats' hunting prowess. But even the wild cats' smaller, domesticated kin, whether the scraggly denizens of an alley or the pampered lap-warmers of a family home, boast exactly the same skills and physical gifts. Felines, from tiger to tabby, are designed for the hunt.

GETTING A GRIP

The claws are the primary weapon in the feline arsenal. In addition to providing an iron grip for climbing, a cat's claws can be lethal, quickly unholstered to slash at an enemy or rip open an underbelly. Although the claws are often described as retractable—as if they normally were extended and then pulled back in by choice—the claws are, in fact, hidden until the cat's paw is extended. Safely sheathed when the cat is relaxed, even while it is walking, the claws stay razor-sharp, ready for action. During a mid-nap stretch or an angry swipe, the tendons controlling the claws are pulled taut, thrusting the talons outward.

The claws of the cheetah, the fastest of all felines, are always partially visible. Its claws are a little straighter than those in other felines and part of the sheath is missing. The ends of the claws give the cheetah valuable additional traction when it runs. The adaptation may be a response to the spotted cat's wide-open African plains habitat, where the cheetah's basic hunting strategy is to outrun its prey; it needs a firm grip on the ground for dead runs and sharp turns.

Felines, seemingly incorrigible scratchers, rake their claws over rough surfaces to both clean and hone them. But the raking motion also sheds the claws' dead and dulled outer layers and helps exercise leg muscles. Just as importantly, scratching allows the cat to leave its calling card, a territory-marking scent released from the paw pads *(page 64)*. Wild cats and domestic felines with access to the outdoors usually choose a tree or fence for these purposes. Indoor cats, unless they are encouraged to use a scratching post, will opt for a piece of furniture or anything else that is stable, rough in texture, and high enough off the ground to provide a good stretch.

Blessed with a flexible body structure, a cat can sleep comfortably while twisted into improbable and seemingly awkward positions.

Opposite: The sinuous arch of the back in a stretching leopard is typical of all cats. Thick cushions of fibrocartilage between each of the feline's thirty vertebrae make its spine extremely pliable.

Overleaf: Bobcat

EXTENDABLE CLAWS

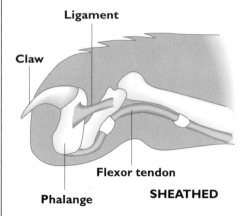

Ligament

Claw

Flexor tendon

Phalange

SHEATHED

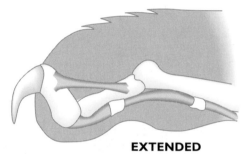

EXTENDED

Cats extend their normally sheathed claws by flexing muscles in the forelegs that pull on flexor tendons in the toes. The tendons tug on the phalanges, causing ligaments to stretch and the claws to extend.

THE FLEXIBLE FELINE

Cats gain another tactical advantage, and the envy of much less flexible humans, from their extraordinary mobility and fluidity of body design. What allows the cat to contort itself into unusual positions? How can the creature comfortably curl into a perfect circle when sleeping, twitching its tail rhythmically across its nose? Human spines are not flexible enough, even in childhood, to bend so generously.

The secret to the cat's flexibility lies in the structure of its body. Between each of its thirty spinal vertebrae—five more than in a human—are thick discs of fibrocartilage that are as pliable as they are resilient. In addition, the cat's shoulder bones, or scapulae, are held to the sides of the body by muscle only, permitting movement in almost every direction. And unlike the motion-restricting collarbone of humans, cats have a tiny, muscle-attached "floating" clavicle. The resulting narrow chest accounts for the exceptionally long stride of cats and explains their talent for squeezing through tight spaces.

Because it may need to break into full sprint at any time, a cat walks on its toes, reducing friction with the ground and extending the length of its limbs. The digitigrade walk, as it is known, is made possible by the intricate "wrists" of the front legs—a collection of small, flexible bones called carpals—and similar bones, called tarsals, in the hocks of the rear legs. The agility afforded by these bones, combined with the cat's shoulder placement and a vestibular system in the ear *(page 36)* that is coordinated with the cat's muscles, enables it to parade gracefully and casually over unnervingly skinny surfaces such as fence rails and porch balustrades.

STEADY AS SHE GOES

The tail, too, is an anatomical marvel. It's a highly specialized tool of communication *(page 70)*, but more importantly, it helps balance the body. Like a tightrope walker's pole, this appendage acts as a counterweight in such feline high-wire acts as climbing trees, walking along a chair back, or tiptoeing across ceiling-high shelves. The tail also serves as a gyroscope of sorts, allowing the cat to maintain its orientation in sharp turns made while on the run, a critical advantage when hunting. In the dizzying, zigzag pursuit of desperate prey, the cheetah, for instance, uses its extra-long tail to stay upright during each abrupt change of direction.

The tails of wild cats often are as much as half the length of their bodies. Domestic cats sport tails that proportionately are even longer. The only wild feline that boasts a tail longer in relation to its body than its domestic cousins is the margay. The margay needs an especially long appendage for balance since it is a tree climber and spends much of its time skipping along precariously slim branches in its arboreal habitat high above the forest floor.

WEIGHING IN

Although wild and domestic cats may be similarly assembled, they differ considerably in their weight ranges. A typical adult house cat tips the scales at about six to twelve pounds. Fully grown wild cats generally are much heavier, and variances are greater from breed to breed. They range from the mighty seven-hundred-pound Siberian tiger to the tiny wild black-footed cat, which at maturity can weigh as little as three pounds and is the only wild feline punier than domestic cats.

PACKAGING DIFFERENCES

Selective breeding has fiddled extensively with the domestic feline's shape, shade, and more. Natural evolution has yielded two dramatically different basic body types, each dictated by environment. The harsh, cold climate in the mountainous regions of the old Persian Empire (such as in the north of today's Iran) produced the "cobby" body, which harbors a heavy, often large, skeleton. This physique features a compact, round, broad-chested

With typical surefooted feline grace, a domestic cat deftly negotiates a precariously narrow fence rail. Odds are the cat will reach its destination without falling. The narrow build of its chest allows careful placement of one paw directly ahead of the other and the tail aids in maintaining balance.

body with a dense coat and thick tail, and is typically found in the long-haired Persians and the shorthaired exotics. Perfect for retaining warmth, cobby bodies are crowned by large, round heads with short, broad muzzles.

If cobby bodies are akin to bulky wrestlers, then "foreign" or Oriental body types are the lanky basketball stars. The hot climes of Africa and Asia produced this lean line, ideally suited to releasing rather than retaining body heat. The narrow foreign body features slender legs, a long, thin tail, and a wedge-shaped head with large ears and slanted, oval eyes. The Siamese is the quintessential foreign cat.

The "semi-foreign," "modified," or "moderate" body type could be described as a bridge between the extremes. With a slender but muscular body and a head shape known as a modified wedge, these cats often bear the oval eyes of the foreign breeds. With little intervention from man, the Abyssinian and Russian blue breeds are the standard-bearers here.

Shapes and sizes of domestic cats vary, but certain breeds are prototypes of the three body groups: the Siamese of the "foreign," the exotic of the "cobby," and the Abyssinian of the "semi-foreign."

COATING: THE TRUTH

Whether a cat wears the equivalent of a windbreaker or a parka usually depends on local climate. African lions do well on the hot savanna in their short, tan coat. The snow leopard of Asia's Far East depends on its thick, light-colored coat to fend off cold and blend in with the snow. What makes fur such a sophisticated heating and cooling system? The answer is as many as three different types of coat hair.

Humans produce only one type of hair, each strand from an individual follicle. In a cat, outer "guard," or primary, hairs also grow individually from separate follicles; long and rigid, they keep the feline warm and dry.

The more numerous secondary hairs of the undercoat, in contrast, grow in clusters from single follicles. This dense, insulating layer is close to the cat's skin and consists of both shorter, bristly "awn" hairs and soft, wavy "down" hairs. Depending on the cat's environment, the double-layered coat works like household insulation to prevent warmth from escaping when it's cold or entering when it's hot.

All wild cats sport two-layered coats made of all three hair types. Domestic-breed coats might have one or two types. When the genetic dice roll, some dramatic permutations turn up. The "hairless" sphynx actually does

Siamese

have a few down hairs—on its ears, face, and tail. Only short, curly awn and down hairs adorn the Cornish rex; the lack of guard hairs leaves the cat vulnerable to temperature extremes. Plush, shorthaired Russian blues are double-coated thanks to awn and guard hairs of the same length.

COLOR

Cat fanciers give out ribbons for perfectly patterned coats. For a feline that must survive in the wild, though, coat patterns are a hide-saving form of protection. With the exception of the cheetah, which has a spotted coat that is easy to detect on open plains, wild cats dress in one basic style: camouflage. The stripes, spots, or blotches help them blend into their environment by obscuring the distinct outline of their bodies. Typically, all cats within a wild species will have similar patterns—a thousand lions will share one basic look. Any group within a species that deviates has evolved a better disguise for its regional habitat; leopards living in jungles, for example, differ in appearance from those residing in high, snowy mountain ranges.

The earliest ancestors of domestic cats are said to have borne color-banded coats that helped them blend in with their surroundings. But as domestication lessened the need for hunter's camouflage, mutations to solid colors such as red, black, and white began to occur. And once cats with these mutated colors started crossbreeding, the color and pattern palette burgeoned into countless variations.

Abyssinian

Exotic

Humans deliberately have done more than their fair share to mix things up, thanks mostly to breeders seeking particular colors, patterns, and even hair length. Some feline associations cite up to eighty colors just for Persians alone! A cat show today offers an instant and dizzying primer on the many coat color and pattern classifications within larger categories. While ticking, tipping, and pattern varieties may seem of only passing interest to the uninitiated, they are worthy of blue ribbons in the world of cat fancy.

The lined or spotted tabby category is the most familiar: Many of the domestic feline's wild ancestors have these same markings—the African wildcat, the house cat's closest relative, is a striped tabby. The gene that spawns the tabby pattern is so dominant that all cats inherit some form of it. Even solid- (known as "self-") colored cats may show faint tabby markings in certain light.

In between its spots or stripes, a tabby flaunts a distinctive salt-and-pepper design. Each hair in these areas is "ticked." It has (usually two) bands of different colors alternating down its length. The outer tip of the hair is dark, followed by a light band, then a dark band, and a light one at the root. This ticking occurs over the top of the cat's head, on its back and sides, and on the outside of its legs. Ticking can create a pattern of its own, also known as "agouti," which is best typified by the Abyssinian.

"Tipping," on the other hand, refers to the shading of a hair. The outer dark color at the end of the hair becomes gradually lighter all the way down to the root. Tipping can be "shelled," "shaded," or "smoked," depending on the way the color is shaded. Shelled hairs exhibit only a slight bit of color at their very tip. Shaded hairs contain slightly more color. Smoked hairs appear to be a solid color for two-thirds of the length, then are white near the skin. So-called bicolored cats are those of any color or pattern in combination with white. Particolors, such as the tortoiseshell, exhibit two colors.

Oddly, while aging grays human hair, it darkens the hair of cats with colorpoint, the other major coat pattern. All colorpoint kittens, such as the Siamese, Birman, and Himalayan, are actually born white, then darken as they age. The striking colorpoint pattern consists of lighter hairs on the cat's torso, complemented by darker "points" on the paws, tail, ears, and face, extremities susceptible to a heat-sensitive enzyme in the cat's pigment cells that restricts full color to the cooler parts of the body.

The ocelot's spotted coat makes it less visible in the dappled light of its South American forest environment. The coats of wild cats often are patterned or colored in response to environmental conditions. The ocelots of the scrub and grasslands in Arizona and Texas, for instance, have lighter coats than their forest-dwelling counterparts.

A PALETTE OF FELINE COLORS AND PATTERNS

When life got cushy for domesticated cats, they began to wear coats more for appearance than utility. Selective breeding, which must mask the tabby-pattern gene found in all cats, has given us hundreds of variations in hair color, pattern, and length. Shown here are domestic breeds that display some of the most common color and pattern classifications.

Bicolor (Manx)

Particolor (Persian)

Pointed pattern (Birman)

Shaded pattern (American shorthair)

Agouti pattern (Abyssinian)

Tabby pattern (Exotic)

THE ATHLETIC
·HUNTER·

Design a "dream machine" for hunting and you'd come up with something very close to a cat. From the smallest domestic to the biggest "king of the jungle," felines are gifted in all the bodily tools and techniques needed to chase prey in the wild or toys in the living room: speed, athleticism, and the killer instinct.

BORN TO RUN

If a cat were an Olympic athlete, the only marathon it might win would be in sleeping. But watch out in the sprint events. The cat would leave its competitors in the dust. Oddly enough, it is the cat's fondness for sleep that makes it such a speed demon. Sleep is its way of conserving energy for the explosive bursts of speed it needs for a successful chase. More often than

Above: An African leopard keeps a watchful eye over the carcass of its most recent victim, stored high to protect it from scavengers. Leopards are the champion climbers of the big-cat world. The powerful legs and gripping claws that make them fast runners, coupled with brawny chest and jaw muscles, help leopards climb—with supper in tow—up the trunks of trees with great ease.

not, these brief, energy-sapping episodes of running prowess are punctuated by yet more slumber. But hunting is not the only arena for showing off a cat's running ability, of course. Sometimes its speed is put to the test when the cat itself is the target of a chase. Felines that survive in the wild, especially on open plains, rely heavily on their ability to run—much more so than domestic cats, the habitat of which puts greater onus on stalking and surprise attack. Given cause, though, all cats are gold-medal winners in high-speed pursuit.

What makes cats so good at running? Observe any feline and you'll find some answers. When they walk, for instance, cats alternate opposite legs. But watch them run and you'll see that the front and back legs work as pairs to attain speed. At a gallop, the cat arches its supple spine as its hind legs propel ahead of its front legs, rendering it airborne for the time between strides. The speed with which cats run comes through an exceptionally long stride and strong back legs. They have the on-toes walk *(page 20)* and flexible shoulders and spine needed for a long stride, the powerful hindquarter muscles to push for speed. In fact, when going all-out, felines bear more than half their weight on the front legs, allowing the hind legs to work mostly at propulsion. The champion of all felines, the cheetah, can explode

Propelled by its powerful hind legs, a Siberian tiger bounds through a marsh. The cat's limbs are also extremely flexible, allowing it to make the quick stops and turns needed to bring down a victim at the end of a pursuit.

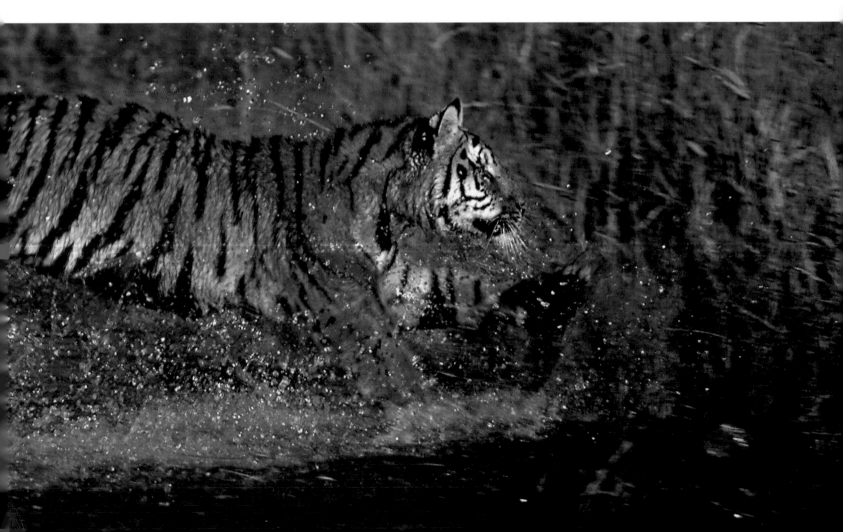

from zero to faster than sixty miles per hour in just four seconds. Even its much less talented domestic cousins can reach speeds of up to thirty miles per hour in just a few seconds. But like most great sprinters, the cat has poor endurance over the long haul; even a sustained trot will exhaust it. It becomes overheated in less than a minute and must stop to pant in order to cool down. And the cheetah, in particular, has a heart only one-third the size of the human organ, relatively speaking. This contributes to its lack of stamina and explains why cheetahs, despite their blazing speed, have a poor success rate in capturing prey.

JUMPING

When it comes to the long-jump and the high-jump events, cats are back in the winner's circle. The same pliable muscles and flexible spine that make them great sprinters allow them to jump vertically or horizontally up to six times their own body length. Wild cats need a well-developed ability to pounce in order to survive, especially those solitary hunters that base successful dining on an element of surprise. Tigers can leap more than thirty feet through the air onto unsuspecting prey. With its exceptionally long hind legs, the puma effortlessly jumps distances of more than forty feet. Even the relatively short-legged lion, a pack hunter without much need for jumping, can spring as far as four-and-a-half times the length of its body— some forty feet. Humans measure in at the low end of the big-cat scale. The average person can barely jump twice his or her body length.

These pouncing, jumping, and leaping talents come from the combination of powerful leg and back muscles, along with a calculating mind. Easy jumps are sometimes made during the course of a trot or run. More difficult leaps, especially where landing areas are short or narrow, call for careful planning. Because a cat pushes off with great force, it first tests the solidity of the take-off point with its hind legs. Next, the cat sizes up the distance to be spanned, then calculates the hind-leg push needed to leap it successfully. Once all these assessments are computed, the cat crouches forward, tips its pelvis, and bends at the hips, knees, and ankles. Then, it's lift-off time. Contracting muscles and extending the joints, the would-be astronaut launches itself. Whether jumping up onto the top of a bookcase or down to the ground beside its unwary prey, the cat usually lands front-paws first and draws its hind legs in behind. A safe landing is assured by its flexible shoulders and solid feet, ankles, and wrists, which absorb the force of touchdown with little or no lateral movement. Padded paws act as miniature shock absorbers.

Not all situations call for the same technique. Depending on the height of the jump, a cat will occasionally keep one leg on the ground for extra balance. To snatch airborne prey, the animal will sometimes spring off all four limbs, rising straight up and slightly backward to swat at a target with

Believed to be as much as seventy times thicker than the skin on the rest of its body, the leathery pads on a cat's paws serve as cushions for walking, running, and climbing, and absorb the shock of landings. The pads also silence its step and provide the traction it needs to negotiate sharp turns in a high-speed chase. Cheetahs' pads are tougher than the standard feline issue, with grooves akin to tire treads to provide more traction for their high-performance running demands.

extended claws before landing on its hind legs. In the wild, the caracal applies this technique to perfection, leaping several feet into the air to knock surprised birds to the ground. This is a polished version of the amusing impromptu upward capriole of a startled kitten, where a sudden springing of the muscles occurs in all four of its legs at once. The cat, thanks in large part to its flexible back, is able to meet almost any athletic challenge it may face in a day.

CLIMB EVERY CURTAIN
Equipped with effective crampons and powerful boosting and balancing systems, cats can go where less acrobatic animals fear to tread. While almost all felines are accomplished climbers, the skills of cats in the wild vary greatly according to body type. Small cats typically are the most talented climbers; however, even the largest of cats can scale heights to some extent.

Poised for take-off, a domestic cat lunges from a log on muscular hind legs. Before committing to the leap, the cat tested its launch pad for resistance and computed the force of the push needed. In mid-air, the animal will take advantage of its flexible spine to extend its body and guide itself to the landing site using its tail as a rudder.

A young cat ascends a tree, its cramponlike claws providing grip. Helpful tools in climbing, a cat's claws hook the wrong way to be of much assistance in gaining a graceful descent.

Opposite: A cat who takes an unexpected tumble rights itself in midair, stretches out its limbs to help slow the descent, and aligns its body for touch-down. The tail helps to provide balance, and the padded paws and flexible leg joints and shoulders absorb most of the shock of the landing.

The leopard climbs with ease, thanks to its particularly well-muscled, broad chest and flexible limbs. Like most felines, its shoulders can rotate so that it can grasp a tree trunk between its forepaws. The cheetah, however, is a poor climber. It has a narrow chest built for speed and shoulder joints that are more limited to the forward and backward movement necessary for the run. Tigers and lions carry much of their bulk on the front part of their torsos and consequently they have difficulty pushing themselves upward. But even these disadvantaged climbers on occasion will scale a tree, especially when seeking shade from the scorching sun.

A climb begins with a running jump, then upward propulsion with the help of those mighty hind legs. Hooked claws maintain a firm grip on whatever is being scaled and the tail acts as a counterweight. The tail and an organ called the vestibular apparatus in the inner ear provide the cat with the balance necessary for such vertical acrobatics. Although cats climb primarily in search of shelter, some hunting cats will lunch aloft. Leopards, for instance, in an impressive feat that is a testament to their powerful jaw muscles, frequently carry their kills up into trees to eat them in peace, away from scavenging hyenas. Other cats, such as the small and obviously highly agile rusty spotted cat found in India and Sri Lanka, take to the trees for some high-altitude hunting of birds and small rodents.

Anyone who has ever witnessed a mewling kitten "stuck" in a tree knows about the flip side to cats' remarkable ability to climb: They aren't nearly as adept at getting themselves back down. Their less powerful front legs cannot support their body weight, and their rigid, downward-hooked claws cannot assist in gripping in a headfirst descent. Occasionally they will go down the trunk headfirst. From a secure perch, they will stretch their front paws as far down the trunk as possible before launching themselves and virtually "running" down the tree. But more often than not, caution wins out and the usually dignified feline is obliged to embark on an ungainly, precarious, and often comical backward descent. The margay, a tree-climbing virtuoso from the rain forests of South America, is the one cat spared such a humiliating experience: The bone structure of its ankles, like that of the squirrel, provides the margay with enough flexibility to reverse its hind feet for an easy, headfirst descent.

Luckily for cats, a sensory mechanism that they develop as kittens helps them to land safely in the event of a fall. In what is known as the "righting" reflex, a cat in airborne descent rights itself to land on all-fours. Messages to the brain from the eyes and vestibular apparatus of the inner ear tell the cat to turn its head and front torso toward the ground. With the help of its balancing tail, the cat aligns its back with the rest of its body and prepares to land. The shock of the touchdown is cushioned by the soft paw pads and flexible leg joints and shoulders. This entire complicated sequence of movements can take place within a vertical distance of as little as two feet.

WIRED FOR HUNTING

Today's owners of house cats may be repulsed by the predatory habits shown by an otherwise docile kitty, but in fact it was the feline's ability to catch and kill disease-carrying rodents in ancient Egypt and in medieval Europe that led to its domestication and popularity in the first place. Cats are born with the instinct to hunt. Their brain circuitry is wired to make stalking and attacking reflex actions. The mother's role is not to show them how to hunt but to bring them prey so they can refine this skill. Play with their siblings also arouses natural hunting instincts. Some cats, even when deprived of this practice when young, can develop into great hunters.

All cats are capable of hunting, but some are not adept at completing the job with the killing coup de grace, the nape bite. A skilled feline hunter will dispatch its prey with one clean bite to the back of the neck, breaking the animal's neck and severing the spinal cord. Many domestic cats, however, are incapable of correctly inflicting the nape bite, probably due to a lack of practice in kittenhood. Often, the result is a protracted, messy, or even unsuccessful kill. In the wild, however, the victim almost always becomes a quick meal. The nape bite is used to dispatch small prey; larger victims are asphyxiated by a powerful clamping bite on the throat. Domestic cats, which have never had to catch their own dinner and are regularly fed by caring owners, sometimes manage to finish off a mouse or bird that happens to cross their path. Even though hunger is not the motivation, the hunting instinct is strong enough to surface and the prey, either dead, mauled, and stunned or alive and kicking, may be deposited at the feet of a usually unappreciative owner.

THE DANCE OF DEATH

Everything about felines makes them perfect killing machines. First the senses come into play: The cat usually detects potential prey by its movement, then identifies it by sound and smell. Next, the feline's athletic attributes allow the cat to chase and subdue its victim. Finally, the cat's teeth and powerful facial muscles are applied to make the kill, then to tear and chew the meat of the vanquished.

Except for lions, who usually hunt in groups, most cats are solitary hunters who will generally attack prey only smaller than themselves. Domestic cats will target small mammals, although their diets can include everything from insects and birds to fish and reptiles. Some wild cats, however, such as the small but ferocious fishing cat of southern Asia, have been known to bring down animals twice their size.

All cats, domestic or wild, take what is known as a "stalk-and-pounce" approach to the hunt. There are several variations of this technique, depending on the prey, the nature of the surroundings, and the particulars of the situation. Once the cat has detected and identified its prey, it sizes up the circumstances and chooses a course of action. Both wild and domestic cats generally catch birds on the ground by stalking. Since birds possess excellent vision and fairly acute hearing, cats must approach stealthily—which, thanks to their soft, padded paws, they do well. To avoid detection, felines often freeze in their tracks for protracted periods before resuming the silent approach. Under cover of long grass, the cat crouches low to the ground, taking advantage of its flexible joints and shoulders. (On the manicured lawns of suburbia, where the cat's success rate in hunting drops dramatically, it's lucky that the next meal is just a can opener away.) Cats use the same techniques for capturing most mammals. Those living underground require different techniques. A cat will lie in wait patiently outside the burrow, sometimes for hours, until its victim pops out its head.

In the final movement of this ballet macabre, the cat judges the vertical or horizontal distance to be broached, then launches itself onto its prey. Unlike dogs and other large predators, which confidently attack teeth-first,

If this African lion succeeds in overtaking the fleeing zebra, it will pull the striped prey to the ground with its powerful claws and dispatch the zebra with a killing bite. Unlike most other cats, lions often hunt as a group, allowing them to target larger prey than they would as solitary hunters.

A bobcat does a victory dance following its successful kill of a jackrabbit. What might seem to be a rather ghoulish celebration relieves tension.

Opposite: An unfortunate bird is quickly recaptured after having been released in the hunting ritual of a domestic cat.

THE DOMESTIC PREDATOR

The natural hunting ability that has made the domestic cat so valuable through the ages as a mouser is now becoming a source of concern for some, especially bird lovers. Several studies have shown that cats have indeed taken a serious toll on bird populations, with some arguing that the cat's appetite for fowl actually threatens the survival of some species—particularly ground-nesting birds. Estimates vary, but even the most conservative ones hold cats responsible for tens of millions of bird deaths in North America each year. And small mammals killed by cats number significantly higher. Leash laws, curfews, and all-out bans on outdoor cats, enforced by fines, are currently on the law books in cities around the world; in many places, though, such proposed laws have been defeated through the intervention of cat lovers.

a cat, especially a small domestic one, dives in paws-first to subdue its catch and avoid being bitten or scratched in the face or neck. When leaping toward prey such as birds, it swats or grabs at its victim; when fishing, it scoops its prey from the water.

Despite good vision, a cat can't focus well close up, and sometimes must release the prey in its mouth to get a good look and a proper grip. Both to prevent the catch from escaping and for the cat's own self-protection, prey is preferably motionless before it is released. Thus the cat, whether wild or domestic, "plays" with its catch. In fact, this is an attempt to stun the victim into unconsciousness. Once confident of the prey's submission, the cat uses its sensitive whiskers to feel for signs of movement before it delivers the killing nape bite. Then, it's back home with the kill if there is a litter to feed. Or, as is the case with most wild and feral felines, it's time for a fast-food meal on the spot.

EARS &
·HEARING·

A domestic tabby swivels one pinna, the conelike external ear flap, to locate and identify a sound. More than twenty muscles move each of the cat's ears (human ears have only six). The same network of muscles bends, turns, and folds the cat's ears in positions that telegraph its mood *(page 70)*.

The cat's ear is yet another marvel of feline engineering. Like a sophisticated satellite dish turning to pick up a signal, the cat's external ear, or pinna, rotates up to 180 degrees to locate and identify even the faintest of squeaks, peeps, or rustling noises.

While dogs are renowned for detecting high-pitched whistles far beyond human hearing, cats actually hear much higher frequencies than canines and are only slightly inferior at the low end of the frequency scale. They also can detect the tiniest variances in sound, distinguishing differences of as little as one-tenth of a tone, which helps them identify the type and size of the prey emitting the noise. This heightened sense of hearing is especially important in wild cats, which depend on hunting for survival. It also enables wild and domestic feline mothers to hear faint squeals of distress from their cubs or kittens when they stray too far away.

A cat up to three feet away from the origin of a sound can pinpoint its location to within a few inches in a mere six one-hundredths of a second. Cats also can hear sounds at great distances—four or five times farther away than humans.

THE ORGAN OF BALANCE

The ears also serve in another way that is vital to successful feline life. The vestibular apparatus, housed deep in the cat's inner ear, is responsible for the cat's remarkable sense of balance. This sense organ's tiny chambers and canals are lined with millions of sensitive hairs and filled with fluid and minute floating crystals. When the cat moves suddenly, the delicate hairs detect the movement of the fluid and crystals and rapidly send messages to the brain, giving readings on the body's position. This is similar in principle to the instrument in an airplane called the "artificial horizon" or "attitude indicator" that tells the pilot the position of the plane's wings in relation to the horizon. When a cat loses its balance and actually takes a spill, the vestibular apparatus kicks in. This helps the cat register which direction is up, and triggers the "righting" reflex that cats rely on to turn themselves in midair, adjusting the orientation of the body so that they land squarely on all four feet *(page 31)*. This organ, together with the tail, which acts as a counterbalance, permits the cat to perform its remarkable signature acrobatics. The manx, a tail-less breed, is thought to have an especially sensitive vestibular apparatus to compensate.

DEAFNESS

Cats, like humans, can experience hearing problems or even total deafness due to disease, infections, outer-ear trauma, inner-ear damage from excessively loud noises, or simply old age. The cat's ability to detect high frequencies particularly declines as the eardrum thickens with age. This condition not only affects the cat's hunting skill; it also can compromise the feline's ability to heed noises signaling danger.

In domestic cats, however, deafness is most commonly hereditary. Although inherited deafness has not been genetically related to specific breeds, the dominant gene responsible for producing white hair is sometimes associated with inner-ear abnormalities that often lead to deafness. Incidences are highest in white cats with blue eyes; white cats with eyes of different colors are often deaf only in the ear on the blue-eyed side.

UNUSUAL AUDIO TOOLS

 Whether they have evolved in response to environmental conditions or occur as genetic defects, ears come in a variety of shapes and sizes in both wild and domestic cats. Most variations are merely slight deviations from the usual large, funnel-shaped ears that help cats draw sound into their inner ears. But some unusual shapes and sizes stand out—sometimes up—from the rest. The African serval illustrates an extreme adaptation to environmental factors: These small wild cats rely on their oversized ears to facilitate heat loss, which keeps them cool, and to detect the little rodents on which they commonly prey in their nocturnal hunting forays.

Wild caracals and their genetic cousins from the lynx family, including the North American lynx, sport long tufts of fur on top of their ears. Although the purpose of these tufts is not universally agreed upon, one theory suggests that these ear extensions accentuate facial expressions, especially the more threatening ones.

Genetic defects in domestic cats have resulted in folded or curled ears. In some instances, these mutations were striking and unique enough to grant the cats the status of individual breeds—thus the birth of the Scottish fold and the American curl. In both these cases, the physical aberration is limited to the outer-ear cartilage and in no way interferes with the cats' sense of hearing.

African serval

North American lynx

Scottish fold

EYES &
· VISION ·

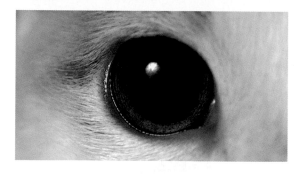

Like the aperture of a camera, a cat's pupil opens and closes to control the amount of light that reaches the retina. As shown from top to bottom here, the pupil dilates from a narrow slit (in bright light) to a fully open orb (in dark conditions).

The belief that cats can see in the dark is an exaggeration. Felines can see no better in total darkness than humans can, but special night-vision adaptations allow them to see extremely well in even the dimmest light, a vital ability for nocturnal hunters. While sensitive hearing may help the cat initially detect prey, its keen, nighttime-adapted vision permits it to identify the location of a potential meal with deadly, laser-beam accuracy.

SEEING THE LIGHT

A combination of ocular features works to first collect, then enhance the amount of light in the cat's eye, providing it with nighttime vision estimated to be six times better than that of a human. A cat's eyes are large in proportion to the size of its head, with correspondingly big pupils that dilate to allow the maximum amount of light to enter them. An extensive and sharply curved cornea creates a large anterior chamber in front of the lens of the eye. The lens, then, is close to the retina and helps concentrate the amount of light collected there. Nocturnal hunters such as the lynx have especially large anterior chambers that help them see well at night, while those of daytime hunters such as lions are considerably smaller.

Once light is concentrated on the retina, it must be refined to create clear images. In both humans and felines, the retina contains two types of photo-receptor cells, rods and cones, that send signals to the brain when stimulated by light. Rods are sensitive to low-intensity light, while cones are triggered by bright light and provide the eyes with both resolving power and the ability to detect color. With a rod-to-cone ratio of twenty-five-to-one compared to four-to-one in humans, cats can see in a fraction of the light we require, but lack the ability to detect fine details.

Shine a light on a cat in a darkened room or look at a photograph of a cat taken with a flash and you'll observe the eerie green or yellow glow reflecting from its eyes. To take full advantage of available light, the back of the cat's retina contains a layer of mirrorlike cells, called the tapetum lucidum, that collects and reflects light back to restimulate the retina's rods—much like the effect seen when a car's headlights shine on a road marker at night. Present in nearly all carnivores and many other mammals, this layer of cells is particularly thick, up to as many as fifteen cells, in cats. Not visible in normal conditions, the tapetum lucidum appears only when light is aimed directly into the animal's eyes.

A cat's vision is sharpest between two and three feet from its face, and its focus is on the center of what the cat observes rather than on the entirety. This is a helpful adaptation when it come to zeroing in on small prey. Cats also can detect motion much better than humans do. Since the many rods in the cat's retina serve as motion detectors as well as light receptors, anything running across a cat's field of vision is more likely to be detected than something coming straight toward it.

Despite the presence of the color-detecting cones, cats have little or no need to distinguish colors. Until fairly recently, cats were widely believed to be color-blind. In tests, however, domestic cats were successfully trained to distinguish blue, green, and yellow (but not red). Their light-sensitive vision also allows them to differentiate among several shades of gray.

The eyes of a fishing cat, native to Asia, emit an otherworldly green glow, evidence of the reflective cells lining the back of its eyes that improve its vision in the dark.

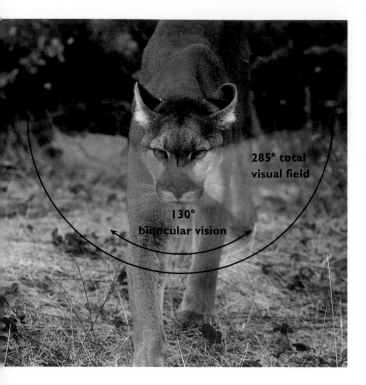

285° total
visual field

130°
binocular vision

Scouting for prey, a cougar focuses on targets that appear in the area achieved by the overlap of the vision range of its left and right eyes.

A domestic cat displays its nictitating membranes, or third eyelids, the white tissues at the inside corners of the eyes. Their visibility—other than when the cat first awakens from a snooze—often signals illness.

PUPIL FLEXIBILITY

Because a cat's eyes are designed for keen night vision, its large pupils must constrict to limit the amount of light entering the retina during the day, thereby preventing them from being dazzled. Domestic cats and many smaller wild-cat species possess pupils that narrow to a mere slit, allowing them to see well even in extremely bright light. Big cats such as lions, which hunt in daytime, possess pupils that constrict into small, tight circles instead; their night vision is not as acute as that of their nocturnally active cousins. In low-light situations, both wild and domestic cats will fully dilate their elliptically shaped pupils into almost perfect spheres to harvest the maximum amount of light. Cats also open and close their pupils during periods of stress or confrontation. A fearful cat's pupils will be fully dilated to create a wider field of vision and take in as much of the surroundings as possible, while those of an aggressive cat are considerably constricted as a threat signal.

BINOCULAR VISION

Predators rely on acute distance judgment and depth perception to time leaps and strike prey successfully. Their eyes face forward, offering a wide field of overlapping sight. In this area of binocular vision, depth perception and distance assessment are keenest. The eyes of prey, on the other hand, are generally placed on the sides of the head, offering them a wider range for detecting approaching predators but less depth perception.

Cats have a greater range of binocular vision than any other carnivores, which contributes to their remarkable hunting skill. This visual ability comes at a price, however. Cats, like humans, have only limited peripheral vision, which means that they have to roll their eyes or move their heads to view anything located on either side of them.

THE THIRD EYELID

Cats' upper and lower eyelids, like those of humans, sheath the eyeballs. For further protection, all cats have an opaque, white third eyelid, called the nictitating membrane, between the lower lid and inside corner of each eye. This layer helps moisten the eye and clear the surface of the cornea of dust. When dozing, this third eyelid closes, perhaps to act as a shade. As soon as the sleeping cat is alerted by any sound, the nictitating membrane flicks back to the inside corner of the eye.

Hidden from view behind the outer eyelids of a sleeping cat and barely noticeable in the corner of the eyes while the cat is awake, the nictitating membranes are sometimes visible in felines that doze with open eyelids. While most cats do sleep with their eyes completely closed, some rest with their eyes partially open. Cats with very short noses, such as Persians, may not be physically able to close their eyes completely because the eyes bulge more, causing the nictitating membranes to be visible during sleep. The membranes also are seen when cats blink, which, quite mysteriously, they do infrequently—sometimes as little as once every few minutes.

The nictitating membranes can become inflamed by foreign objects such as dirt or dust particles. Their visible presence when a cat is awake can indicate sickness or a condition such as intestinal parasites, thus signaling the need for a visit to the vet. Some illnesses can shrink the fatty tissue behind the eyes, causing the eyeballs to retreat into the orbits, exposing the membranes. Weight loss and dehydration can also bring on protrusion of the third eyelids by causing the eyes to fall back into the orbits.

"MY, WHAT BEAUTIFUL EYES YOU HAVE"

 All domestic kittens are born with beautiful blue eyes that usually change color at around twelve weeks of age. Genetics determine whether the cat will end up with copper, gold, green, orange, or blue eyes. Those eyes that remain blue do so because of a genetic link with hair color. A cat's white coat is due to a lack of pigment in the hair, and blue is often associated with white or pigmentless cats. (Similar to human albinos, cats may also manifest white hair and pink or red eyes.) Thus, blue eyes normally are present in cats with little or no color in their coats. Many white cats have blue eyes.

The eyes of Siamese cats always are blue, but for a different reason: Since this breed originates from regions in northern Asia that receive little sunlight, blue eyes may be the result of an environmental adaptation for better light absorption.

The range of eye colors in wild cats is quite limited; generally their eyes are brown, hazel, or copper—or some variations of these shades that may appear more green or yellow.

There is also a fair amount of variation in the shape and placement of feline eyes. Wild cats usually possess oval eyes that are slightly slanted, while in domestic cats, eye shape ranges from round to almond. For the most part, the semi-foreign or oriental cat typified by the Siamese has slanted, almond-shaped eyes, while breeds from the West, such as the Persian and the chartreux, have larger and rounder eyes.

A green-eyed tabby

A copper-eyed British shorthair

The startling blue eyes of a Siamese

A white cat with different-colored eyes ("odd-eyed")

SMELL & ·TASTE·

Whether in a natural or an urban jungle, a feline constantly monitors the aromas around it to assess the risks and seize the opportunities presented by its environment. A discriminating sniff will help a feline determine if a morsel of food is fit to eat, just as surely as the whiff of a predator provides advance warning of trouble. Even procreation in cats owes much to the olfactory sense: The message that a female is ready to mate is delivered to the tom via the odor of her urine *(page 60)*.

THE SCENT SENSE

A cat's reliance on its sense of smell is well placed. The back of its nasal chamber is lined with a layer of cells covered with some twenty million scent-sensitive nerve endings, at least twice as many as humans have, poised to rush messages about surrounding smells to the cat's brain. A cat sniffs to deliver a greater volume of air, and odor, to the nerve endings than it would receive from routine breathing.

The sense of smell develops in kittens and cubs well before hearing and sight, which enables newborns to sniff out the location of their mother's nipples for suckling. Later, when diet becomes more varied, cats routinely sniff food before tasting it. This practice is particularly important in the wild, where there is no provider of safe, nutritious food. Spoiled food, which could sicken the animal, is easily detected by the cat's super sense of smell because the food emits nitrogen, the signal to abstain.

In addition to their sensitive nasal nerve endings, cats, like most carnivores, are also equipped with a scent organ located on the roof of the mouth near the nasal palate. Called the vomeronasal or Jacobsen's (after its discoverer), the organ sharpens odor detection and identification. In a strange combination of gape, grimace, and grin known as the flehmen response, a feline opens its mouth, wrinkles its nose, and curls back its lips. This unique facial contortion blocks off the cat's normal breathing route and channels odors to the pouchlike Jacobsen's organ, which then telegraphs odor information to the brain. Cats typically employ the flehmen response to interpret the urine spray of other cats in a territory, particularly male cats assessing the sexual status of females. The urine of females ready to ovulate contains chemicals called pheromones that, when detected by the Jacobsen's organ, send a powerful message to sexually mature toms. Interestingly, a chemical similar to the pheromones in female cat urine is present in catnip. This likely explains

Hungry kittens jockey for places at their obliging mother's built-in feeding station. Although the newborn offspring of other species show no attachment to specific nipples, suckling kittens usually return to the same one, based on its particular smell. Loyalty to a nipple may even indicate the beginnings in the formation of a hierarchy, with places nearest the mother's head assumed by the dominant kittens.

Opposite: A young lion pulls back its lips and opens its mouth in the characteristic flehmen response, directing odor to the Jacobsen's organ where it is interpreted.

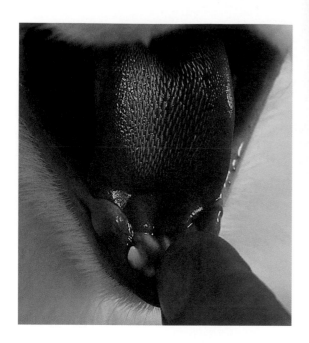

A feline bares its tongue, exhibiting rows of papillae, the fleshy barbs used in eating and grooming. An adult domestic cat possesses approximately 250 papillae on its tongue.

Above, right: Ever vigilant, a tiger drinks at the edge of a pond. All cats sport a ladlelike tongue, curled at the tip, that laps water into the center before the animal swallows. A cat may lap five or six times between swallows.

why male cats are generally more responsive to the charms of this vegetation than females. Their wildly ecstatic reaction is sexual in nature.

TASTE AND TONGUE

Discriminating taste buds have earned cats an unfair reputation as fussy eaters. Cats aren't picky just to be difficult; they've simply evolved tastes that help them distinguish what is good for their health from what isn't. Rows of small hooked projections, called papillae, cover the tip, sides, and back of the tongue and throat—and each papilla can house from a few dozen to several thousand taste buds. (A dog has only about two thousand taste buds in its entire tongue.) Like other carnivores, cats prefer salty, bitter, and sour foods, while eschewing sweets. They have trouble digesting sugar and often end up with diarrhea when they eat it. Some domestic cats will occasionally succumb to a sweet tooth, favoring particularly chocolate (which is poisonous for them) and raisins. In general, though, cats prefer the fats and amino acids found in meat, though they often eat only certain parts of an animal, based on taste, or will choose a certain dry cat food by taste, if it has little aroma. When a cat does overrule its better judgment and samples something unpleasant or poisonous, it will salivate heavily to expel the offending tidbit. Domestic cats sometimes react to medicines this way.

Cat tongues are more than mere organs of taste, though. Anyone who has ever been treated to a licking knows that cats' tongues are rough. The backward-facing papillae that scratch your skin when the cat licks you are used as a built-in "comb" during grooming and to scrape meat off bones when consuming prey.

ARMED TO THE TEETH

 In a cat's role as hunter, the mouth is a lethal weapon, finely tuned for killing, filleting, and eating. Wild and domestic cats alike often use their canine teeth to break the prey's neck with a lethal nape bite. Their small incisors serve to strip off feathers or tear away tough skin, preparing the prey for eating. While a dog's jaws have the power to chew and grind meat, a cat's jaws lack the lateral mobility and crushing teeth required for these actions. Instead, the sharp and long third upper and second lower premolars, called the carnassials, slice through flesh and bone, shredding them into bite-size chunks. Although domestic felines don't need to rip through their prepared food, they often revert to the technique by instinct, tilting their heads to one side for powerful slicing bites.

Carnassials

Incisors

Canines

A female lion sinks its teeth into a fallen African buffalo. Three types of teeth fulfill separate functions: Canines kill, incisors fillet, and carnassials slice food into manageable pieces.

SENSE OF
· TOUCH ·

Of all the cat's finely tuned senses, its sensitivity to touch is perhaps the most sophisticated and wondrous. An array of pressure-sensitive touch receptors and a network of message-carrying nerves keep a feline in constant contact with its physical environment. Whether a cat is hunting, eating, playing, or simply sleeping, this unbroken communication with the world contributes mightily to its split-second reaction time.

WHISKERS

At the front line of the cat's sensory system are its tactile vibrissae, less formally known as whiskers. Facial whiskers complement the cat's already keen eyesight. Shorter carpal vibrissae, less prominent behind the wrists of the cat's front legs, help tree-climbing felines land safely and feel for prey while hunting. Any of these supersensitive antennae will be triggered into action at the slightest touch of an object, or even the subtle change in air current passing around it, whisking information to the cat's brain.

Located above the eyes, on the cheeks and muzzle, and on the chin and lips, the facial vibrissae are especially useful in the dark. Just as a cat's owner might rely on outstretched hands to grope around a pitch-black room, a feline navigates through the darkness of night with its whiskers leading the way. Whether in the wilderness or the family room, the facial vibrissae will register any minute shift in an air current, helping the cat skirt round a tree or the leg of a chair. These whiskers also serve as guides to the distance between two objects, telling the cat whether or not it can squeeze between them without getting stuck. Because facial whiskers are so closely related to nocturnal vision, those sported by domestic cats and wild night-hunters such as leopards are proportionally longer than those of daytime hunters such as cheetahs. Losing or breaking a whisker can diminish hunting prowess in a cat; the animal may even bump into objects at night until a new whisker grows to replace the absent one.

Cats can control the movement of their whiskers, especially the long and rigid whiskers, called mystacials, that protrude sideways from the muzzle. Because their eyes cannot focus well on close-up objects, such as prey they hold in their mouths, cats will rotate these whiskers down and around to check the captive for signs of life. The chin and lip, or mandibular, whiskers help the cat direct the killing nape bite. When eating or fighting, cats pull their whiskers back and out of food or harm's way. At night, they push the

Short whiskers located behind the "wrists" of the front legs, the carpal vibrissae help the cat to negotiate soft landings and feel for signs of life in prey trapped between its paws. Although these whiskers can be colored or even striped, they are almost always white, rendering them virtually invisible.

Opposite: Teeth bared, an aggressive Bengal tiger boasts the full glory of its abundant facial whiskers. Longer in nocturnal cats than in daytime hunters, the cat's facial whiskers serve as sensory aids for moving about in total darkness.

mystacials and mandibulars forward to use as sensors while they navigate through the darkness.

The superciliary whiskers above the eyes and the genal whiskers on the cheeks are less rigid and distinctly less mobile than the mystacials. They play an important, but less spectacular role. Whenever these whiskers are touched, they cause the lids to blink, thus protecting the eyes from injury.

SENSITIVE COAT AND SKIN

Scattered among the regular hairs of a cat's coat are larger single hairs, called tylotrichs, that pick up sensory information in the same way that whiskers do. Feline skin is covered by millions of touch receptors that are hypersensitive to pressure, air currents, and temperature. Considering the sensitivity of these receptors, cats have a surprising tolerance to heat. They even revel in it. The cat's African ancestry is often used to explain its pen-

A hungry bobcat twists its mandibular whiskers down to feel for signs of life in a trout just plucked from the water. As well as standing in for eyes, these whiskers also act like built-in tape measures, gauging the space between two objects to tell a cat how tight the opening is.

chant for warm firesides and hot car hoods—provided the temperature does not exceed 125 degrees Fahrenheit, or 52 degrees Centigrade. (Humans generally cannot withstand heat over 112 degrees Fahrenheit, or 44 degrees Centigrade.) Similarly, cats have a high pain threshold that can make it difficult for their owners to detect injuries.

The feline's nose and paw pads are very sensitive to temperature. Adapted for the hunt, the paw pads are loaded with touch receptors, but have little insulation against temperature extremes. Felines wield their sensitive paws to evaluate the texture and density of potential prey. After dispatching a victim, both wild and domestic cats are often observed pawing it to check for remaining signs of life before picking it up in their mouth. The extreme sensitivity of the cat's paw has led to some speculation about the feline's ability to feel vibrations or tremors in the ground preceding phenomena such as earthquakes. Animals have been known to exhibit strange behavior before such events, possibly because their highly refined sensitivity enables them to sense minute vibrations in their limbs.

A cat's reaction to physical contact depends on where it is touched. As any cat owner soon learns, cats enjoy being rubbed under the chin, behind the ears, and down the back to the base of the tail. Even in the wild, these are the same places cats nuzzle or groom each other. Touching tails, bellies, or feet, however, may provoke an unwelcome response. Contact with these areas is believed to produce discomfort, and no cat worth its salt puts up with human-induced discomfort for more than an instant before responding with a scratch or nip.

A domestic cat examines a fallen bird, checking its victim for signs of life. To avoid a surprise counterattack, a cat will paw its prey and brush it with downturned whiskers to make sure it is dead or stunned before picking it up in its mouth.

THE
·LIFE STAGES·

Very young kittens spend most of their time basking in the warmth of the feline huddle; hampered by a lack of mobility, they don't have much choice. But even once they are able to scamper away from their littermates, they still appreciate a group nap.

The taming of the miniature tiger has provided humankind with more than furry and loving companionship. Sharing our lives with the domestic cat has thrown open the window to the compelling and mysterious feline world, exposing the cycle of cat life to us so we may enjoy and learn from it firsthand. The cat's life span fits neatly, perhaps sadly, within a portion of our own. We can observe the development of cats from rambunctious kittenhood to the serenity of old age, with all of the ups and downs between. Often these stages mirror those of wild felines; sometimes they contradict.

At birth, for instance, a domestic kitten may weigh a mere two ounces. Its wild cousins weigh in at anywhere from five ounces for a lynx or bobcat to two or three pounds in the case of a tiger cub. Wild or domestic, though, newborn felines are entirely dependent on their mother for the first few weeks of life. Although the larger wild cat species, such as lions and Bengal tigers, typically are born open-eyed, albeit with immature visual capabilities, the eyes of most small cats usually remain shut for the first five to ten days. Nearly deaf, yet able to smell and sense heat with its nose, a newborn feline can sniff its way to the mother's nipples and zero in on the particular one that it calls its own. The babies will partake in one or two days' worth of immunity-building colostrum, followed by weeks of rich, nourishing mother's milk. In their first few days out of the womb, they may suckle for as long as eight hours at a time.

GROWING UP

For the first few weeks, both small wild and domestic newborns gain about three ounces in weight per week, while big-cat cubs gain proportionately more. For example, Siberian tiger cubs pack on the same amount in a day as their smaller cousins do in a week. To stimulate milk flow, kittens start to tread on the mother's breasts almost immediately after birth. They will continue to employ kneading as a comfort mechanism right into adulthood.

Feline mothers, both wild and domestic, are among the most protective in the animal world. They keep their kittens warm and clean, licking them head to toe—even the genitals are licked, both to clean them and to stimulate urination and defecation. To keep the nesting den clean and free of odors that might attract potential predators, the dutiful mother goes so far as to consume her litter's bodily wastes.

The helpless newborn cubs and kittens spend nearly all of their time on their bellies, their heads pressed against the ground. They don't have the strength to stand. The intensity of their early feeding, however, brings quick physical results. Although their limbs will not fully support them for some time yet, week-old domestic cats may crawl as much as a few feet at a time, usually to rejoin siblings in the perpetual huddle for warmth. Most cats can stand at around three weeks of age. At about the same time as the kittens' first teeth emerge, domestic mothers begin to wean their fold to solid foods. When they start to eat solids, the mother stops consuming their bodily waste and the kittens begin to bury their excretions in the ground or litter box. Not yet fully coordinated but with decidedly more stable limbs, domestic kittens at about four weeks of age slowly but surely begin to walk.

Like all cats, North American lynx kittens take their first uncertain steps at around four weeks of age. Gaining confidence on their feet, they quickly move from walking to running, jumping, and climbing.

Their tails, until now limp and of little use, also may become upright, assisting the new walkers in maintaining their balance on shaky feet. Before long, as their bodies fill out, the kittens start to run, jump, and climb with frenetic intensity. By six or seven weeks of age, domestic kittens usually are fully weaned and eating only solid foods. At eight weeks of age, many are taken from the litter to new homes, but twelve weeks is a better time for this separation—the extra time spent with the feline family is important for social development, as long as there is also interaction with humans.

THE SELF-TAUGHT CAT

By the age of four or five weeks, the physical skills of domestic kittens have progressed to the point where their play exhibits all of the energy and techniques of the hunt, complete with high-speed chases and pouncing. Around this time, if the mother is allowed to go outdoors, she may bring home dead prey to present to the litter. The sight and smell of the prey often triggers an innate reaction in kittens, causing them to become focused and considerably more aggressive. As the kittens mature, the mother will offer them stunned or injured prey, introducing live prey

A pair of African lions mate in what might be but one of a hundred such encounters in a day during the female's estrus. Growth of the male's distinctive mane starts when he is about three years of age. Related to his body's production of sex hormones, the mane recedes as he ages and disappears altogether if for some reason he becomes neutered.

once they are weaned to stimulate their interest and provide them with the opportunity to develop their killing skills.

EXTENDED KITTENHOOD

Although wild cats' physical development roughly parallels that of domestics, most of them achieve independence much later: at around three-and-a-half months of age, although the period can vary dramatically among species. Wild mothers must take a more cautionary approach in rearing their young. Because their survival is so closely linked to successful hunting, wild cubs need to master the art of stalking and killing before going off on their own. The animals preyed on in the wild are generally larger and far more combative than the domestic's field mouse or bird, so wild mothers take a sober, gradual approach to their offspring's hunting practice sessions, but the steps are the same as those of a suburban house cat. At first, the mother will bring prey back to the den and eat it in front of her young. Eventually, she will share some of her catch with them. As her offspring reach about three months of age, she will bring home stunned or injured animals for them to kill. Once their bodies have matured and their mouths are equipped with teeth, the cubs begin to accompany adults on hunting trips. Some species, such as tigers, take down prey, then stand aside to let their cubs move in for the kill.

Lion cubs have a cushier youth than most other types of wild cats, thanks to living in prides. Since food generally is provided for them by the adults, lion cubs seldom kill on their own before reaching twelve to fifteen months of age. Cheetahs, too, are late bloomers, reaching independence at about eighteen months of age.

STILL GROWING

At eight to ten months of age, domestic cats have completed most of their physical development. The breaking up of litters and the growing aggressiveness of what was once play weaken the ties that bind kitten siblings together. By the time they're about eighteen months old, they are drifting into adolescence. Cats will continue to play throughout their lives, but the frenetic energy of kittenhood gradually yields to a considerably more mellow, routine pace.

Like adolescent humans, cats continue to grow and develop through to adulthood, becoming sexually and intellectually more mature along the way. Because domestic cats are provided with food and shelter and usually are spayed or neutered while kittens, an artificial environment is created for them, a perpetual kittenhood of sorts. Depending on one's point of view, "fixed" domestic cats are either spared from or robbed of what would otherwise be a preoccupation defining much of their adolescence and adulthood: sexual activity.

A female domestic shows the swollen and low-slung belly of advanced pregnancy. Her breeding period is slightly longer than that of her wild cousins and is related to the amount of daylight. Cats near the equator are fertile almost all the time. Farther away from the equator, fertile periods are usually linked to spring and summer, when the days lengthen.

AGE OF DOMESTIC CATS IN HUMAN YEARS

Cat age	Human equivalent
6 months	10 years
1 year	15 years
2 years	24 years
3 years	28 years
4 years	32 years
5 years	36 years
6 years	40 years
7 years	44 years
8 years	48 years
9 years	52 years
10 years	56 years
11 years	60 years
13 years	68 years

Cats age quickly in human years when they are young, a process that slows as they get older.

A European lynx finds safe ground for her kitten. Such wild cats, especially those in the north, coordinate breeding with the availability of prey. When food is scarce, the females do not ovulate.

Just as they grow from helpless kittens to skilled hunters in a relatively brief period, cats quickly become sexually mature. The testes of males may become visible as early as four weeks of age. In domestic cats, males reach full sexual maturity, if they remain unaltered, between nine and twelve months of age. Most females reach sexual maturity at around ten months of age, although instances of much earlier pregnancies have been recorded. Many domestic breeds reach sexual maturity much later in life. Persians, in particular, may have trouble mating until well into their second year. Wild cats mature later as well. Cheetahs are sexually mature at close to two years, leopards at about thirty months, and tigers don't reach full maturity until three to five years of age.

Any breeding difficulties felines experience are usually the result of cats' solitary nature—a lack of available partners—rather than from physical incapability. The cycle of female sexual receptiveness is closely linked to exposure to daylight. Cats living near the equator can become pregnant at any time of the year. Dwellers of temperate climates are called seasonally polyestrus, meaning that they have many periods of heat, or estrus, within a certain season. These periods, which vary substantially among breeds and species, last for as little as two days and as long as two weeks. The Scottish wildcat, needing to give birth in the summer months when prey is plentiful in its northern environment, mates only in the early spring. In most of North America, domestic cats experience five- to six-day periods of estrus every twenty-one days from late winter through to mid to late summer.

For all cats, mating season can be hazardous. Depending on the density of the local male population, the competition for females can be fierce. Ferocious fighting often occurs between competing males or incompatible males and females. Especially among the big cats, serious and sometimes fatal injuries are quite common.

GROWING OLD

For domestic cats, improvements in veterinary medicine and care by owners have helped extend life expectancy well into the teen years, sometimes into the twenties. But cats age quickly in terms of human years. By the time they are six months old, they are the human equivalent of ten. Although cat-to-human age comparisons can vary, after the age of two, cats take on about four human years for every cat year. An eleven-year-old cat is the approximate equivalent of a sixty-year-old human, right down to the onset of aches and pains, health problems, declining fertility, and weight gain or loss. But in terms of changes in diet and health care, cats are considered "senior" at about eight years of age, equivalent to middle age in humans. Unless they live in zoos, where they receive regular veterinary care and a good diet, wild cats rarely live more than ten years. Malnutrition, parasites, and a host of other factors serve to shorten their decidedly harsher lives.

Large wild cats such as the African lion exhibit a greater variety of physical changes in their first few years than domestics and smaller wild cats. Their life expectancy also is much shorter; few live longer than a decade.

CAT
BEHAVIOR

· · ·

"A cat is a lion
in a jungle
of small bushes."

◆

ENGLISH PROVERB

Once a mother, always a mother. Older kittens still have some of their bathing done for them if they are living with their mother. Even unrelated cats may engage in mutual grooming. Through licking, cats exchange scents, which is thought to strengthen bonds. Allergy sufferers may rue cats' cleanliness since their reactions to cats actually are triggered by the high concentration of allergens released into the air from the saliva on the hairs, not by the hair itself.

Overleaf: Black-footed cat

SELF-
· GROOMING ·

Somewhere, far back in the evolutionary process, cats must have been imprinted with their own "golden rule" concerning fastidious cleanliness. When they are not sleeping, hunting, or eating, cats are likely to be primping meticulously. Felines, wild and domestic, are believed to spend up to one-third or more of their waking hours on preening. Far from being a vain preoccupation with appearance, however, the self-grooming vigilance of cats is a natural, reflexive behavior that is vital to their hygiene, health, and comfort.

TONGUE POWER

Grooming begins at the moment of birth. Immediately after delivering their litters, both wild and domestic females lick off the layer of membranes covering each cub or kitten, simultaneously cleaning and warming the newborns. By two or three weeks of age, the youngsters have the physical skills and the motivation to groom themselves.

The papillae-spiked tongue is a feline's primary preening tool. The moistening saliva and the rough tongue work together to scrub and align the hairs of its coat. And thanks to the incredible suppleness of its spine, a cat can lick almost every part of its body, except for the head and the face. To clean these places, cats lick their paws, then rub them over the face and head. If frustrated by a particularly rough, sticky, or dirty patch on its coat, a cat may resort to using its teeth to tear or bite off the offensive material— along with the hairs. As a consequence of all this grooming, felines ingest a considerable amount of dead hair, which they occasionally vomit as hairballs. Longhair domestic breeds are prone to impacting of hair in the intestinal tract and may need regular doses of a hairball remedy to avoid serious problems. Frequent grooming of both longhair and shorthair cats by owners helps by removing loose hair before it is swallowed.

WEATHERPROOF CAT

Grooming also regulates body temperature. In warm weather, the saliva acts as a coolant that can reduce a cat's body heat by as much as a third. In lower temperatures, the rakelike tongue aligns the hairs of the coat so that they retain heat and keep out cold. The licking and tugging at the coat hairs also stimulates the sebaceous glands on the surface of the skin to secrete a water-repelling oil that helps keep cats dry even in inclement weather.

Depositing saliva on the coat has yet another interesting purpose. When a cat scents itself with its own saliva, it may relieve its anxiety, offering a source of reassurance at tense moments. Cats appear to dispel fear, nervousness, and pain by seemingly inappropriate or frantic grooming—much like the human displacement behavior of nail biting or other nervous habits to overcome anxiety. A domestic cat's fall after a poorly timed jump, for instance, is often followed by impromptu preening.

High stress levels can cause cats to overgroom to the detriment of their health. The boredom of being confined indoors can drive a feline to excessive preening, sometimes to the point of baldness. A cat's stomach, lower back, and inner thighs are parts most at risk. An anti-anxiety medication from a vet may help, but getting to the bottom of the problem and finding ways to alleviate it are better solutions over the long term.

Licking a massive paw, a Bengal tiger prepares to wipe its face. Wild cats are as fastidious as domestic cats in their grooming. As a rule, a disheveled coat signals poor health. The dense, lush coats of some longhair domestics require daily brushing or combing by the cats' owners.

COMMUNICATION BY
·MARKING·

More than a simple feline manicure, scratching a fence, a tree trunk, or a couch releases scent from glands in the paws. Such marking by domestic felines isn't restricted to the setting of territory boundaries. Cats also will lay claim to other cats and to people, rubbing faces or other body parts to strengthen emotional bonds.

Self-preservation is at the root of almost all cat behavior. And if the feline's master plan—eat, procreate, and be merry—results in what may seem to be odd or unpleasant habits, so be it. Cats must assure themselves of sufficient food, avoid life-threatening conflicts, and promote their chances of successful mating. And one of the ways they accomplish these goals is to avail themselves of a highly specialized system of communication, one perfectly suited to their largely solitary lifestyle.

Since direct contact among felines in the wild seldom occurs, they must rely almost entirely on indirect methods of transmitting messages. Through a series of scent and visual markers, cats post their own distinctive "Keep Out" signs or "Welcome" mats to announce their own happy hunting and breeding grounds. Potential trespassers coming across such a marker must retreat or enter at their own risk. Outdoors in rural areas, the suburbs, or the urban jungle, domestic cats mark territory in much the same way.

All felines, wild or domestic, will mark territory for themselves, no matter how small. The size of the territory is dictated primarily by the availability of food. Where it's scarce, cats must stake out large tracts to satisfy their appetites. Where it's plentiful, a small territory will do. Social factors, however, also play a role in territory size. Sexually intact males will roam territories up to ten times larger than those of their female counterparts in order to find mates. Even domestic males who have been neutered exhibit some degree of the greater wanderlust demonstrated by males in the wild.

LEAVING THEIR MARK

At key locations, usually at the perimeters of a physical territory, cats leave declarations of their presence, some subtle, some not so subtle. But marking does more than simply lay claim to a space. It conveys messages that inform a stranger of the physical, social, and sexual status of the cat that made the mark and even tells how long ago the messages were left.

Spraying urine is the preferred marking method of all felines. The practice is most common, and the urine most pungent, in wild and unaltered domestic males, serving to keep the sexual behavior of less dominant males in check. The location of the penis near the male's posterior enables it to aim a spray of urine backward at strategic locations on a specific object, at a height a passing cat won't miss, or in a sheltered area where rain can't wash it away. Female cats spray, too, most notably to broadcast their presence in a

Caught in the act, with its tail held high, a serval emits a stream of pungent urine to mark its territory, an act that the males of this species can perform as many as forty-six times an hour. Female servals spray at about half that rate, more often if seeking to attract a mate.

Below: Cats are not especially known as tree huggers, but this Bengal tiger embraces a tree to mark it, rubbing to activate sweat glands on the paws and chin. This is one of the ways in which a single tiger may claim as much as 250 square miles of territory. Like all other cats, tigers will remark spots where they detect the smell of an interloper.

LAYING CLAIM

Feral cat colonies are an interesting example of felines claiming territory. With no human contact before the critical age of eight weeks, the offspring of stray domestic cats go wild and remain fearful of humans. These cats band together and occupy a certain area. While their fate commonly is to be caught and euthanatized, animal welfare groups such as Alley Cat Allies have created programs of trapping, sterilizing, and releasing the cats back into their territory, with caretakers making sure they get enough to eat. Their numbers grow very little, and they form a stable population in their own territory. This prevents a new group of ferals from entering the area, with the resulting cat fights and smelly marking behavior that cause a problem for people living nearby.

Feral cats partake in a meal put out by a concerned benefactor.

territory and their readiness to mate. The appearance of a new feline in the neighborhood often triggers a spate of spraying by all the others. Sterilizing domestic cats at six months of age or earlier—before they reach puberty—will short-circuit this smelly behavior before it becomes a habit more than 90 percent of the time.

In a similar behavior, some larger and more dominant wild cats may openly display their droppings, marked by scent glands near the anus, in prominent locations. Smaller wild felines usually bury their solid wastes to avoid being tracked by larger predators, but may leave them exposed, particularly in a disputed territory, as a show of ownership.

All felines possess scent-producing glands on their head and muzzle, on their neck and shoulders, at the base of their tail, and on their paws. As the cats patrol their territories, they will rub against objects with these parts of their bodies, stimulating the glands to deposit their personal scent. When

Although they aren't true communal hunters like lions, related young adult male cheetahs will sometimes hunt in packs when food is abundant.

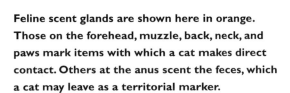

Feline scent glands are shown here in orange. Those on the forehead, muzzle, back, neck, and paws mark items with which a cat makes direct contact. Others at the anus scent the feces, which a cat may leave as a territorial marker.

quite at ease within its territory, even a big cat such as a lion, a tiger, or a cheetah will roll in delightful abandon to mark the ground.

Rising on its haunches to scratch a tree, a fence post, or even a piece of furniture, a feline not only hones its claws, but releases a faint scent produced by the glands between its toes. The claw marks draw attention to the scent. Wild and domestic cats will scratch the same object routinely to strengthen the scent on it. This behavior is deeply ingrained, but most house cats can be taught to use a scratching post instead of furniture.

ALL IN THE FAMILY

What happens if more than one cat claims the same territory? If food is plentiful enough to sustain all of the felines within it, the area may be shared quite peacefully. Lions are likely to have formed prides because of the number and size of their prey. The members of a pride can cooperate

Communicating intimidation with its body language, a defensive cat will literally back away from the aggressor, which is often lord of the domain. Neutering male cats reduces their territorial aggressiveness.

in taking down larger, often combative prey, such as a three-thousand-pound giraffe, and still have enough food to sustain themselves until the next hunt. The largest prides, often containing as many as twenty to thirty lions, can be found in East Africa, where prey is plentiful. In desert regions, where food is much harder to come by, lions live in smaller groups or even just in pairs.

Occasionally, other cat species also break the mold of the solitary hunter. Male cheetahs and tigers, for example, are known to group with others of their own kind. In these units, called coalitions, the fearsome duo or trio claim territory together, especially where prey is scarce but large in size and the hunt must be carried out in wide-open, potentially dangerous terrain.

SCRAPS WITH LITTLE SCRAPING

Territorial disputes are at the root of many conflict between felines, wild or domestic. Altercations between domestics are far more common than confrontations in the wild because of the artificially dense environments of the cities and suburbs where most cats reside. Sexually intact males are involved in the greatest number of disputes, but all cats, wild or domestic, male or female, may become embroiled in conflicts.

In almost all feline flare-ups, one cat is the aggressor and the other is the defensive cat. Because these fights can be extremely violent and possibly life-threatening, even the aggressor seems to realize that it's better to avoid a dispute than to risk injury from combat.

When two cats cross paths, the aggressor frequently asserts itself immediately, often boldly approaching the interloper to sniff its tail. Through hissing, spitting, bared teeth, and other intimidating or defensive postures, cats consciously and unconsciously reveal their intentions, all in slow motion. The apprehensive cat may betray its fear in a series of defensive displays, including drawing back slowly from the aggressor. Many feline flaps degenerate into nothing more than lengthy face-offs until the defensive cat eventually breaks eye contact to flee. While scurrying from the scene of the showdown, however, the vanquished may receive a decisive bite on the tail.

LAST-DITCH COMBAT

Sometimes the call to arms can't be denied. Most outright fights occur when the defensive animal is cornered and unable to flee or fails to communicate through body language that it is backing down. The aggressive cat expects the defensive cat to hiss, spit, or snarl. And when the fearful cat lies down and turns onto its back, it is taking up the typical defensive posture. With outstretched paws and claws bared, the fearful cat is in the best position to defend itself and inflict the most damage on its opponent. Circling menacingly, the aggressor will angle its body so that it appears to be larger, all the while searching for an opening to lunge at its prone opponent. This odd crablike sideways dance may continue for quite some time. Depending on

WAYWARD CATS

Both wild and domestic cats display an amazing homing sense that allows them to navigate easily through and beyond their sometimes vast territories. In fact, many different animal species demonstrate varying levels of this ability, from homing pigeons and migrating birds to sea mammals and even bees. Although not much is known about this built-in, biological radar system, an innate sense of time and direction as well as the ability to navigate by using the stars and the sun are thought to be possible explanations for it. Recent studies on felines reveal that older cats, in particular, may be guided by the influence of Earth's electromagnetic fields on traces of iron contained in their brains. Too numerous to be dismissed as mere coincidences, dozens of well-documented stories abound about domestic cats somehow journeying incredibly long distances to find their way back home to loved ones.

Spirited play or premeal tension can provoke scraps between domestic cats of the same household. The feet-up pose of the cat at right above is typical of a defensive cat.

Opposite: Rearing tigers take paw swipes at each other in a fierce battle, potentially inflicting wounds deep enough to be fatal. Male lions vying for a pride's leadership sometimes fight to the death.

the defender's ability to maintain its guarded position, the aggressor might actually tire of waiting and give up. If not, the fight is likely to be brief but furious, marked by piercing cries, scratching, and biting. The aggressor will attempt to grasp its opponent by the head and bite its neck. Frantically pedaling all four legs, the defender will try to toss the attacker aside. At the first break, the defensive cat usually bolts, with its proverbial tail between its legs.

Equally aggressive felines, whether wild or domestic, wage war in a straightforward, more violent fashion. After a face-to-face confrontational show of strength, one cat attacks the other. An intense, ferocious battle ensues, remarkable for the loud shrieks, the vicious bites and raking of back claws, and the short period of time between bouts. Cats can be thrown surprisingly long distances during these titanic struggles. The fur literally flies. Some felines stubbornly persist in warring with each other several times over an extended period until one of them either leaves the territory or learns its lesson and avoids the other.

CAT
· LANGUAGE ·

A quick look at this open-mouthed domestic cat tells you everything you need to know: He has a complaint. One can almost hear his sharp vowel-filled, "Meow!"

Listen to cats. You may be surprised by how much they can communicate despite their limited vocalizations. Along with their long-distance olfactory dialogues and close-up exchanges of body-language signals, felines possess their own vocabulary of sounds. Long considered as a marginal element in the communication system of cats, their spoken language is surprisingly evolved and effective, especially in domestics.

In the wild, big cats roar to lay claim to territory and intimidate interlopers. Small wild felines prefer less conspicuous ways of communicating that won't alert predators to their presence. Even if they did yearn to let loose an earth-shattering roar, they couldn't. The bony composition of a structure called the hyoid that attaches the larynx to the skull severely limits the small cat's vocal range, domestic as well as wild. In big felines, the hyoid is composed of cartilage and allows for a flexibility that, coupled with a large chest cavity, produces far greater resonance. But despite volume limitations, small cats still vocalize. When confronting rivals before or during a fight, all felines find some combination of growls, high-pitched threats, spits, and hisses to tell their opponents exactly what they think.

SPEAKING CAT

Studies disagree on the actual number of feline vocalizations, but three categories of sounds generally are recognized: vowels, murmurs, and high-intensity sounds. The classic "meow," originating in the kitten's plaintive or anxious "mew," contains vowel sounds. Adult cats express variations of this vocalization to state their demands for food or attention, register complaints, and convey bewilderment. A slight alteration in the tone, pace, or punctuation changes the meaning. Murmurs are usually happy sounds, purrs, trills, and chirrups of greeting or contentment, uttered through closed mouths. The feline's repertoire of high-intensity sounds, such as angry or fearful hissing, spitting, growling, and shrieking, is most often directed at other cats. And the ultimate purpose of the wail of a female in heat is to attract males.

Making allowances for our inability to read their visual and odor clues and obliging of our penchant for vocalizing, domestic cats have adapted remarkably well to human social impositions by turning their normal volumes up a notch for our benefit. Not such a hardship, when all is said and done, since we respond by offering food, opening doors, and administering caresses and satisfying ear scratches.

The ability to roar distinguishes big cats from their diminutive counterparts. A roaring male lion emits the loudest sound that a feline can make—as high as 114 decibels, as loud as a blaring car horn.

AUDITORY "PURRFECTION"

 We might like to interpret a cat's purr as tuneful expression of gratitude for our constant care and affection, but the soothing rumblings stem from more practical origins. Purring is believed to arise from the feline mother's need to comfort her newborn kittens. Mothers emit purrs and elicit them from their young as a form of mutual reassurance. In the wild, where predators pose a threat, this feline auditory version of a pacifier or a security blanket keeps cubs composed and quiet so that they escape detection. It is also in the mother cat's best self-interest to have a calm, reassured group of sucklers since the sharp young claws of boisterous or anxious kittens can injure teats during feeding.

Like the other closed-mouth murmur sounds of cats, purring is created by the resonating of the "false" vocal chords alongside the larynx. Most cat species can emit some sort of a purr. Cheetahs purr in much the same way as small cats. But instead of the continuous double-stroke purr with which we are most familiar, other big cats such as the tiger generate a booming, single-stroke purr, a sound that is sometimes called chuffing.

Although purring is widely taken to be the cat's way of conveying contentment, sick, injured, or fearful cats sometimes purr also. Researchers are not sure why cats purr in these stressful situations.

BODY ·LANGUAGE·

A fearful and defensive mountain lion snarls and flattens its ears. Often the backs of the ears are turned forward, signaling aggression. The communication is even more dramatic among cats with distinctive ear markings, such as the pronounced tufts of lynxes, caracals, and several domestic breeds, and the white "eye" spots of some tigers.

Unlike the extremely social pack-dwelling canines, felines in their natural environment often go for lengthy periods without face-to-face encounters with others of their kind. They have very little need for a system of direct visual communication. But when cats do happen to meet, a universal feline body language communicates information.

Most of what we know about the feline's body language stems from the observations of cats, wild or domestic, in conflict. The usually aloof animal sends out a variety of physical messages when it confronts another feline. Its nervous system automatically registers stress levels and produces physical signals that reveal whether the animal is relaxed, tolerant, fearful, apprehensive, defensive, or aggressive. Properly interpreting these reactions tells us when and how to approach and handle cats *(page 105)*.

FIGHT OR FLIGHT

Feline body language is not intended to deliver refined signals. The messages are broad, such as, "Leave me alone." Triggered by fear, a rush of adrenaline causes the cat's back and tail to arch and the hair to bristle. This familiar Halloween-cat pose makes the frightened feline appear more physically imposing. Although the raised hackles may outwardly convey strength and a readiness to do battle, the communication is really designed to dissuade rather than provoke potential attackers. When cats, wild and domestic, are fearful or nervous and defensive, their ears flatten or twitch and their eyes dilate fully to take in as much of their surroundings as possible.

The body language of confident, aggressive cats is exhibited in response to direct confrontations, with intruders on their territory, perhaps, or run-ins with smaller cats. The pupils narrow to slits for better depth perception as they stare down opponents; their ears stand up, facing forward or folded so that the backs are seen head-on. With its rear end held high and tail slung low, an aggressor will often approach the defensive cat in a prancing sideways motion that creates the illusion of being larger.

Not all feline body language is straightforward, however. Messages sometimes seem to be mixed or conflicting. Since most of a cat's body language is not intentional but a reflexive response to stimulus, anger and fear may elicit the same physical response. It is not unusual, for instance, for a fearful feline to display signs of aggression and vice versa.

Above: A domestic cat strikes an intimidating pose. Triggered by reflex, arrector muscles cause its hairs to stand on end. The raised hackles, coupled with the arched back and sideways stance, produce the illusion of a larger, more imposing cat.

The tolerance, even affection, of these young African lions is evident in their relaxed ear positions, facial expressions, and postures. Since lions coexist in prides, they are more practiced and comfortable with body language than their solitary feline counterparts.

FELINE
·INTELLIGENCE·

Most kittens will find the litter box through exploration on their own, without any input from another cat or a human. They eliminate in litter, soil, or sand because these materials can be pushed around by their paws and thereby feel right for this purpose. The scratching that comes after (and often before) is an innate behavior, meant to hide the waste from predators.

Pet owners love to boast about the cleverness of their furry companions. Dog and cat lovers, in particular, seem to relish unending debates over which animal is "smarter." Dog owners often cap their arguments with the fact that dogs have the ability to perform tricks, while cat people counter with the claim that their pets are too intelligent to perform on command. In truth, such methods of pet comparison are futile animal-world versions of mixing apples and oranges. Dogs are pack animals, motivated by a strong need to follow and please the pack's "top" dog (or a human master) in order to receive praise. The solitary cat answers to no one and is motivated by the need to survive. And while trainability may not be the feline's forte, cleverness and adaptability certainly are.

Incredibly resourceful and self-reliant, the species has survived thousands of years in radically different environments and living conditions. Even domestic cats will show a crafty, strong-willed, and versatile nature. In cases where they are cast out or abandoned by uncaring and irresponsible owners, some of these strays actually continue to survive and multiply, although due to disease, malnutrition, and injuries, they live for only a fraction of the life span of a cat that is properly cared for. Are these feline survival traits the markings of an unintelligent creature? Not in the least.

PRACTICE MAKES PERFECT

Many of the cat's remarkable mental and physical abilities are dismissed as simply instinctive. However, just as humans are born with innate communication skills but must learn over time to master a language, cats refine many of their inborn abilities through practice. The widely-held belief that they learn through observation and imitation of their mother or other cats is now being called into question. Cats do learn, but in a different way than do humans or dogs; they have a special kind of intelligence.

Cats are preprogrammed to interact with the environment in certain ways, and they have exceptional skills for survival, such as in tracking prey. The feline mother plays a role by giving her kittens or cubs chances to learn. In the case of hunting, she brings prey to them, first dead, later alive, thereby providing them with the raw materials needed to practice what their instincts prompt them to do. They are learning by themselves, and even cats without these opportunities as kittens can become proficient and efficient hunters through practice on their own.

Cats go through a "sensitive" period of socialization between the ages of two weeks and about two months, where they have a tendency to accept and socialize with other animals with which they are raised. This period of familiarization with people and other pets (cats, dogs, and even mice and birds) is vital for domestic kittens so they will peg these classes of animals as potential companions, rather than as prey or to be feared, for the rest of their lives. The mother will have some influence here, bringing species to be considered as prey for her young to eat.

The well-known curiosity of cats is another aspect of feline hardwiring, and they figure out much about their surroundings through this investigative tendency. A cat's first forays from its mother and littermates prove to be fertile learning grounds. Early explorations teach the cat valuable lessons about which objects, or even other animals, can be approached and inspected and which should be avoided altogether. However, this same curiosity can get cats into trouble and owners need to be watchful, especially of kittens as they explore the home.

All felines, wild or domestic, are playful by nature. Through play, kittens not only refine their physical skills, but also practice and perfect their hunting instincts. By the time they're five to seven weeks old, kittens are physically developed and coordinated enough to begin playing harder.

A mother cheetah presents her offspring with a young impala. These babies will develop prey preferences based on their mother's diet and from their experience of the prey she provides for them. The young cheetahs will not actually hunt with their mother until they are much older.

A domestic kitten toys with a dead mouse. Through practice, young cats develop their physical skills and perfect their hunting techniques, at the same time releasing some of their boundless energy.

Play-fighting with other members of the litter is the most natural outlet for the kitten or cub's newfound energies and physical abilities. Although the high-spirited roughhousing of littermates may not always seem like play, especially between young wild cats, injuries are extremely rare. Even at this tender age, all cats know the difference between play- and real fighting. During these frenetic wrestling matches, cats first develop the techniques that they will use for the rest of their lives. The pounces, paw swats, and scoops they will later use in taking on prey and in defending or attacking in territorial disputes are used first on the chins and tails of littermates. Stalking behavior often first surfaces as stealthy attacks on the twitching tail of an unsuspecting playmate. Domestic kittens taken from their littermates early in life need extra attention from their owners to make up for the lack of feline stimulation. Toys can be used to rouse a kitten's interest, uncovering inborn hunting behaviors for refinement through practice.

A CAT NEVER FORGETS

Once attained, even if by accident or trial and error, most knowledge is retained for life, thanks to the cat's excellent memory. Even hunting techniques buried under years of neglect in the brain of the well-fed house cat will be recalled with ease should the feline ever have to fend for itself for some reason. Cats are quite easily frightened, and they retain a very strong memory of the incident. All it takes is one face-to-face encounter with a growling dog to convince a feline that the entire canine species is best avoided forever. However, positive experiences are just as easily stored and recalled, particularly if they have to do with food or play. As any cat owner knows, domestic felines do respond to familiar sounds, such as can openers, the rattling of their dry-food bags, or the crinkly noise of a favorite toy. Many of them also have an uncanny ability to know the hour of their regular breakfast time, waking up their owner if he or she tries to sleep in.

TRAINING AND TRICKS

As the feline psyche has become better understood, animal handlers have had more success in training felines to perform in film and television, once the exclusive domain of the dog. Although they won't perform for pats on the head and "good-cat" praise from their owners, some felines, if properly motivated, can be trained to do a wide variety of tricks, from opening doors and jumping through hoops to turning on lights. In what psychologists call operant conditioning, a cat will repeat a behavior for a food reward. This is best achieved if the desired behavior is fun for the cat, even more so if the person doing the training is its usual food provider. More amenable to rewards of food than domestic felines, large wild cats such as lions and tigers have performed in circuses for centuries. Sadly, there were times when unspeakably cruel punishment was used interchangeably with rewards of fresh meat to "tame" these unpredictable and potentially dangerous wild felines into performing desired tricks.

"A cat bitten once by a snake dreads even rope."

◆

ARAB PROVERB

Peering through a hoop, a domestic feline eyes a food treat held out on a stick. With patience, practice, and continued temptation, the cat may eventually jump right through the ring to collect its tasty reward.

SLEEPING
·FELINES·

Cats are the undisputed sleep champions of the animal kingdom. Only the notoriously slow-footed sloth, which sleeps away an estimated 80 percent of its life, catches more shut-eye. Although the number of hours a cat spends sleeping can vary considerably among individuals, felines spend an average of sixteen hours per day in slumberland. No one is quite sure why, but the solitary cat's lifestyle, punctuated by frenetic, energy-draining bursts of hunting and playing, is thought to necessitate this form of energy conservation. In fact, sleeping wild cats are often described as "resting for the hunt." Because they consume so much energy in taking down large, wily prey, wild cats usually sleep even more than domestic cats. Female lions, the primary hunters of the species, have been known to rest or sleep as much as twenty hours a day.

The cat's diet is also thought to be a contributing factor to its ability to sleep so much. Large grazing herbivores need to feed for hours on end to get enough nutrition to survive and generally only have time to sleep four or five hours a day. The protein-rich diet of the feline, on the other hand, requires no such investment of time for daily sustenance. Instead of eating all day, the cat can stock up on sleep for its short, high-energy chases.

ON THE PROWL

As some sleep-deprived cat owners already know, many felines like to wander a good part of the night. Because the small rodents it naturally preys on are most active at night, the cat also became a nocturnal creature, complete with night vision and a sleep pattern that reserves a good part of the daylight hours for dozing. Of all the wild-cat species, only the lion and cheetah hunt during the day.

Because we have modified much of their behavior by providing food and locking them indoors for hours on end, the greater part of a domestic cat's periods of wakefulness is now distributed throughout the day. But during the bewitching hours around both dusk and dawn, when the call of the wild is at its strongest, cats instinctively take up positions near windows, pace the corridors of confinement, push open cat doors, or harass humans. Pet owners who leave their cats at home alone all day are more likely to be disturbed by night prowling. Already inclined to snooze away part of the day, cats will sleep even more in a boring environment. It's not unusual for cat owners to return home from a day at work to find their

Seemingly sound asleep, a domestic cat actually is still on the alert, capable of detecting the slightest motion or sound. Should the need arise, a feline will awaken in a flash to appraise its surroundings, then just as quickly fall back to sleep.

Opposite: This group of slumbering African lions must believe in there being safety in numbers. Solitary wild felines aren't likely to risk sleeping out in the open, especially in broad daylight.

Above: All felines stretch out in an effort to cool down and curl up into a tight ball to retain heat. But only a very secure cat, such as this young domestic shorthair, will sleep with its vulnerable belly exposed.

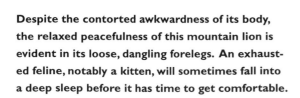

Despite the contorted awkwardness of its body, the relaxed peacefulness of this mountain lion is evident in its loose, dangling forelegs. An exhausted feline, notably a kitten, will sometimes fall into a deep sleep before it has time to get comfortable.

sleepy-eyed pets curled up exactly where they were in the morning. But all this daytime sleep makes cats ever more alert and ready for action come nightfall, just when the human members of the household want to curl up.

CATNAPS

It's no coincidence that your cat seems to wake you from a deep sleep with a paw poke on your nose at exactly the same time, usually very early, every single morning. Like most animals, cats are affected by circadian rhythm; their daily activity patterns are biologically attached to the rotating Earth's twenty-four-hour cycle. But the similarities end there. Humans and most other mammals sleep an average of eight hours out of twenty-four, and usually all at once. Cats don't have these prolonged periods of sleep, but scatter their sixteen or so hours of shut-eye throughout the day and night in what are popularly referred to as catnaps. However, like slumbering humans, the cat's sleep pattern consists of a cycle of light and deep sleep *(see at right)*.

SLEEPERS AWAKE

As solitary hunters, most cats in the wild have had to evolve into very alert sleepers for their own protection. Their extraordinarily well-developed senses of hearing, touch, and smell are never turned off by sleep. At the slightest whisper in the grass or the faintest scent on the breeze, a feline awakens and is ready to spring into action. After a quick evaluation of the situation, the cat can either drop off to sleep again or further investigate the reason for its disturbance.

When they do emerge naturally from a sleep, most cats go through a waking ritual of sorts. They usually start with a big yawn, then they stretch the limbs, scratch behind the ears and arch the back. Often they will work out on a natural or man-made scratching post and may groom themselves for a while after waking.

CRASHED CAT

For comfort and security, most cats choose the places they sleep very carefully. Depending on the season and environment, they may select dozing areas for keeping either warm or cool. House cats are particularly renowned for huddling under heaters and on top of radiators or even heat-emanating television sets. Outdoors, their concern for their own safety may mean they head for a hiding spot in tall vegetation. Inside, cats often lie on the beds or even on the clothing of their owners. It is thought that the familiar scent makes them feel secure, but the attraction may just be the convenience and softness of the pile of clothes. Domestic cats, to the delight of their human companions, sometimes satisfy the desire for both safety and warmth by napping in a friendly and familiar lap.

THE SCIENCE OF SLEEPING

 Because they are such great sleepers, cats have long been the favorite subjects of scientists studying brain activity during sleep. French researchers recently attributed the onset of sleep to a hormone called melatonin that is released in the brain by the gene responsible for controlling circadian rhythm. Once triggered, the sleep cycle of the cat follows a pattern similar to that of humans—both are marked by phases of light and deep sleep. Light sleep lasts anywhere from ten minutes to half an hour. During this period, the cat is still very alert to its surroundings and its muscles have not yet fully relaxed. Deep sleep follows light sleep, but lasts only seven to ten minutes. Brain monitoring still shows a surprising amount of activity in the cat's brain during deep sleep. During deep sleep, both humans and cats display body twitching and rapid eye movement, or R.E.M., which characterize periods of dreaming. Although any attempt to interpret cat dreams is pure speculation, cats likely replay the day's events in their mind just as humans do. After deep sleep, the cat returns to another period of light sleep. The light-sleep/deep-sleep cycle continues until the cat wakes up naturally or is rudely awakened by a sudden change in its environment.

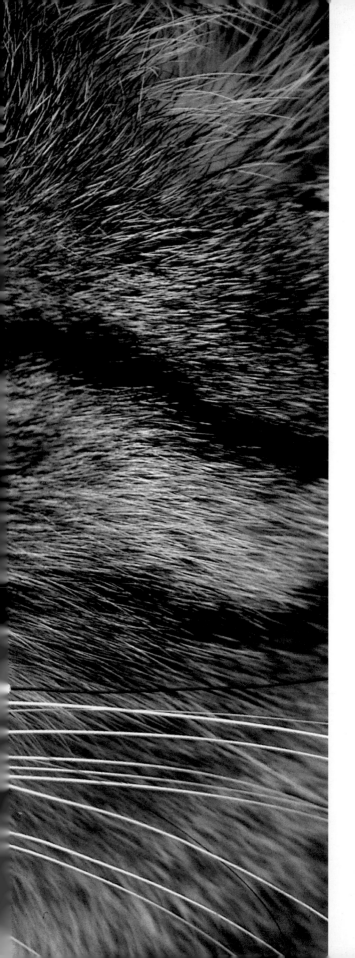

CHOOSING

A

CAT

· · · ·

"I love cats because I love my home,
and little by little
they become its visible soul."

·

JEAN COCTEAU

BEING

· RESPONSIBLE ·

Are you ready? Any doubts? Now is the time to consider what's involved. Before adopting any pet, cat or otherwise, you must realize that you are making a long-term commitment. You have to be prepared to care for the animal for its entire life. Even when things change in your life, be it deciding to live with someone, relocating to another city or country, or having children, you should be willing to make the necessary concessions to ensure your pet continues to have the kind of life to which it becomes conditioned. Even going on vacation means making arrangements for someone to look after your pet. If you work an inordinate number of hours or travel often, it may be better to wait until your life is more settled, or you might consider adopting more than one cat so they'll have company and stimulation. It's true that most cats accept being left alone much more easily than dogs, but rarely are they the aloof, completely independent creatures that many people seem to believe they are. Cats thrive on attention and affection that comes from *you*.

WEIGHING THE CONSEQUENCES

Don't make a hasty decision. Even if you've decided you're ready to open your home and your heart to a pet, do some research to see what having a cat is all about and whether a cat is the ideal pet for you. Don't choose a cat by default. If you really want a dog, for instance, but feel that it would be too much work, perhaps you should put on the brakes. The worst thing you can do is adopt an animal and find that it doesn't live up to your expectations. This often leads to neglect or a sad visit to the humane society to give the cat up. If you need to learn what having a cat is all about, spend some time with friends who have cats and pump them for information. Offering to cat-sit or fostering for your local animal shelter are excellent ways to practice all aspects of feline care and to spend time interacting with a cat. You may also find out whether or not you're allergic to cats before you take the plunge. But a word of warning: Sometimes allergies don't surface until you've lived with a cat for a while.

While every cat has a distinct personality, all tiny tigers have certain common characteristics—and you pretty much have to accept them. Your cat may or may not develop bad habits, such as biting, but certain behaviors come to domestic cats in a straight genetic line from their wild relatives: scratching and climbing. Although you may be able to modify some behavior *(page 116)* by introducing such things as scratching posts, you must be prepared to live with other habits. For example, your cat may like to jump from

Who said cats are standoffish and independent? The fact is they usually want to be where the action is, and often get up on the table to "help" you with whatever you are doing. This family pet is the very embodiment of contentment, eyes squeezed shut and head pressed against his human friend.

Overleaf: Silver tabby domestic shorthair

the sofa to a position of security atop the nearby bookcase in order to survey his domain. Rather than discouraging him, you should give in to his need to get up high; just be sure to remove any breakables from the top shelf. Also keep in mind that having any kind of a pet involves a certain amount of mess. In the case of a cat, this means hair shed on the furniture and on your clothes, litter tracked out of the box, and the occasional hairball left on the carpet. Are you willing to put up with these annoyances in exchange for the companionship and amusing antics of a cat?

Your pet will count on you to provide a safe environment, stimulation and exercise through play, good-quality food, a clean litter box, grooming, and regular veterinary care. But all this costs money. Aside from the initial expenses for accessories and the vet care a new cat requires (vaccinations and neutering or spaying), you'll likely spend at least four to five hundred dollars a year on food, litter, a veterinary checkup, professional grooming, and teeth-cleaning by a vet. This doesn't include potential emergency vet care, which can run into hundreds of dollars or the additional veterinary expenses of an older cat. And cats often live from fifteen to twenty years.

A cat can be a wonderful playmate and friend for children, and will give you the chance to teach youngsters to love and respect animals. One word of caution: Never get a cat for your children unless you want one yourself. The bottom line is that *you* are responsible for the cat's well-being. While children can help with cat care, they often go through stages where other interests take precedence over caring for the cat. An adult must be in charge and prepared to take over all the chores whenever necessary.

A feline friend will enrich your life, bringing you years of pleasure. But remember, you are inviting a living, sentient being into your home. The commitment is real, so remember the rule: Resist impulse!

A GUIDE TO CHILDREN'S CAT-CARE RESPONSIBILITIES

AGE	DUTIES
Up to 5	Putting premeasured amount of cat food into bowl; helping adult with brushing; helping buy or make cat toys; playing with cat (with adult present to teach gentleness).
5 to 8	Helping with grooming; playing with cat; putting out food and water bowls under adult supervision.
9 to 12	With adult overseeing: feeding and refilling water bowl; grooming; removing waste from litter box. Also observing cat to help in early detection of physical abnormalities or changes that might require veterinary attention.
Teen years	With adult checking up to make sure tasks are done: taking over feeding and grooming; removing waste from litter box; regularly washing and refilling litter box. Accompanying adult to vet and helping to administer any care or medication required.

LIVING WITH CAT ALLERGIES

 The primary allergen in cats is found in their saliva and is spread by their constant grooming. A secondary type of allergen is produced in the sebaceous glands and secreted onto the skin and fur. These cells are shed as "dander" and add to house dust.

Does being allergic to cats mean that you can never live with one? Not necessarily. There are differing degrees of reactions and you should see an allergist for advice and possible treatment. While severe reactions such as asthma usually rule out life with a cat, there are things you can do to lessen the effects.

◆ Wash your hands after touching the cat.

◆ Buy allergy-proofing products that can be applied to the cat with a damp cloth, or bathe the cat weekly.

◆ Keep your cat out of your bedroom, or wash the bedding very frequently.

◆ Try to keep your cat out of carpeted rooms and away from upholstered furniture. If that's not possible, remove carpets and cover furniture with sheets that you can launder easily and often.

◆ Vacuum frequently, preferably with a vacuum equipped with a HEPA (high-efficiency particulate air) filter, wearing a dust mask.

◆ Wash the cat's sleeping blanket often.

◆ Leave grooming and litter-box cleaning to nonallergic members of the household.

◆ Invest in an air purifier.

THE SELECTION
·PROCESS·

If there is a trick to choosing the perfect cat, it is to think through what is best for you and your living situation before even laying eyes on any irresistible bundles of fur. The goal is to avoid an impulsive decision that you may later regret. Start by taking your lifestyle into account. How much time do you really have to devote to looking after a pet? If you aren't home much, a pair of shorthaired adult cats may be ideal for you. They can amuse each other when you're not there and they don't need much grooming. Longhaired cats might not be a good idea for you. They need a regular grooming routine. Aside from hair length and number of cats, you will also need to consider such factors as age, gender, and personality type and whether you want to allow your cat to go outdoors.

Cats come in all shapes, sizes, and colors, virtually all of them appealing. But when you decide to bring a cat into your life, don't be swayed by appearance alone. Consider the whole package and choose the kitten or cat that best suits your situation and lifestyle.

The curiosity of a kitten combined with its energy and athletic skills means that it will be into—and up—everything. If you adopt a kitten, you must be prepared to have a furry whirlwind sweep through your house—that is, until it falls into a deep slumber, often in midstride.

The ideal companion for a senior is another senior, but of the feline variety. An adult cat, with its calmer disposition, is usually a much better choice than a kitten for the older owner.

KITTEN VERSUS ADULT

If your first instinct is to adopt a kitten rather than an adult cat, you aren't alone. Kittens are cute, playful, and just about as appealing as you can get. But a kitten's seemingly limitless energy is not something you can turn off when you've had enough. Because everything is new and fascinating to them, kittens get into more mischief than adults. Their tiny needlelike claws can do some serious damage when they climb the curtains or scale your leg to join you up on your chair. And a very young kitten, like any baby, requires a lot of attention and mothering, and may be prone to health problems.

One of the reasons people prefer kittens to adult cats is that they fear an older cat may already have some bad habits; they think they will be able to "train" a kitten as if it were a dog. The truth is that the majority of excited, unruly kittens are not very receptive to any type of behavior modification, much less actual obedience-training. An adult cat may, in fact, be more receptive to patient correction of bad habits than a frisky kitten (page 116).

There are several advantages to choosing an adult cat. First and foremost, it will be calmer, a real plus if there are young or elderly members of the household. Small kittens are generally too fragile to be handled by a youngster, and are more likely to scratch or bite the child, especially one who is too young to read the kitten's signals. As a rule, if you have children four years old or younger, consider only kittens more than six months of age. Kittens eight months old or older are even better with youngsters; and even at this age, they are still very playful. Senior owners often find kittens

OUTDOOR CATS

The risks to letting your cat roam freely outside increase if you live in a busy, urban area with heavy car traffic and stray cats. If you deem your area to be safe, protect your outdoor cat as much as possible. First of all, the cat must not be declawed. He may need to defend himself. Do not let him out until he is very familiar with your house, which becomes his territorial base. Also ensure that all necessary vaccinations are up to date. Outdoor cats—who could catch diseases from other cats—need some inoculations that indoor cats do not. Also look into flea control. An outdoor cat must be sterilized so that you do not contribute to the problem of cat overpopulation. This also helps males stay closer to home; and since they won't venture off in search of female cats,

they will be less likely to get into fights with other males competing for the same mate.

It is best to keep your cat in at night, which is the most dangerous time for cats to be out. Get him used to staying in after you give him supper.

Make sure your cat is properly identified in case he gets lost: A collar and ID tag combined with a microchip implant covers all the bases *(page 206)*. Buy the breakaway or elastic-type collar to avoid strangulation and keep it on him at all times.

Before allowing your cat to set off into the outside world, be aware of the risks he'll face and make sure he is protected as much as possible.

"The cat is domestic only as far as it suits its own ends."

♦

SAKI

---

too active, whereas a placid adult or senior cat, while still playful, can be the perfect companion. Remember, too, that the ultimate temperament and personality are already quite evident in an adult cat, so you know exactly what you are getting. And with an adult cat, there won't be any surprises about the eventual size of your pet.

If you have children, you should test the cat's reactions to them. If he cowers, runs away, or tries to hide when one of your young ones makes a noise or moves quickly toward him, you know you have to keep looking. You want to find a cat who is unperturbed by children and, even better, one who is curious and willing to interact.

WHICH GENDER IS BETTER?

Whether a cat is male or female usually doesn't make much of a difference once he is neutered or she is spayed—unless you plan to have more than one cat *(page 88)*. The personality of the individual cat is more telling than the sex, although in general males are more outgoing than females. If you speak to several cat owners, though, you'll hear many exceptions to this rule. The behavior of unsterilized cats is more markedly different. An intact male, for instance, will be more territorial, be more aggressive with other male cats, and will want to roam far afield in search of females. When an unspayed female is sexually receptive, or "in heat," she will display annoying behaviors, such as yowling and pacing anxiously, in search of a mate.

INDOOR VERSUS OUTDOOR

A cat kept indoors will most likely live a long, healthy life, usually up to at least fifteen years. While the great outdoors truly awakens the wild hunting instinct present in all cats and makes for a more interesting existence, a cat that is allowed to roam freely outside may not survive to old age. Aside from the most obvious dangers inherent in roaming outdoors—getting lost or hit by a car—a cat may also fight with other animals and end up with abscesses or serious wounds. Fleas and other parasites and diseases are easily picked up outdoors and some, such as roundworms and toxoplasmosis, can be transferred to humans. (Immunosuppressed cat owners especially are advised to keep their pets indoors.) And once a cat is roaming the neighborhood, the owner can't supervise what it might eat—poisonous products are an ever-present danger. Sadly, there are also a few cruel people who take pleasure in hurting animals, and some who steal pets.

While an indoor cat can be quite happy, the best compromise on the indoor/outdoor issue is to build a secure enclosure in your yard. Or, if you already have a perimeter fence, look into cat-proof add-ons that will keep your cat on your property and bar entry to other cats. Alternatively, you might tether your cat with a harness and leash, but only under supervision, to be sure the leash doesn't become tangled around his neck or keep him from escaping from other animals that might enter the yard or swoop down from above. Hawks and owls, for instance, have been known to prey on cats. Many cats, even adults that once were accustomed to going out, live very fulfilled lives exclusively indoors, especially if their owners spend the time to stimulate them through play and provide them with play structures and window seats, maybe even a feline companion.

PERSONALITY TYPES

The range of feline personalities is nearly as wide as it is for humans, with shy and fearful at one end of the scale, sociable and affectionate at the other. A number of other traits are part of the package. The cat may be active or sedate, bold or timid, aggressive or passive, confident or anxious. Some facets of a cat's temperament may even seem to be contradictory. A cat may be very friendly and happy to be near you, but never want to be picked up or sit on your lap. Sometimes, with encouragement and patience, such a cat will learn to cuddle, but, as is usual in dealing with cats, the human, not the cat, most often does the adapting.

A roofed-in outdoor enclosure allows your cat to enjoy the best of both worlds and relieves you of safety concerns. When installed against the house, you can leave a window into the structure slightly open so the cat can come and go from house to outdoor area as he pleases. A variety of easy-to-assemble kits are available, or you can plan and build your own, filling it with climbing structures and perches.

Because environment plays a role in shaping a cat's personality, knowing the life history of a particular kitten or cat makes it easier to predict what he will be like. In general, kittens grow up to be better adjusted cats if they were gently handled by humans from the age of two weeks on and if they stayed with their mother and littermates for at least eight weeks. An adult cat that has lived in one home with caring owners is more likely to have a good nature than one who has had uncertainty and neglect as its life companions. But even this isn't foolproof. If you are choosing a purebred cat (Chapter 6), you can be fairly certain that his personality will fit the profile for that breed; for instance, Maine coon cats are known to be placid and very friendly, while Burmese are very lively, inquisitive, and amiable. Purebred or not, any cat is as much a product of upbringing as genes and will have a distinct personality. Whether you know the cat's background or not, assess how he reacts to you. And even if a cat develops one or two annoying traits or habits, his endearing qualities will most likely make up for them.

COAT TYPES

Keep in mind the old adage "beauty is only skin deep" when selecting your cat. The coat is probably the first thing you will notice—both the color and length. You may have a preference for a certain color, but try to look past that and evaluate the whole cat. The character, not the look, is what you will come to appreciate most of all. And in practical terms, that stunning longhaired cat will require frequent grooming, typically at least three times a week, so be realistic about the time you are willing to put into coat care. Both longhaired and shorthaired cats shed the same amount, but the hairs from a longhaired cat will be more visible around the house.

MORE THAN ONE

The joys of living with more than one cat and watching them interact almost always outweigh the extra expense. And if you have an indoor-only cat, a feline companion can do wonders in staving off the boredom that can result in stress or destructive behavior. Even when two cats never become good friends, it's rare that they don't eventually call a truce. At least they have another live being around for distraction when you're out—and chasing and tussling are good forms of exercise.

If you already have an adult cat, a kitten (or another smaller adult cat) is usually easier to integrate into the household than another full-sized adult. He'll be considered less of a threat by your resident cat. But there are no hard and fast rules. Many people have introduced adult cats with great success. The chances of having the integration work are even greater if the newcomer is already sterilized, is already accustomed to living with other animals, and has a personality similar to your cat's. Cats of opposite sexes often get along better, although again, there are countless exceptions to this rule. Don't bring unneutered males together; territorial conflicts may trigger offensive urine spraying.

Plopping down a new cat in front of your resident feline rarely makes for a smooth introduction. A better approach is to keep the cats apart at first and let both acclimatize gradually, which will take some patience on your part. Set up a separate room for the new cat, with food and water bowls, a litter box, toys, a bed, and places to hide. Make sure the food and water bowls are set away from the litter box. Take the new arrival straight to this room, and for the first day only go in to check on his food and litter box. Let your resident cat smell the carrier you used to transport the new arrival so that he gets used to the stranger's odor. Keep the newcomer isolated long enough for him to adjust to the new situation without the additional stress of meeting another cat. This may take as little as a day, but sometimes more

Longhaired cats are beautiful, but they are high-maintenance pets. The cat at left is a good example of feline grooming, while the cat above needs a good brushing to keep mats (tangled clumps of fur) from developing. If you plan to let your cat go outdoors, a shorthaired animal is usually a better idea. Long hair picks up sticks, burrs, and other debris and takes longer to dry when it gets wet.

than a week; you'll know he is ready when he comes out of hiding and shows an interest in exploring what's on the other side of the door.

As soon as possible, take your new cat to the vet for a checkup, shots, tests for diseases (which means continued isolation until you get the results), and, if the cat has not been altered, a decision on when to sterilize. Over the next few days, pay lots of attention to your original cat and try not to change his routine, but gradually spend more time in the room with the new cat. You can expect to find your resident cat at the door to the new cat's room, possibly hissing or maybe sticking his paws under the door.

The next step is to shut your resident cat in another room and let the new cat out to explore the house for a short period of time. If he simply runs back into his safe room, try again later. Once he's comfortable with the rest of the house it's time for the cats to meet. Experts usually recommend waiting until there has been no hissing or growling from either side of the door for a day or two. Clip the claws of both cats and allow the new cat to come out of his room. Try not to greet his presence with any fanfare. Allow the two cats to interact. An arched back and puffed-up tail, hissing, and snarling from one or both cats on these first face-to-face meetings are nor-

Although a kitten will bond more easily to another cat, even adult cats can become friends, but it may take a while. One word of caution: While a very young feline housemate may bring out the kitten in a senior cat, more often than not the nonstop antics of an energetic little one will be annoying to a sedate older cat that is set in his ways.

INTRODUCING CATS AND DOGS

 Cats and dogs often can become pals, or at least learn to tolerate each other. The younger the dog or cat, the better, but make sure the dog is well trained and test him with friends' cats to make sure he doesn't have a tendency to attack them. If the cat is the new arrival, let the cat adjust to the house first with the dog in his crate or shut in a room. If the dog will be the interloper, give your cat lots of attention away from the dog and make sure he has dog-proof hiding spots (especially up high, so he can observe from a safe vantage point).

For the initial introduction, first trim the cat's claws. Keep the dog on a leash so you can control him. The cat will likely hiss and put his back up, may lash out at the dog, and will probably run away. Continue this routine, increasing the length of each meeting until both animals seem comfortable.

Before you unleash your dog, make sure he will obey your verbal commands to stay away from the cat if it looks like he might do harm. Do not leave the dog and cat alone together without supervision until you are confident that it is safe to do so.

A well-trained dog can be introduced to a cat as long as the cat is safely out of reach and the dog is restrained by a leash. After a few such sessions, you can try unleashing the dog if you can be sure he will respond to your "Stay!" command.

mal reactions. But be prepared to separate them should a serious battle break out. Try distracting them with a loud noise, spray them with cold water, or drop a box or laundry basket over the aggressor and place the other cat in a closed room. Never reach into the melee to pull fighting cats apart; you'll be clawed or bitten for your trouble.

Even if things seem to be going smoothly, play the psychologist. Fuss over your resident cat, but don't pay a lot of attention to the new cat in front of him. Put the new cat back in his isolation room after a short session. Continue this routine until the cats appear to be more comfortable with each other, letting the new cat stay out for longer and longer periods of time, but only when someone is around to supervise. Cats usually work things out by themselves, although it can take from a few days to several months. Usually the existing cat is the one that takes longer to accept the presence of the other cat. The best thing you can do is to leave them to it; as they grow to accept each other, you'll need to separate them less and less often. When you feel the time is right, leave all the rooms open. The final step is to start gradually moving the new cat's litter box and food bowls closer to those of the other cat. They will probably end up sharing litter boxes, but keep food bowls well separated. Cats can become anxious when they eat too close to each other.

SHOPPING
·AROUND·

At cat shelters, the friendliest cats usually sit near the front of the cages, ready to stick out a playful paw and choose you as you walk by. A slightly less confident cat will sit a bit farther back, but look content as it observes the goings-on around it. Timid or frightened cats generally huddle at the back of the cages or even in the litter boxes in response to the hectic environment. In quieter surroundings, their true personalities may emerge.

When you begin looking for a feline companion, you'll quickly discover there is no shortage of candidates; in fact, there aren't nearly enough homes for all the available cats. You'll find an almost overwhelming selection at animal shelters and small-scale private animal rescue groups, pet stores, veterinarians, and breeders. You can also go the informal route, taking a kitten from the litter of a friend's or neighbor's cat or bringing in the stray that shows up at your door. Newspaper ads are another source, especially if you are looking for an inexpensive adult cat that has already been fixed and vaccinated. But wherever you start your search, remember the golden rule: No impulsive decisions. If you have any doubts about the kitten or cat, keep looking until you find the right one.

ADOPTION OPTIONS

Animal shelters and pounds can be upsetting to visit, but choosing a pet there will save at least one animal's life. Some shelters are tax-funded, while others depend on donations and volunteers. Usually the animals have been seen by a vet and vaccinated, and sterilization is often included in the adoption fee. Workers should be able to help you choose the best cat for your situation and give you as much background as possible about the candidates that interest you. Information such as whether the cat lived with other animals or with children (and how it reacted to them) can help you make your decision. There should be a contact room where you and your family can spend some time interacting with each of your potential choices. Many shelters will want to know about you, too, to ensure their cats will be cared for properly.

If you are choosing a kitten, try to look beyond the cuteness; all kittens are adorable. You should observe each kitten's behavior. Is it bold or shy? Friendly or defensively aggressive? Unless you are prepared to deal with potential behavior problems, opt for the friendly, outgoing one. If a timid kitten is the one who captures your heart, you will need to take extra time and handle him very gently to bring him out of his shell, but it is possible. You should pass up any kitten that cowers and looks terrified. If you're choosing from a group of kittens, hold out your hand and see which ones come to investigate; then, pick up each in turn. Hissing and panic can be bad signs. Well-socialized kittens will rest in your arms or may squiggle to be let down. Separate the one that interests you from the others. Handle the

Both of these cats are beautiful, but which is the purebred and which came from the animal shelter? A random-bred, or "domestic" cat, such as the one at left, can be just as attractive as a purebred, such as the Maine coon cat above. Domestic cats are available in a huge variety of colors and coat lengths, and many are just as engaging in personality and as beautiful in appearance as their more expensive purebred cousins.

Most strays look grubby for a reason: Washing up is usually done after eating, and regular meals are rare for homeless cats. Once in your home, a cat usually does a good job of cleaning himself.

cat, dangle a toy, and see how he fares on his own; some apparently retiring kittens liven up when away from their siblings, or may just have been sleepy.

The personality of an adult cat is usually easier to read; you can gauge his temperament by how he reacts to you when out of his cage. Even so, aggression or timidity may just be a reaction to the stressful shelter environment. Spend some time with him to try to get a sense of his true character. If this is your first cat or if you have children, select a cat that is friendly and outgoing after a few quiet minutes alone with you. While even a less well-adjusted cat will come round eventually, you may not have the time and patience to wait it out.

Although pet stores often house darling-looking kittens, they are not your best option. The stores count on impulse purchases, the worst reason to acquire a pet. The kittens may not have been checked by a vet or vaccinated and may be unhealthy, especially if they have been acquired from one of the unscrupulous operations known as kitten mills. These are large-scale breeding farms where the animals are bred indiscriminately, housed in terrible conditions, and often sick. Why support needless increases to the pet population when millions of cats in shelters are euthanized each year because of a lack of homes? Even pet-store kittens labeled "purebred" may be suspect, as the better breeders only sell to individuals they deem suitable for one of their kittens, never to strangers through pet shops. There is an exception to this pet-shop boycott. Pet-supply stores that cooperate with local shelters or rescue groups to showcase a selection of available kittens and cats follow shelter guidelines for placing a cat. The store's payback comes from selling food and supplies to new owners.

Some kind-hearted veterinarians serve as clearinghouses, offering kittens, a stray they have nursed to health, or the cat a client can't keep for some reason. The vet may already have examined the cat for serious health problems and if it is not already altered, the vet may give you a discount on the surgery. Many vets that don't have animals on site may have a bulletin board listing cats and kittens needing homes.

Adopting from a friend or neighbor or through an ad in the paper usually means you will know more about the animal's background and previous treatment. You should still spend time interacting, using the same criteria as you would when adopting from an animal shelter.

If your heart is set on a particular breed of cat, find a responsible breeder. Visit cat shows or contact cat associations for recommendations. Once you have a selection of breeders, visit the catteries to ensure they are clean, and the kittens have been raised with their mother and siblings, and a lot of gentle handling by humans. A good breeder will provide you with the pros and cons of the breed as well as the background of a particular kitten's bloodlines. Responsible breeders won't force a sale and, in fact, may refuse you if they're uncertain you will provide proper care for one of their "babies."

It's important to sign a contract with the breeder, outlining the responsibilities of both parties. Make sure you understand the conditions, and if the breeder is reluctant to explain, go elsewhere. There should be a health guarantee in the contract, both for immediate health problems and for genetic problems that may show up only much later. Have the kitten checked by your vet within the time period stipulated in the contract to identify any long-term health concerns. Breeders usually require proof of sterilization before they will supply the registration papers. Some breeders have a stipulation against declawing put right in the contract; others simply recommend against it. Still others permit declawing as a last resort, but insist that the kitten be kept indoors.

Responsible breeders care about their cats for life, and will be happy to help you with any behavioral problems that may arise. Many will take the cat back, even years later, if for some reason you can't keep him.

Purchasing a purebred cat can be a sizeable investment. Breed rescue groups and even animal shelters can offer less expensive alternatives to breeders. Shelters often have purebred or nearly purebred cats for adoption, a sensible option if you are looking for a pet and not a show cat. If you would like a particular breed but can't afford breeder fees, track down a breed rescue group through a cat association or on the internet. These groups pick up cats from shelters, or from owners who are abandoning them, clean them up, and, if necessary, nurse them to health. They usually charge only enough to cover their veterinary costs. The disadvantage of this arrangement, however, is that these groups often have a waiting list, especially if the breed they care for is a popular one.

HOW'S HIS HEALTH?

Even before visiting the vet, give the animal you are considering a once-over yourself for obvious signs of illness. Runny nose or eyes may mean an upper respiratory infection (in other words, a cold). A very round, protruding stomach often points to intestinal worms. Visible third eyelids or a dull, dry, or patchy coat reflects general poor health. If you see a dark discharge in the ears, you are likely dealing with ear mites. You may spot fast-moving fleas diving for cover, or their calling cards, tiny black specks in the fur or scabs from their bites. Many of these are not serious problems and don't necessarily mean you must reject your choice, but be prepared to spend some time and money at the vet to get the cat into top condition. Kittens are generally more fragile than adults and minor problems can become more serious. And remember that any animal, particularly those that have been outside, may already have contracted a serious, even fatal, disease. Even if the previous owner provides you with health records for the cat, take it for a checkup. No matter how good a home you provide, you won't have a happy cat unless you have a healthy cat.

These purebred Scottish fold kittens are the picture of health, with their clear, bright eyes and soft, shiny coats. A good cattery, one that produces robust, friendly kittens, will be clean and properly ventilated, and have large cages containing well-maintained litter boxes, fresh water, toys, and comfortable sleeping areas.

CAT·PROOFING
· YOUR HOME ·

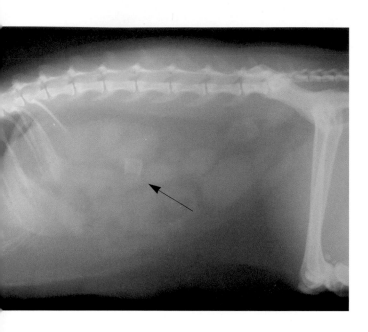

The breastbone's connected to the...doorstop? Cats will eat almost anything they can swallow, and they can swallow almost anything. The rubber doorstop tip shown in this x-ray had to be surgically removed, or the cat could have died from an intestinal blockage.

"Curiosity killed the cat. But satisfaction brought it back."

♦

PROVERB

A cat, as one saying goes, has nine lives; curiosity, another tells us, killed it. This built-in curiosity is an evolutionary device that works well in the jungle: Wild felines need to know their environment in order to survive. Somehow, though, this doesn't always translate well into the domestic scene. Your house can be a hazardous place for cats that have no idea of the dangers lurking in such benign-looking household items as electrical cords, plastic bags, and potted plants. To make your home safe, you'll have to think like a cat and remove or mitigate things that pique curiosity but hold danger. In truth, cat-proofing your home is a lot like childproofing it for a toddler.

Cats, like a lot of youngsters, will eat almost anything. And they will play with anything that can move. Strings, yarn, dental floss, elastics, and especially needles and thread are highly enticing, but if swallowed they can do serious, often fatal, damage. Store anything stringlike and any items small enough to swallow in a drawer or somewhere that feline paws can't penetrate. Chewing an electrical cord can be fatal and pulling on it may bring down an appliance—in the case of an iron, possibly a *hot* appliance. Hanging cords, such as those for curtains, blinds, and lamps can be strangulation hazards. Bundle all cords or tie them off out of reach.

Try to get all family members into the habit of leaving the toilet lid down. Cats, especially small kittens or less agile older cats, can fall in and drown. Make sure all windows are covered with sturdy screens and, if your cat will be an indoor pet, watch that he doesn't scoot out as you enter and leave the house. Keep garbage, a source of such dangerous items as bones and sharp tins, in a latched trash can. Stow all breakable items, utensils, and hazardous objects safely in cabinets, cupboards, and drawers; if your cat figures out how to open doors (some do), use baby-proofing latches to keep him out. Thoroughly clean up puddles of car fluids on your garage floor or your driveway. Gasoline, oil, and brake fluid are all highly toxic, and the sweet smell of antifreeze can attract a cat, with fatal results. *(See page 200 for a list of other poisons.)*

Cats will investigate anything they can fit into, and they can fit into tight spaces. Always check your dryer before starting it. Its warmth and darkness make it an attractive nest. Also check furniture with mechanisms—recliners and sofa beds—before using or closing them. Plastic bags are as dangerous for cats as they are for small children. And don't forget your car. Cats often crawl up under the hood for a warm nap in cold weather. Get into the habit of banging on the hood before starting the car to rouse any stowaways.

Cats are more delicate than sheets and towels: A spin in a dryer will likely prove fatal. Keep the dryer door shut and always check for any feline stowaways before you turn it on.

POISONOUS PLANTS

Cats chew on leafy greens to aid in their digestion, just as cats in the wild do. However, many plant sprays and common household plants, such as dieffenbachia and aloe vera, contain toxins and other noxious substances. They may even send your cat to the emergency room. There are some ways to save your precious houseplants and your even more precious cat.

First, try to satisfy the need for greenery. Prepared (just add water) gardens for cats are available at pet stores or you can make your own. Plain grass, wheat, or oat grass are easy to grow and contain useful fiber and nutrients. *(See pages 201 to 202*

for more about how to grow a cat garden and lists of safe and dangerous plants.)

If your cat is still chewing your plants, spray the leaves with a mixture of water and a dash of cayenne pepper or ginger strained through cheesecloth. To prevent cats from using the soil as their litter box, you can put large (one-inch-wide) glass decorator pebbles or gravel on top of the soil.

Low-fat, high-fiber, nutritious, delicious—the occasional leafy snack proves irresistible to most cats.

FIRST
·DAYS·

Peering out from under a table, this young arrival is waiting for the opportunity to explore his new surroundings. Often cats feel safer coming out of hiding at night to explore the house when it is quiet.

Cats are creatures of habit. Bringing one into a new environment can be very stressful. Although kittens tend to be less upset by change than adult cats, moving can still be overwhelming. From the kitten's point of view, everything is new at this stage in his life. Moving is just one more change. Normally he will adapt fairly quickly. An adult cat, on the other hand, may strut around his new quarters confidently, as though he has always belonged, or he may cower under a bed or at the back of a closet, bewildered by the change of surroundings. One way to make this transition easier for both you and the cat is to be prepared before the cat arrives, both with supplies and a plan.

GETTING READY

Before you bring your new cat or kitten home make sure you're ready to take care of his basic needs. First, find a vet who suits you *(page 100)*. Your new arrival should be examined as soon as possible after you bring him home. Also make time to poke around a pet-supply store for food and litter and their containers and a few other essentials.

You'll probably be amazed by the range of cat foods available; there are different types for different life stages as well as brands that vary in quality and price *(page 132)*. Ideally you should continue feeding the cat whatever food he is accustomed to. If it is of low quality, however, you may want to gradually introduce a better food. Your vet will offer advice. Buy only a small quantity to start with; or even better, ask if the store or your vet offers free samples.

Food bowls may be made of plastic, metal, ceramic, or glass. The disadvantage of plastic is that the bowls may become scratched, creating a breeding ground for bacteria. Even when they are washed frequently, the bacteria often remains on the bowl's surfaces. It's best to have a separate water bowl, again preferably not made of plastic. Wash the food bowl after each meal and keep fresh water available at all times. Bowls don't have to be fancy or even designed for cats; you can save money by buying mismatched, but not cracked, china at discount stores or garage sales. Some cats prefer a low bowl or even a saucer so that their sensitive whiskers are not rubbing against the sides of the container.

Think about where you will be placing the litter box: Location may affect its size and shape. Although there are many new and fancy boxes on the market, there's nothing wrong with the standard open pan. If you're concerned about odors and litter being scattered by an enthusiastic digger, a covered box is a possibility, although these raise some health concerns, especially if you are using a litter that is dusty. *(For a full discussion of boxes and litter, see pages 136 to 139.)* No matter what kind of box you use, some litter will always be tracked out of the box. A mat can minimize tracking around the room.

The choice of litters is even more confounding. Purchase a small bag initially in case it takes some experimentation to find the type your cat prefers. Plastic litter-pan liners can help make cleanup of the box easier, although some cats tear the liners to shreds while scratching in the box, thus defeating the purpose. A sturdy scoop completes your feline toilet kit.

A scratching post is another "necessity." Have one in place when your cat arrives so you can encourage him to use it right away *(page 121)*. If you wait until he has already dug into the furniture, you'll have a hard time luring him to the post.

Unless you can borrow a carrier to transport your cat home, invest in one before picking him up. A carrier is indispensable for trips to the vet and, lined with a towel, can double as a bed. If your cat sleeps in the carrier, he'll be less terrified when you need to transport him in it.

Pet stores have an amazing array of cat-related accessories. Keep yourself in check. You don't really need to spend money on a fancy wicker bed with a quilted cushion, for instance. A simple cardboard box or plastic bin lined with an easily laundered towel will serve just as well. Limit your extra purchases to one or two toys until you know your cat's playtime preferences *(page 113)*.

ARRIVAL STRATEGIES

To ease your cat's entry into your home, set up a special "isolation" room for him to inhabit for the first few days. This room is especially important for a kitten or a timid or frightened adult; they only have to get used to one small area. Set up the isolation room with food and water bowls, a cozy bed, litter box, scratching post, and a few toys. Place the litter box away from the food bowl. Understandably, cats do not like to eat right next to their toilet. If you have a kitten, put the box about six feet from his bowl, closer (two to three feet) if he's less than fourteen weeks old. Kittens sometimes forget where the box is or may not be able to reach it in time if it's too far away.

After a day or so in a safe isolation room, most cats will begin to check out the surroundings. You'll know you're making progress when you can enter the room without causing the newcomer to dive under the bed.

If you can't create an isolation room, at least block off any areas with potentially dangerous hiding places, such as the basement. And make sure your house is fully cat-proofed *(page 96)*.

If possible, isolate the cat in the room where the litter box will be kept permanently so the kitten or cat won't be thrown off when the box is moved. (If you do have to move a litter box, do it gradually, a few feet at a time.) The ideal place for a litter box is in a quiet area, off limits to children or your dog. Your cat will want to go about his "business" undisturbed. Laundry rooms are not necessarily good locations; many cats are afraid to use the box when noisy machines are in operation. Once the cat has the run of the house, make sure the box is always accessible; use a stopper to keep the door to the room partially open or create a cat door by cutting a hole through the door.

THE NEW ARRIVAL

Immediately confine your new cat or kitten to the safe room, with water in the bowl, but no food at first. Whether young or old, he will almost always recognize a litter box and in this small area should have no trouble finding it. Then, tempting though it may be to stay in the room and play with your new pet, leave him alone to settle in. After a few hours, give him some food and then, unless he is a very shy or frightened cat needing socialization *(page 88)*, he should be more relaxed and open to some interaction. Always let the cat initiate contact. Hold out your hand, palm down, and let him sniff and rub against it. If he seems quite comfortable with you, have other family members come in, one at a time so he won't be overwhelmed, to spend time with him.

A young kitten may cry piteously when alone, particularly if this is his first time away from mother and siblings. Spend time handling and playing with him and consider letting him sleep on or near your bed. When you're away, make sure he has interesting toys for distraction; even cardboard boxes are fun to clamber into. Leave on a radio at low volume set to a talk station.

Before long the cat will begin to show an interest in what's on the other side of the door. Once he is eating well, using the litter box, and no longer hiding, let him out of the room to investigate the rest of the house. To make this step as stress-free as possible for your cat, the house must be tranquil. If you have children too young to understand that they must be quiet and not interfere with the cat while he prowls around, arrange for them to be out of the house or in bed for the evening. A very confident cat will have no inhibitions when going from room to room, but most felines adopt a strange crouched position while exploring. They will smell everything and may frequently hide. Once they determine there are no dangers, they relax. This can take a while for some cats, but be patient; your cat needs time to adapt to this new living situation and human family. A routine makes cats feel secure, so stick to regular times for feeding, grooming, and playing to help banish feline angst.

KIDS AND CATS

Your child must learn to respect the cat and treat him gently. Your influence as a role model is essential here. Supervise any interaction between your child and the cat until you are confident both are behaving properly.

Your child should be sitting calmly for the initial meeting in the isolation room—any fast movement will send the cat into hiding. Bring the animal to the child and help your youngster pet him, stroking with the fur, not against it. Show your young one how to play gently; no tail pulling.

Teach your child how to hold the cat so that he is properly supported (*page 111*). And more importantly, your child should know when to let the cat go. Most youngsters can learn to read body language: If the cat is wriggling or his tail is lashing and his ears are back, it's time to put him down. Kittens are delicate and can be injured by a child's overly tight hug; or, they might lash out with teeth and claws. And don't allow a child to tease the cat, or to disturb him when he is eating, using the litter box, or in a deep sleep.

The gentle way this youngster handles the cat, without restraining him, bodes well for a good relationship between the two.

IN THE

COMPANY

OF

CATS

• • •

"By associating with the cat,
one only risks becoming richer."

•

COLETTE

READING
·YOUR CAT·

Every feline possesses its own distinct personality, just as people do. Even purebred cats of breeds known for a certain character profile don't always match the description. Your Siamese may not be as boisterous as the majority of his relatives; your British shorthair, a breed known for its calm and self-possessed manner, may be quite skittish. But like a bonding parent who learns to read the subtle body nuances of a newborn, you can become attuned to your cat's temperament and idiosyncrasies, making for a more harmonious relationship.

BODY LANGUAGE

A cat's posture, tail, ears, eyes, and hair all speak volumes. But frequently, because we fail to understand and interpret the signals correctly, we blame the cat—unjustly. Understanding the body language of felines can be difficult, even counterintuitive, since it is meant to convey messages primarily to other cats. Signs of fearfulness or irritation can be easily misread as playful excitement because a cat's associated behaviors appear to be similar. And misinterpretation of cats often arises out of confusion with the body language of dogs, which is sometimes opposite in meaning.

A cat's tail is its signal flag. Held high, the tail is a banner communicating confidence. Curling around another feline's tail or a person's legs, it offers friendly greeting. In motion, it usually indicates excitement. The cat is either in predator mode, having sighted a bird or a mouse, or is feeling playful, hiding behind a chair ready to pounce on a passing person or cat. And while the rhythmic wagging of a dog's tail signals happiness, the agitated whipping of your cat's tail means that he is perturbed or upset. Don't startle a cat in this state. Your reward may be a claw swipe or a bite.

Cats are affectionate and love to be touched, but only on their own terms. They may greet members of their household fondly with cheek rubs, but they prefer to initiate this contact. Cats may exchange quick eye-blink hellos with each other, but they seldom stare. Instead, they will respond to a long stare from you by freezing movement and then alternately looking at you and looking away.

Huddling with its tail wrapped around its body, a cat may be telegraphing that it is cold. A similar body position, but with a relaxed cat, signals its dreamy contentment. A feline that feels very secure may become so limp that its sleeping nook seems filled with a furry liquid. A sick cat often doesn't

A bobcat (opposite) and a domestic feline (above) deliver the same message: Turned ears, squinting eyes, bared teeth, and a paw raised defensively mean, "Go away!"

Overleaf: Calico domestic shorthair

Tail raised and legs outstretched in a long stride, a self-assured, proud cat struts its independence.

Bristling fur on the back and the tail are signs of fright. While appearing to lick its nose, a cat blocks its nostrils with its tongue to activate the scent-interpreting Jacobsen's organ in its mouth.

curl up, but lies in the position requiring the least energy. An alert, attentive cat scans wide-eyed, ears pricked and rotating, tuned to threats, prey, and other felines. Spotting something of interest, the cat stares intently, pitching its ears and its whiskers forward. A startled, fearful, or defensive feline may strike the pose of the classic Halloween cat to make itself look larger and more threatening. It turns to one side with back arched, hackles raised, ears turned back, and teeth bared.

Sensing a potential threat, a cat tenses its body, lowers its tail, and raises the fur on its back and tail. On its toes, it is ready to flee the instant the need arises. If it is preparing to attack, the cat will crouch or lie on its side or back, narrow its eyes to focus on its target, hiss, and bare its teeth and claws. A feline that takes this posture isn't interested in your affection; it means business. You're best to stay out of the way.

Few felines are truly aggressive by nature, but even the gentlest of kittens may lash out if annoyed, threatened, or over-excited by play, seeming to lose control beyond some threshold of arousal. Claws and teeth can be dangerous, especially to small children, so take signs of impending assault serious-

Exposing a vulnerable tummy is a playful sign of trust. Mistaking it as an invitation for a belly rub can earn you an unappreciative bite or scratch.

A cat's rapt interest is evident in its stillness and the directed focus of its ears, eyes, and whiskers.

ly. Keep a youngster who seeks to shower kitty with affection from hugging it, kissing it, and lugging it around. While a cat that's in the right mood may put up with a moment's snuggle, it won't appreciate—and may not tolerate—being confined or roughly handled. A squirming cat that switches its tail, turns back its ears, or growls is making a clear statement: It wants to be put down. Heed the warning.

VOCAL VOCABULARY

Felines express a surprising variety of sounds, each carrying one or more messages. On sighting a bird, a cat may clack its teeth in a chatter of excitement. A rhythmic purring usually signals contentment, but a cat also may purr when injured or while giving birth. In response to a threat, a feline may growl or grumble, often as a prelude to hissing or spitting. Owners should read hissing as a defensive, "Keep back. I'm scared right now."

Cats speak to people primarily with meows, which come in many forms and carry many different meanings. You will quickly become an expert translator of your cat's meows. Easiest to interpret is the meow of request, which is usually accompanied by a head-held-high, front-paws-together begging posture. Sometimes a meow expresses complaint, anxiety, or confusion. Other easily recognized cat sounds include the hissing, spitting, and caterwauling of battle-readiness and the sharp yelp or scream of pain. And there certainly is no mistaking the yowl of a feline in heat or the boisterous uproar of mating cats.

BONDING WITH
·YOUR CAT·

Why do cats love to lie on our beds, especially if they're rumpled and unmade, or in the full laundry basket? It may be that they take comfort from items suffused with our smells, a substitute for the solace they derived as kittens from their mother's scent. Or, they may just like the softness of laundry and bedding.

Opposite: A lion cub snuggles with its mother, a physical manifestation of the bonding universal to felines. This rubbing of faces, kneading, and licking are ritual honors that a cat will bestow on you as it transfers its allegiance.

One reason cats make such good pets is that they're quite content to be cared for by humans. Their notoriety for being aloof and independent doesn't mean that they are antisocial or unresponsive. On the contrary, most cats thrive on human interaction and come to depend on their owners. With basic needs for food and shelter satisfied, cats seek out human affection, which also indulges our desires to nurture.

Ideally, a cat begins life amidst its siblings in the care of a doting mother. It huddles in a furry jumble for warmth, rubbing its mother and siblings to exchange scents. As your cat gets to know you, he will regard you as a member of his family, perhaps even as a surrogate mother, and you will become the recipient of his affection. Even an older cat may retain kittenlike rituals, settling in to knead your lap, reminiscent of the motion used to stimulate his mother's milk when nursing, or being lulled into a dreamy sleep by a neck rub. Your petting can be a soothing reminder of being groomed by his mother's scratchy tongue.

To ensure that kittens adapt comfortably to people, they need to be handled gently for short periods of time once their eyes are open. But because they benefit so much from the presence of their mother, kittens should stay with her until they're at least eight weeks old. Interact at first with both the kittens and the mother, then gradually spend more time with each kitten on its own. A kitten that is given the freedom to approach you, climb on you, and play with you will feel most secure around people. Kittens need to explore their environment in order to build confidence and cope with change and different surroundings. Small, dark hiding places, such as behind the couch or in the corner of a shelf, provide safe havens of retreat should the youngster encounter an apparent threat while exploring. When kittens leave their mother for new homes, they should take with them some bedding made of material with which she has been in contact; her lingering scent may comfort little ones in their unfamiliar environment. In time, your own scent will become as reassuring as that of the mother.

Your bond with your pet may become so strong that the cat attempts to parent you. For instance, a cat may bring you its quarry: a real mouse or bird captured outdoors or a plaything hunted indoors. When actual animal prey is involved, a cat will bring you the animal dead, as an offering of food, or alive, as an apparent opportunity for you to make a kill. Your cat even may try to nudge you into doing what he wants you to do or going where

PREPARING YOUR CAT FOR A BABY'S ARRIVAL

 The sounds and smells of a new baby can be disconcerting to a cat. Accustom your cat to the sounds of a baby beforehand by playing taped recordings. When the baby's room is set up, let the cat investigate it as well as the infant's accessories so they won't be a novelty once the baby arrives home. Before the baby leaves the hospital, bring home a blanket or an item of clothing the child has worn so your cat can get used to the baby's smell. After the baby arrives, keep to your cat's set routines as much as possible.

Sit calmly with your baby and encourage your cat to introduce himself. Supervise interaction between the two to prevent the baby from grabbing the cat and him reciprocating with a scratch or a bite.

he wants you to go. Some cats will treat you like they would another adult cat, rubbing their face against you in greeting as they would a feline ally.

PROMOTING FELINE FRIENDLINESS

Many cats need time to adapt to change. Only after they feel at home will their full personalities bloom. If your newcomer appears shy, be patient. Even the most unfriendly of cats can become more sociable if treated with gentleness and understanding. Cats may be timid or anxious around people because of previous bad experiences. They simply need to be shown that humans can be trusted. On the other hand, some cats are timid by nature and there may be a limit to what you can expect from them. Sometimes our own prejudices about cats dictate a negative outcome: If we expect aloofness and act impatiently, we unwittingly encourage antisocial behavior. Children eager to make friends with a cat may unintentionally antagonize it, picking it up improperly, giving it unwanted hugs, or coercing it into play. Animosity or ambivalence shown toward a cat by any member of the household, human or animal, may cause it to retreat socially.

As your cat acclimatizes to your presence, move in closer. You can imitate a mother cat by stretching out on the floor where the cat can sit or lie beside you. Talk to the cat in a calm, soothing voice. Pet your cat slowly at first, giving him a chance to respond, but be prepared to back off if he seems uneasy. If the cat drifts off to sleep, simply rest your hand against him. Stroking or scratching might waken the cat in an ill temper. Never force your cat to be close to a person or another animal. This may make the problem worse.

Spending periods of quiet time with your cat can help banish his human antipathies—and offer excellent therapy for you. A cat can be a natural sedative, relieving stress and calming nerves. Although they are more reserved than dogs, which once held the monopoly on animal-assisted therapy, cats are now being used in hospices, at seniors' residences, and with autistic people. Their calming influence has mental and physical benefits, easing stress, lifting spirits, and lowering heart rates and blood pressure.

Cats like to sleep next to warm bodies, both those of humans and other cats, especially in cold weather, and most of them love to share a person's bed. The valley created by two people side by side or the enclosure formed by a pair of bent legs is a cozy hollow just perfect for a cat to sleep in.

Grooming and playing are also helpful in bonding with your cat. Setting up a schedule is one of the best ways to make your cat feel secure. Try to feed, groom, and play with your cat at about the same time and in the same place every day. Your cat may be quite content when you aren't around; he will probably sleep. But while they're awake, cats need both mental and physical stimulation. Play is a good source of excitement and exercise, as well as an excellent way for you and your cat to interact. Change the toys and games every so often, bringing out different items to spark interest.

DO YOU TALK TO YOUR CAT?

Chatting to your cat isn't a sign that you're losing your sanity; perfectly normal people converse out loud with their cats all the time. Although your cat may not understand everything you're saying, at least you have an audience that won't contradict with more than a bored blink of the eyes. Cats sometimes seem very intuitive about human moods. Many an upset cat owner has looked up to find his or her feline companion sitting quietly close by, as if offering emotional support. Such responsiveness may result from a feline ability to interpret human body language, a natural talent considering that all cats communicate among themselves in this way. In fact, cats probably read human body language better than they interpret human speech.

Nonetheless, your cat may learn up to as many as twenty different words. Typically this vocabulary will include his name; repeated often enough, the cat usually makes the connection. If you chant, "Come here," at mealtimes, the reward of food reinforces the command's meaning; your cat eventually may respond even when his stomach is full.

A cat will come to associate an entire package of words or phrases, your tone of voice, and your gestures with specific activities and things. For a good relationship with your cat, learn to understand his unspoken language *(page 105)* and the different sounds he makes *(page 68)*. Eventually you'll be able to interpret even the subtle distinctions in your cat's meows and know what he is asking. And if you enjoy having your cat talk to you, be sure to encourage him by always responding favorably to his sounds.

HOW TO PICK UP A CAT PROPERLY

Correct handling of your cat will build his trust in you. Take hold of your cat from behind, reaching underneath just to the rear of his front legs with your open palm. Cup your hand and lift first the cat's chest, then raise his hindquarters, tucking his tail underneath. Be sure to support the cat's entire body, cradling it in the crook of your arm with paws propped on your other arm. Or, place the front paws up on your shoulder. Keep in mind that kittens need to be treated with extra care since their bones are still hardening.

Some cats simply don't like to be handled. If your cat squirms or frets when you pick him up, put him down gently and let him go, gaining his trust—and saving yourself a few nips and scratches. Never try to pick up a cat or, for that matter, a kitten, by the scruff of the neck. This privilege is reserved for the mother cat and may actually harm an adult cat. If restraint is necessary, however, you may grip the loose skin on the back of a cat's neck if the body is fully supported. In this hold, the cat cannot turn his head to bite you.

Properly supported, your cat will relax while being held in your arms.

CATS'
·PLAYTIME·

Through play with their siblings, kittens act out the rudiments of the hunt and pick up social skills and self-sufficiency. They refine the stalking and pouncing, as well as the coordination and timing, required to make a kill. They learn about their environment through rambling and climbing, finding the best spots to hide and the ideal places to lie in wait for victims. A kitten's development is speedy: At three weeks, it will begin to paw at things tentatively; only five weeks later, it is capable of catching and killing a mouse—or doing the equivalent to a toy.

Play stimulates your cat mentally, alleviating boredom, keeping him alert, and helping to decrease the likelihood of behavioral problems. If your cat is prone to boisterous nighttime romps or sneak attacks on your hands, or, at the other end of the scale, depression-like lethargy or apprehensiveness, add more play sessions to his schedule. Play also offers an opportunity for adult cats to get needed physical exercise. Indoor cats, in particular, are at risk for obesity, which may lead to more serious problems such as diabetes, liver disease, and undue stress on arthritic joints. Play also is a wonderful way for you to enjoy the marvels of feline nature.

TOY SELECTION

Start your cat with a small collection of simple toys: lightweight balls (ping-pong balls are excellent); stuffed toys for sinking teeth and claws into; and interactive pole-type toys (enticing objects suspended by elasticized strings from hand-held wands). See how your cat responds to these and if you notice a preference for a certain type, such as toys that make a crinkly sound, get more along the same lines. Many ordinary household items, ranging from wine corks to paper bags, can provide your cat with hours of delightful amusement *(page 205)*. Make sure plastic bags are out of reach, and either cut through or remove completely the twine or plastic handles on any paper shopping bags you let your cat play with. It's easy for cats to end up with the handles round their necks, and frantic attempts to escape can tighten handles more, leading to tragic results.

Kittens and adult cats alike incorporate hunting moves into their play. Whether or not they have ever actually hunted, they capture prey by pouncing, swatting in the air, or using a scooping motion. When you are choosing toys or playing with them with your cat, think about typical feline prey—the sounds they make (squeaks and rustling noises) and how they

Playtime is no more important for lion cubs in the wild (opposite) than for an Abyssinian kitten kept indoors (above). Through play, felines learn about their environment and hone the skills they will need through adulthood.

CAT TREES

One thing indoor cats really miss is tree climbing, but you can fulfill this need with a cat tree. These gyms can vary from a simple carpeted or wound-rope scratching post, with one or two platforms, to an organic-looking, multilevel, three-dimensional maze, complete with many platforms and even small enclosed rooms or tubes.

Ideally, place the structure in front of a sunny window with interesting scenery (meaning small animals and birds, even human traffic). Your cat should be able to be near you and survey his indoor domain, too, so place the tree in a room in which you spend a lot of time.

Simple, robust construction and natural materials are best. Wood wrapped with sisal rope or a log, complete with bark, affords the rough texture preferred by cats. Carpet also makes for a good grasping surface for claws. The tree should have at least as many platforms as you have cats, all at different heights. Cats like variety and may have individual preferences, so an assortment of resting places at different heights is a good idea.

In a multi-cat household, a tree with many platforms may keep the brood happy by giving all cats a chance to climb and perch. Cat trees can be expensive, though, unless you can build your own. An alternative is to place soft towels or cushions on a number of places that would make good resting areas.

move (darting and hiding, slithering)—and attempt to make the toys act and move this way. And, most importantly, allow your cat catch the toy frequently; otherwise, you're just teasing and frustrating him, and he'll quickly lose interest.

Many cat toys contain catnip *(page 43)*, which usually excites cats and adds to the attraction. Revive an old toy by rolling it in the dried herb, if you don't mind some catnip residue on the floor, or apply a catnip spray. Some toys feature a pocket expressly for catnip.

Check all toys for safety. A toy should be big enough that your feline can't possibly swallow it and sturdy enough that it won't break into smaller pieces. Avoid toys with small parts that can be bitten or pulled off, such as buttons, beads, or rivets, or remove them right away. A ball of wool is about the worst toy possible. Once in your cat's mouth, the wool gets stuck on the backward-facing papillae of the tongue; the cat can't spit it out and just keeps swallowing more and more wool, resulting in serious, sometimes fatal, intestinal problems. Toys with strings, elastics, or ribbons are great fun, but pose similar problems and should be used only under supervision. Beware of laser pointing devices; they can cause damage if they hit a cat's eyes. Instead you might use a flashlight in a darkened room to create a moving spot of light for your cat to chase.

PLAY GUIDELINES

Try to play with your cat for ten to fifteen minutes at least twice each day. A romp before you leave in the morning can ease your absence during the day. Another in the evening can help minimize sleep-disturbing nocturnal play. In addition, try dangling an interactive toy during television commercials or while you talk on the phone. If your cat spends a lot of time alone, leave out some safe toys, such as balls or toy mice, for him to play with. Rotate your cat's toys to avoid monotony and hide some in easy-to-find spots so your cat will come across them unexpectedly. A good majority of the toys will end up under the couch or behind the bookcase, but you can make toy searches part of the fun, with your cat waiting expectantly while you use a long stick to dig out his playthings. If you have more than one cat and the more aggressive one always gets the toy, you may have to play with the cats separately so each gets a turn with you.

If your cat is getting on in years, is out of shape or obese, or seems simply to have lost the will to play, reawaken his youthful spirit by encouraging him to exercise. First, visit the vet to make sure that activity will not create or exacerbate any medical problem. Then, using interactive toys with which you can control the intensity of activity, try to hold and build the cat's interest. You may need to change the toy fairly often to hold the cat's attention. But be sure to match the pace of the play with your cat's condition; you don't want to overtax your older or overweight pet.

> **"When I play with my cat, who knows whether I do not make her more sport than she makes me?"**
>
> ◆
>
> **MICHEL DE MONTAIGNE**

Sniffing loose catnip prompts this feline to flop down and roll. About half of domestic cats respond to catnip, some with aggression, most in playful bouts of tension-letting. Wild cats also respond to this naturally stimulating herb. Lynx, jaguars, pumas, and leopards have been observed exhibiting the same kind of unfettered behavior while "under the influence."

TRAINING
· YOUR CAT ·

Some cats take well to leads, which permit safe outdoor exercise. Cats may slip out of a harness, though, even if it is properly fitted, so be sure your cat also wears a collar with an identification tag.

Opposite: Front paws outstretched for scratching, a bobcat scars and scents a log, making the wood a territorial signpost and sharpening its claws at the same time. For the same reasons, your cat will claw the couch or other furniture unless he is encouraged to satisfy this urge on a scratching post.

Banish all thoughts of training your cat as you would a dog. Although it's feasible at the hands of a professional trainer, it isn't very practical or affordable. You will want your cat to behave well, though, and you should be able to stop him from such undesirable practices as jumping up on the table to join you at mealtimes. Your coexistence will be a lot more pleasant and fun if the cat can be persuaded to come when he is called and to sharpen his claws on a scratching post instead of shredding the furniture.

Be realistic in your expectations. Certain behaviors are deeply rooted in the feline psyche and can't be altered. Nighttime romps and furniture climbing, for example, are carryovers from nocturnal hunting and territory surveillance in the wild. Out of respect for the feline nature, you will need to make some accommodations yourself. If your cat wakes you up at night, try having a good play session with him before bedtime. Sleep with ear plugs until the cat realizes you won't be roused in the middle of the night for an extra feeding. Don't simply scold the cat for scaling curtains and other household items. Satisfy the feline instincts to exercise and to survey the surroundings by investing in a cat tree.

Behavior problems aren't as likely to arise if you understand the working of the feline mind (*Chapter 2*). Understanding what underlies certain behavior will help you determine whether you should try conditioning your cat or whether you'll have to settle for changing your home environment or your own conduct. Modifying your cat's behavior will take *consistent* encouragement or discouragement, most likely a combination of both. Take a gradual approach and be patient, bearing in mind the feline's natural resistance to change.

TRAINING TACTICS

Since cats, unlike dogs, rarely do things merely to please their owners, you will need a feline-based system of positive reinforcement and possibly some form of aversion stimulus in order to achieve a change in your cat's behavior. The best way to encourage a cat to continue a behavior is with an immediate food reward, whether a full meal or a tasty treat. If at the same time you say, "Good!" the cat will come to associate the word with a positive event, even when food isn't forthcoming. Anything your cat loves will also work—a good scratch behind the ears or a play session with a favorite toy may work as well as a food treat.

Tired of moonlighting as a doorman? With a cat door, your feline is free to come and go as he chooses. One high-tech variation recognizes your cat by means of a device worn on his collar so unwelcomed guests can't enter.

Many cat owners try to discourage their cats from undesirable behavior with sprays of water from a plant mister, loud shakers, or any startling sound such as a hand clap or a whistle. If your cat is jumping onto the counter and you stop him by spritzing him with water, in actuality you are reinforcing jumping *off* the counter when the real problem is jumping *onto* it. While spritzing and other such methods can often discourage unwanted problems temporarily, they may also cause additional problems. Some cats actually like getting sprayed and chased. They think it's a game. For them, spritzing provides positive reinforcement for the undesirable behavior, which is then likely to increase. Other cats, particularly those that tend to be excitable, are threatened by such methods and become defensive, which can lead to serious aggression problems. Aversion methods that don't frighten or excite the cat are much safer. Putting sticky two-sided tape on the counter, for example, should provide enough discomfort for most cats to decide that the surface isn't a fun place to explore. And this method works whether you are there to witness the behavior or not. When you are present and see the unwanted behavior beginning, say, "No!" in a stern tone; your cat may, after a while, obey the vocal command alone. Never hit your cat. Injury can result and physical punishment won't change his behavior. The cat will simply become afraid of you and the stress may provoke further misbehavior. Reward your cat when he performs a desired behavior in place of the undesired one. Such a payoff will usually clinch the deal.

Some household items may simply be just too tempting for your cat to stay away from. Put up physical barriers to areas and surfaces you want your cat to avoid. For instance, if your cat is always getting into the garbage, you may have to get a container with a heavier or tighter-fitting lid. If he opens and enters cupboards, install childproof latches. After a while, the cat will probably lose interest in these forbidden locations and avoid them of his own accord.

CAT PERSUASION

One of the most basic things you can teach your cat is to respond to his own name. Say his name out loud whenever you greet or pet him, repeating it often as you do things together. To train your cat to come to you when called, start by saying his name as you put down the food bowl. Then, begin calling his name at mealtime before you do anything that makes a noise the cat might associate with food, such as opening the refrigerator, using a can opener, or scooping dry food into his bowl. When the cat appears, reward him immediately.

With perseverance and patience, you may be able to get your cat to accept wearing a harness, either to go for walks or to run around safely in the yard. Admittedly this undertaking is a lot easier to do if you start while the cat is still a kitten. Approach the wearing of the harness gradually, with food rewards each step along the way. Start by leaving the harness out on the floor so your cat can smell and become acquainted with it. Once the harness is no longer perceived as dangerous or threatening, place it on the cat's back without fastening it. It may help to distract the cat with a treat until he gets used to the feel of the harness. As the cat begins to accept the apparatus, fasten it for a short period of time, taking it off immediately when the cat seems perturbed. Gradually increase the length of time you leave the harness on and only once the cat seems to have forgotten that it is there, add the leash. Let the cat walk around dragging the leash, making sure it doesn't get caught on anything. Then, hold the end of the leash so the cat becomes used to feeling pressure on it. The final step is to familiarize your cat with the exciting, and possibly frightening, sights and sounds of the outdoors. Start off in your backyard or in a quiet area close to home, holding the leash tightly in case the cat tries to bolt. Gradually increase the length of these exercises until your cat is comfortable.

Installing a cat door will give your feline access to the outdoors whenever he wishes. But getting your cat to use it may require some encouragement. A cat door may make no sense to your cat at first; having to push open the flap with his head can be off-putting. Hold the door open and tempt the cat through the door by offering a treat on the other side. Once the cat jumps in and out of the opening at will, gradually close the flap, continuing to reward each exit and entrance.

SOLVING PROBLEM BEHAVIORS

You can eliminate or reduce many problems by setting up physical hindrances and exercising ordinary common sense. If your cat starts eating the foliage of your houseplants, for instance, hang them up or put up barriers around them. If the cat enjoys digging in the potting soil, cover it with aluminum foil or large pieces of gravel.

Some cats, especially kittens, develop the bad habit of chewing household objects. This may be an instinctive reflex transferred from the wild, where felines must work through skin, fur, or feathers and tear meat off bones, but around the house this behavior can be deadly—especially if your cat gnaws through electrical wires. Hide chewing targets or make things such as cords either taste, smell, or feel unpleasant. Wires, for example, can be wrapped in double-sided sticky

Sucking wool or other fabric, a behavior oddity most common to Oriental breeds, can be problematic and difficult to stop. So strong is the attraction that the cat seems to enter a trancelike state. Try to dissuade your cat by using a piece of the material sprayed with a foul-tasting repellent and ask your vet about adding fiber to his diet.

tape or coated with a commercially available cat-repellent spray.

Many cats occasionally eliminate outside the litter box. Any change in your cat's toilet habits is cause for concern and may signal a health problem. Pain when voiding, for instance, may give your cat an aversion to the litter box. Visit the vet as soon as possible to determine if an underlying illness is to blame.

Assuming the vet gives your cat a clean bill of health, start looking for other causes of his behavior. Is the litter box dirty? Cats have a much stronger sense of smell than humans and will tend to avoid an area where they can smell buried waste, be it their own or another cat's. Remove the waste at least once or twice day and empty and wash the box frequently —litter-pan liners can make this job easier. Have you changed the type of litter? Your cat may be averse to the consistency or fragrance of a new brand. Many cats dislike scented litter or litters composed of hard pellets. It's usually best to stick with unscented litter of the type your cat is used to; if you must switch, do it gradually. Where is the litter box situated? If the box is located in a noisy or busy area or if your cat was frightened by

Consistently prevent your feline from jumping onto kitchen countertops and eating tables; if you do it only when there's food around, you'll confuse the cat. To discourage leaps onto surfaces when you're not around, lay out sheets of aluminum foil or apply strips of double-sided tape. Most cats will quickly catch on and thereafter abide by the rule.

something while using it, move it to a safe cat-friendly site *(page 137)*. Leave a bowl of dry food at sites where you want your cat to stop eliminating; as a rule, cats don't eliminate at spots where they eat. You may need to move the litter box to its final location gradually or enclose your cat in the room where it is kept until he begins to use it again.

Another possibility is that your cat is spraying urine outside the box. Your cat will stand, tail raised high and quivering, and back paws often stepping rhythmically. Such behavior is usually sex-related, so if your cat, male or female, isn't already sterilized, have it done at once. If you catch your cat in the act, a scolding, "No!" may stop it that one time, but won't solve the problem. In fact, it may compound things by stressing the cat.

If you have recently adopted another cat or a dog, or if a newcomer has joined the household, even just temporarily, your cat may be reasserting its territoriality. Properly reintroduce the cat to the new pet *(page 89)* and try assigning a different member of the household to feed and play with each animal.

Are neighbors' cats hanging around outside, possibly spraying urine themselves? If so, this may trigger your indoor cat to respond in kind. Close off rooms that allow your cat to see and smell the cats outside. Talk to the owners of unneutered males about getting their cats fixed. Call your local animal control agency to report any strays. When a cat marks in response to stress, brought on by any kind of change in the household, a return to all established routines usually gets things back on track quickly.

The feline scratching reflex is simply too deeply ingrained to be eliminated. Declawing your cat won't do it and should be avoided if at all possible *(page 166)*. In addition to making furniture and other items less attractive to the cat by using physical barriers and other commercially available products *(page 167)*, encourage him to use other alternatives, such as a sturdy scratching post. To be effective, the post must be tall enough to allow the cat to stretch to full height without tipping it over and covered with rough, easily shredded material such as sisal rope, cardboard, or tree bark. Some cats love carpet-covered scratching posts, although their claws often get stuck; the more tattered the carpet, the better. Others like the feel of the carpet's underside. While most cats prefer vertical posts, some take to horizontal surfaces, so plan to experiment with different types and materials. Place a scratching post in an open area of your home where the cat's claw marks will be readily be seen. Since most cats enjoy a good scratch when they wake up, situate a second post near your cat's favorite sleeping spot. Rubbing your cat's paws up and down the post may attract him to it once his scent is deposited on it, but many cats will balk at having their paws held. Make the post more alluring by placing a favorite toy on top to climb to or by rubbing or spraying it with catnip. Reward your cat for scratching the post, either with affection and approval or a food treat; if he claws the furniture, apply repellent or double-sided tape to his target and move the post closer to the favored piece of furniture.

Instinctively compelled to mark his territory and shed layers of claws, your cat will seek out household items to scratch, even if his claws have been removed. You can apply double-sided tape to protect furniture or apply commercially available repellents, but the real solution is to provide a scratching post and then persuade your cat to use it.

CAT THERAPY

If your best attempts at discipline fail and your cat's behavior is prompting thoughts of eviction, it's time to seek professional help.

Start by consulting your vet to rule out any physical causes for your cat's behavior and to solicit advice on handling the problem. If the problem persists, your next step is to find a *certified* applied animal behaviorist or a vet who is board-certified in behavior to get to the bottom of the problem.

A trained animal behaviorist will often visit your home to witness the behavior in context. He or she will then design a suitable behavior modification program.

KEEPING
· THE PEACE ·

There's a natural social hierarchy in the feline world. Just as one lion cub will assume the best position for surveillance in the wild (opposite), one cat in a household will take over the highest vantage point in a room (above).

The antics of two or more cats are better entertainment than television. And what surer way is there to ease your guilt about leaving your cat alone during necessary absences than to know he has feline companionship? Whether best of friends or merely resigned cohabitants, cats will at least provide stimulation for each other, even if only in heated chase.

Some cats will be completely nonplussed by a new arrival. Others will consider the turn of events as nothing less than an encroachment on their space and an affront to their status. When another cat enters the scene, your first cat loses his territorial monopoly. A hierarchy will need to be established: Being first into the home doesn't automatically earn a feline the status of "top" cat. You can expect some conflict as both cats adjust to the new circumstances, even if initial introduction goes well. In time, however, most cats will come to a mutually acceptable arrangement. Be prepared to make allowances for both cats through the adjustment period, which can last for a week or two to many months.

SPLITTING UP THE TERRITORIAL PIE

After introducing the cats *(page 89)*, establish conditions to minimize possible friction, principally ensuring that each feels secure about his source of food. Just as felines in the wild exercise territoriality over the availability of prey, your cats may turn quite aggressive if at the sound of the can opener they fear they won't get enough food to eat. Such stress can easily lead to such behavior problems as fights and territory-marking contests.

Make sure each cat has access to his own resources: a feeding station, including a water bowl, set at a comfortable distance from others; and his own safe area to retreat to in case of hostilities. One cat may seem to be taking over, finishing his food first and nudging the other cat away from his bowl, or consistently displacing the other cat from a favored sleeping spot. While it may seem unfair not to intervene on behalf of the "under" cat, it is best to let the animals work out their own arrangement of which one rests where, as long as there is no serious aggression. Just make sure each cat is getting enough food, attention, and play.

FELINE RELATIONSHIP COUNSELING

Some arching of backs, hissing, and spitting are to be expected. These behaviors, along with occasional spats, are the cats' natural ways of renego-

Some cats, particularly kittens, aren't bothered by eating close to each other or even by sharing the same bowl. To prevent conflict and eliminate tension at mealtime, though, you may need to space food bowls far apart, possibly in different rooms, and provide each cat with his own water bowl.

tiating their relative social positions. But if a real fight breaks out, complete with ear-splitting screams and bodily injuries, it's time to intervene. Also step in if one cat is reduced to a bundle of nerves and hides all the time, overgrooms, stops eating, or stops using the litter box. You'll need to take action if any cat begins to spray, having him sterilized as soon as possible.

If trouble breaks out, separate the cats, giving each of them access to all his necessities in a stress-free safe room. Once each feline returns to normal on his own, go through the introduction process again. Before actually letting the cats meet face to face, you may want to add a step, allowing them only to see and smell each other from behind a barrier—for example, a screen door or a gate. This way, there's no risk of injury if one cat reacts aggressively. Continue this until the cats no longer behave antagonistically toward each other.

If one cat waylays the other en route to the food bowl or litter box, he is only mirroring the hunting behavior of a wild feline. A cat learns the paths of his prey, then hides in a convenient spot for an ambush. Most household ambushes involve play, at least on the part of the pouncer. However, if the pouncee isn't in the mood, aggression can result. This is a common problem when a younger cat lives with an older one. It can take a long time (perhaps even longer than their natural life span) for one cat to accept that the other doesn't like to play this way. The victim may become discouraged from eating or using the litter box if the attacks continue. Place food bowls and litter boxes in areas with clear, unobstructed views and remove any items that provide hiding spots for the antagonist. If you witness one cat stalking the other, about to pounce, chase, or attack—even if in a friendly or playful way—distract him, then reward him for stopping. If the aggressor is persistent, you may have to separate the cats for a few days, then reintroduce them. Let the assertive cat roam about while the other spends some time in his safe room, allowing the rambunctious cat to reestablish his self-esteem and confidence without resorting to aggression.

If all else fails, speak to your vet or a certified applied animal behaviorist for advice on remedying the situation. Sometimes medication can be effective in calming aggression until the cats can adjust to each other. If all these efforts fail and you feel the quality of life of one or both cats is being compromised, you may need to find a new home for one of them.

CAN DOGS AND CATS LIVE TOGETHER?

You'd love your cat and dog to become great companions, but you're willing to settle for having them just put up with each other. When introducing a new cat or dog into your household, start with the all-important meeting process (page 91). Next, set up the cat's food and water bowls in a dog-proof location. Place them high up or in a room barricaded by a gate that your cat can easily jump over or by a door with a cat-sized opening cut in it. Do the same for the litter box. Aside from providing for a stress-free toilet for your cat, this will keep your dog from adopting the revolting habit of chowing down on the box contents.

Even a nonaggressive dog may play a bit too rough for your cat. If so, brush up on your dog's training to discourage this and reward gentle interaction. If your cat stalks and attacks your dog, it may be a defensive reaction to a perceived threat. Punishment usually makes the problem worse. It is better to try to distract the cat with food or a toy.

"Fighting like cats and dogs?" Not these two. Many dogs and cats can coexist peacefully, but keeping some of one's natural behaviors from irking the other takes discipline and a little creative thinking.

THE TRAVELING
· CAT ·

The safest way for a feline to travel is inside a carrier. Having your cat ride on the ledge of the rear window may seem like fun, but it can spell disaster. The cat could jump out an open window or distract the driver and cause an accident. And consider the serious injuries both sustained and caused by a feline missile if you have a collision.

Cats get very attached to their surroundings. Add the fact that most car trips result in humiliating (and sometimes painful) sessions at the vet, complete with pokes, prods, and injections, and it's no wonder your cat disappears at the sound of his carrier being brought out. While many dogs like nothing better than to accompany their masters on car outings, travel with a cat can be difficult. Even if your cat is a decided homebody, there are ways you can help him cope a little better.

Cats tolerate carriers and the travel implied by them much more easily if they have been acclimatized at a young age. If you take your cat for frequent short drives to the store, to visit friends, or even just for the occasional spin around the block, he won't be as likely to associate travel with unpleasantness, such as those traumatic visits to the vet. If your cat is trained to a harness and leash, take him on car rides to check out nature a bit farther away than your backyard. When your cat becomes accustomed to these trips, you can begin to try longer ones.

THE DREADED CARRIER

A carrier is essential for transporting your cat. Get one to bring your new cat home in; the earlier he starts using one, the sooner he'll accept it easily. Put the carrier in an area where the cat normally sleeps and line the bottom with bedding that carries his scent. He may investigate the carrier on his own or you may be able to lure him inside with a favorite toy or a treat. Whenever the cat enters, give him verbal praise and a food reward; then, start to do the same with the door closed.

When the time comes to actually use the carrier, your cat may still be hesitant or unaccustomed to it, or simply may not like being coerced into it. If you try to nudge the cat in headfirst, he will probably straddle the door opening with all four paws, sending the carrier off on a slide across the floor. The best approach is to pick your cat up gently and distract him by repeating his name in a soothing voice. With the carrier against a wall to keep it from moving, back toward it and slowly put the cat in tail-end first. Close the door quickly so the cat doesn't dart out, then offer a treat and a few soothing words. Another option is to place the carrier end-up and swoop your cat in back-feet-first before he has a chance to realize what's going on. A panicky, struggling cat or one that turns aggressive during this exercise may need to be wrapped in a towel or put in a pillowcase for restraint until you can get him securely inside.

WHEN YOU CAN'T BE THERE

If you're going away, your cat will probably tolerate parting with you better than traveling along. The best-case scenario is to have someone who already knows and loves your cat move in for the duration. When this option isn't feasible, you can settle for two visits a day by a friend or sitter—one visit a day is acceptable, but only if necessary. Not only should these visits include feeding, changing the water, and dealing with the litter box, but spending some quality time with your cat, playing or cuddling. Ideally this cat sitter is someone your cat knows well and trusts, such as a friend, relative, or neighbor. Your next option is to ask friends or your vet for a referral. Check this person's references and call your local Better Business Bureau and animal protection agency to see if any complaints have been filed. Interview the person in your home to gauge the level of care your cat will be provided and, most importantly, to see how the cat and the sitter interact. If anything doesn't feel right, for whatever reason, find somebody else.

If you have no choice but to relocate your cat for your time away, see if any of your friends can keep him in their home. Since this isn't a permanent move, you can avoid some of the stress your cat might undergo in getting accustomed to a large new environment by having your friends confine him in a single room, particularly if they have other animals. If your cat is very confident and sociable, however, he may not need to be isolated.

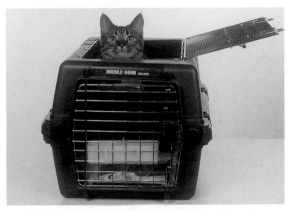

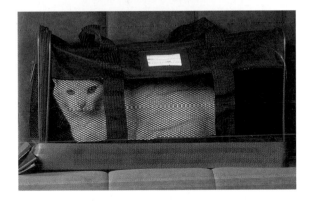

A carrier should be just large enough for your cat to stand, turn around, and lie down and also provide adequate ventilation. A rugged, high-impact plastic shell with a metal door (top) gives best protection. A top-hatch type (center) is easiest to get a cat into and out of. A soft-sided carrier (bottom) collapses for easy storage but is suitable only for short trips.

HOME ALONE: A CAT SITTER OR A KENNEL?

Sitters and kennels each have benefits and drawbacks. The primary advantage of a sitter is that your cat gets to stay in his secure home environment. Sitters can also give your home the "lived-in" look burglars avoid by taking in the newspapers and mail and turning different lights on and off. The main drawback comes if the sitter is not someone your cat already knows, but a stranger who he has to get to know and trust.

A kennel is a strange and potentially high-stress environment and your cat is likely to be confined for most of his stay. Contracting disease is also a possibility, especially if your cat is weakened by anxiety. In some of the better boarding facilities, however, your cat may get more attention and care than a sitter can provide with two daily visits.

Some kennels offer a variety of rooms, from simple cages to multilevel suites. Some are veritable palaces, offering television, piped-in music, lounge beds, and gourmet meals, possibly better accommodations than you'll get wherever you'll be staying.

As a last resort, you may have to find a kennel or a vet where you can board your cat. The same basic rules apply to finding a boarding facility as to finding a sitter: Interview thoroughly, check references, and question authorities. Ask friends which places they have used, and how they and their cats liked them. There is usually plenty of choice in kennels, so be choosy. Check the premises for hygiene and general upkeep, and make sure the owners demonstrate a sincere concern for the pets under their care. If they don't ask about your cat's temperament, feeding schedule and preferences, special needs, or general health, try another place. Be sure your cat will receive personalized care, have space of his own large enough to move around in and away from other animals, and be let out frequently into a play area to exercise. You should be asked to supply proof of vaccinations to decrease the possibility of a disease spreading from cat to cat and there should be an isolation area for any cats that have infectious diseases.

Whichever option you choose, leave emergency contact phone numbers for yourself, your vet, and a friend or family member whom you have authorized to make decisions if you can't be reached. Check in frequently with a sitter or a kennel. If you're trying out a new cat sitter in your home, have a friend or neighbor look in on your cat every few days.

TAKING YOUR CAT ALONG

If you will be away quite a while and feel the stress of traveling can be offset by the pleasure of you and your cat being together, you may consider taking your cat along. Or, perhaps you've taken your cat on progressively longer rides and feel he can cope with an extended trip. If you are leaving the country, call the animal authorities in the jurisdiction to which you are traveling to find out about special vaccination requirements, what documents you will need, and any other regulations concerning animals. International traveling papers can take time to process, so apply for them well in advance. If a quarantine is required, forget about taking the cat; the stress isn't worth it unless you're moving permanently. Visit the vet for a checkup and shots, advice on any sedatives, and details on fasting before the trip. Make sure your destined lodgings allow cats.

A collar and identification tag with your cat's name, your name, and the address and phone number of both your home and place of destination is essential. Your cat will also need his harness and leash; his usual food (to avoid stomach upsets); a bottle of his usual drinking water (gradually substitute local water at your destination); his bowls, litter box, a supply of litter, and a scooper; first-aid and grooming supplies; health records, including vaccination certificates, and medications; and a few favorite toys from home. Don't forget cleanup supplies, including paper towels and spray cleaner. Lining the bottom of the carrier with disposable diapers will soak up any "accidents" and simplify cleanups.

When traveling by car, place the carrier in a secure spot where it won't wobble or shift around. If your cat is nervous, drape a towel over the carrier, but don't obstruct ventilation. Soft music on the radio can help calm your cat, as can reassuring words from you. Drive as smoothly as you can and at rest stops, harness the cat before opening the doors to let him have a stretch and use his litter box. Always be on the watch for heatstroke *(page 173)*; never leave your cat unattended in the car.

If flying to your destination, the best place for your cat is in the cabin with you, in range of your scent and comforting voice. Try to book a direct flight during a slow period, such as a weekday evening, to minimize travel time. Be sure to let your travel agent know that you will be taking along a cat. Most airlines limit the number of animals they allow per flight and will charge a fee for a pet to travel in the cabin with you. Ask about specific regulations such as the size of carrier that will fit under an aircraft seat.

If your cat must travel in the plane's cargo hold, check with your vet about sedation and make sure heat and oxygen will be controlled. Since you won't be with your cat, take extra precautions: Be sure the carrier is sturdy, in good condition, and rated for air travel. It should be boldly marked "Live Animal" on the top and sides. Line it with soft bedding, topped by disposable diapers. For a long trip with connections, fasten a bag of dry food to the top of the carrier, along with written instructions for feeding and watering.

Cats often sense something is afoot as soon as the packing begins and will either try to help out or go into hiding. Confine outdoor cats to the house; the stress of the change may make them run away. If your cat is especially anxious, consult your vet; sedation may help calm him until you are settled into your new home.

MOVING

Relocation means serious upheaval to a cat and is a time of great stress. On moving day, set up a safe room for your cat with food, water, litter box, bed, and toys. Lock the door to the room or post a large sign to prevent someone from opening it and letting your cat escape. Once at your new home, your cat will have to investigate everything in the same way a newly adopted cat does in its first days *(page 98)* and confining him to a small area at first may be helpful. However, rediscovering familiar household items can ease the transition, as will getting back into your cat-care routine as quickly as possible. It may take several weeks before an outdoor cat knows his new territory enough to be trusted to return home, a period of opportunity to convert him to being exclusively an indoor cat *(page 204)*.

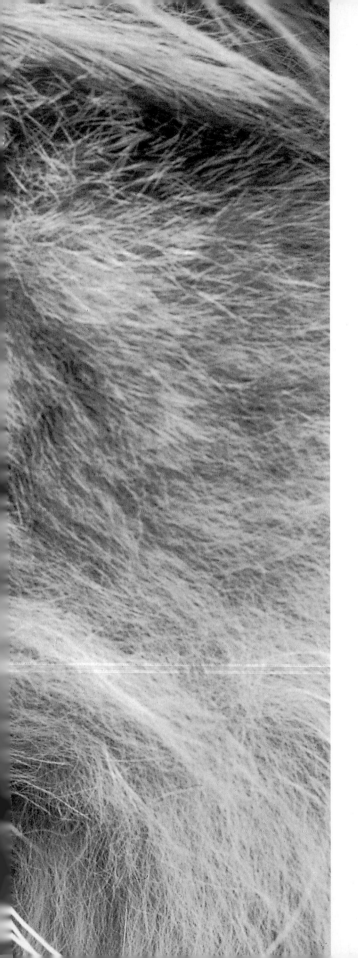

CAT
CARE

◆ ◆ ◆

"A home without a cat,
and a well-fed, well-petted
and properly revered cat,
may be a perfect home, perhaps;
but how can it prove its title?"

◆

MARK TWAIN

FEEDING &
·NUTRITION·

Despite its long hair, this cat looks thin. Checking a cat's ribs is the best way to judge if it is undernourished. The ribs should be covered by a thin layer of fat, but easily felt by pressing your hand against its side. If the ribs are prominent, the cat is underweight and should be seen by a veterinarian.

Overleaf: Silver tabby Persian

Standing in front of the vast selection of cat food available at pet-supply stores, you may feel you need a degree in feline nutrition to choose the appropriate food for your pet. Don't worry; it's not as complicated as it might seem. Start narrowing down your choices by selecting from products appropriate for your cat's age. Many manufacturers have a food formulated for each stage of a cat's life: kitten, adult (regular and diet), and senior. Kittens, for example, need more protein and fat than adult cats, while older cats need fewer calories.

If your cat has any health problems, this will affect your choice. An overweight cat can benefit from a diet food, but check with your vet before making a switch. If your cat is pregnant or has kidney or heart disease, your vet may suggest a special "prescription" diet available through the clinic. This may be temporary, although in some cases your cat will have to be on this food for the rest of his life.

Choosing between canned or dry food is largely a matter of convenience and preference. While you may find yourself holding your breath as you scoop out canned food, most cats love this mucky stuff, and the high nutrient content in the better brands means your cat can eat smaller quantities to meet his dietary needs. But any portion left in the can isn't very tasty if served straight out of the fridge. Heat it up a bit first, but only to body temperature. Dry food is easier to serve and won't spoil if left out for the day. It's also considerably cheaper.

For the long-term health of your cat, a premium brand is worth the investment; ask your vet for some recommendations. You may want to alternate among a few of the high-quality brands, serving one kind for a couple of months, then changing to another. If your cat becomes so used to one type of food that it's all he'll eat, you'll be in a bind if ever it isn't available. But because cats' digestive systems can be delicate, radical changes of food may cause diarrhea. Introduce new food or alternate brands gradually, adding more of the new food while decreasing the proportion of the original food until the changeover is complete.

An ample supply of clean water is also key to your cat's well-being. To make the watering hole appealing to fastidious feline tastes, keep the bowl clean and change the water at least twice a day. While cats eating canned food consume a fair amount of water in their diets, cats eating only dry food will need to drink more.

Obesity is often a problem with older, sedentary cats and can lead to a host of medical problems. To combat this weighty issue, a wide range of dietary cat foods and foods specifically designed for mature cats is available. Some owners actually "kill with kindness" by overfeeding, possibly because they feel guilty about leaving their cat alone most of the time. Fitting in regular play sessions or acquiring a companion cat would be a much better solution.

MEALTIME

While leaving out dry food so your cat can eat whenever he's hungry may be convenient, "free feeding" leads some cats to overeat, often out of boredom. The alternative is scheduled feeding: Two or three meals a day at set intervals is a good pattern. (One big meal may encourage your cat to bolt down the food and more than three meals per day can overtax the digestive system). Feed your cat in the same place every time—a quiet spot that's out of traffic routes and well away from the litter box or your cat may refuse to eat there. Leave the food out for a set period of time (fifteen to thirty minutes), then remove the bowls until the next scheduled feeding time.

Mealtime becomes more complicated when you have more than one cat, since their appetites and eating behavior will probably vary; they may even eat different foods. Use separate food and water bowls for each cat, set well apart, always placed in the same locations. Feed the slowest eater first and

While a group of kittens or very well-adjusted adult cats will happily eat close together or even from the same bowl, in general cats should be given their own food and water bowls and personal dining spots. As creatures of habit, they will come to know their own feeding stations. Place mats will help keep your floor clean—many cats remove food from the bowl in order to have a better go at it on the floor.

the fastest eater last. If one of your cats gulps down his share and immediately bulldozes his way into the neighboring bowl, discourage him, removing him from the room if necessary. Or, if you have a cat that doesn't eat his entire portion in one go, cover his bowl with a plate, then uncover it later for him to finish (refrigerate the leftovers if the food is canned).

An occasional healthy treat in addition to regular meals won't cause any harm and can, in fact, be a useful training tool. But the key words here are "occasional" and "healthy." Limit between-meal extras or you'll eventually have an overweight cat on your hands. Avoid foods intended for humans; they don't contribute to a complete and balanced cat diet. Fish, for example, is not only high in unsaturated fat (which cats have trouble metabolizing), but in sufficient quantities will sap the body of vitamin E and lead to steatitis (a painful skin condition). Pet-supply stores offer a variety of healthful treats; ask your vet which ones would be good for your cat.

Be careful about milk. Many adult cats are lactose-intolerant, so diarrhea may result. If you really want to give liquid treats, you can try milk in very small amounts, but stop the practice if it causes an intestinal upset.

FAT CATS AND FINICKY KITTIES

In most cases, if you feed your cat high-quality food in quantities suggested by your veterinarian and if he gets sufficient exercise, he will maintain an ideal weight. But if your cat becomes overweight or is underweight, it's time to take action. You can judge your cat's correct weight by his ribs: If they are clearly visible, he's too thin; if they are difficult to detect by touch, he's overweight. Take a look at your cat from above: If his sides bulge out, he's overweight; if they are concave, he's too thin.

Obesity, the most common food-related problem, is easy to correct. First, talk to your vet about the weight-loss program that's right for your cat. In many cases, this will involve switching to a high-fiber, low-fat diet and scheduled feedings. Introduce any new diet slowly—suddenly placing an overweight cat on a strict diet can cause fat to accumulate in the liver, leading to liver failure. Along with a change of food, it's also a good idea to encourage a sedentary cat to become more active through play *(page 113)*. A scrawny cat that doesn't gain weight should be seen by the vet. If there is no health problem, ask for a good food to bulk up your bag of bones.

It's not a big deal if your cat skips a meal every now and then, but a finicky cat that repeatedly turns up his nose at his food is another story. If he's holding out because a new food is being introduced, make the change even more gradual. Some cats simply don't like a variety of foods and may not eat again until they get their favorite dish. It will become more dangerous to hold out, in the hope that your cat will come around to the new diet, than to feed the same food daily. Don't let your cat go without food any longer than twenty-four hours before you take him to the vet; disinterest in food may be the first sign of a serious illness.

Just as wild felines cover the remains of a kill with leaves to hide it from predators so they can come back for more later, your cat scratches around his bowl in an attempt to cover any remaining food.

YOU ARE WHAT YOU EAT

Without a complete and well-balanced diet, your cat is susceptible to a variety of health problems. Premium cat foods are well formulated and provide the necessary nutrients, while lower-quality diets can have dangerous, even life-threatening, consequences. At the first sign of any health problem, contact your vet.

◆ Some cats are prone to the formation of crystals in the bladder, which can result in a urinary blockage, a very serious condition that most often occurs in males. Aside from stress, obesity, inactivity, and low water intake, other contributing factors appear to be the magnesium content of food and pH of the cat's urine, which is directly influenced by diet. Ash content was once believed to be a factor, but while cat foods may be labeled "low ash," this is no longer considered to be important. Ask your vet to recommend the food that will be best for your cat.

◆ Flaky skin and dull, dry hair may indicate a diet poor in either protein or fatty acids and possibly zinc.

◆ Retinal degeneration can be caused by a deficiency of taurine, found in meat, poultry, and fish. Cats need much more taurine than dogs, so dog food, which is low in taurine, is not acceptable for cats.

ALL ABOUT
· LITTER ·

There's no way around it. If you have a cat, you need a litter box. And if you have a litter box, you have to clean it—often. Even outdoor cats that prefer to heed the call of nature outside will occasionally have to "go" indoors. But litter boxes don't have to be a messy source of bad smells. With the right type of box and litter, and, most importantly, diligent cleaning habits, you can keep the odor down with a minimum of fuss and prevent your cat from using the carpet rather than a smelly litter box.

THE DIRT ON KITTY LITTER

Until the introduction of clay litter in 1947, cat owners had to make do with messier options such as sawdust, wood ash, or sand. Clay litter proved so effective at absorbing moisture and odors that the popularity of cats as indoor pets rose sharply. In the 1980s, the arrival of clumping litter was a

The rule of thumb for multi-cat households is to provide one litter box for each cat, plus an extra one, whether you're using the covered boxes and standard pans shown below or one of the many new litter-box designs. This formula is not based on the concept that each cat will use one box exclusively, although this may happen, but to make sure there is a sufficient quantity of unsoiled litter available at all times.

huge breakthrough, much appreciated by cat owners, doubly so by those in charge of multi-cat households. Taking advantage of clay's binding properties, this type of litter dissolves as it absorbs urine or the moisture in feces, encasing the waste in a hard lump. The lumps can then be quickly removed (some types are even flushable), keeping odors to a minimum. Clumping litter has skyrocketed in popularity, and while it is more expensive by weight than the conventional clay type, it doesn't have to be completely replaced as often.

Perhaps the greatest problem with clumping litter is that just as it sticks to the moisture in cat waste, it sticks to anything else that is moist—wet feet and wet fur—and gets tracked around the house. Manufacturers now offer products with slightly larger granules that don't track as easily. Concerns also have been raised in recent years over the possibility that clay-based clumping litter, particularly brands using sodium bentonite as the binding agent, may cause dangerous or even fatal intestinal blockages if ingested. To date, however, no clinical evidence of this has emerged and most experts agree this fear is simply the product of misinformed rumors. But to be on the safe side, don't use this type of litter until your kitten is at least four months old or past the stage where he tries to eat everything. Another health concern related to any of the clay-based products is the possibility that the crystalline silica dust in them may be dangerous if inhaled. Dust is a particular problem in covered boxes. Some veterinarians believe inhaling the dust in an enclosed space contributes to respiratory diseases such as asthma in cats.

Along with these potential health problems, concerns over the environmental impact of clay strip-mining have had litter manufacturers scurrying to come up with alternatives. A wide variety of organically based, silica-dust-free litters derived from renewable resources ranging from orange peels to wheat are now on the market (page 139). All these products absorb reasonably well, control odor, and demonstrate varying degrees of clumping. Wheat litters, for example, form hard, unbreakable clumps on contact with moisture, making them ideal for households with more than one cat, where a box user often steps on a clump. And some of these types of litter fit the bill for cats recovering from declawing surgery, with little dust that could cause infection and without the sharp edges that could cause pain when digging.

WHO DECIDES WHAT'S BEST?

When it comes right down to it, your pet will make the final choice. While some happy-go-lucky cats will accept whatever product is on sale this week, most are more fussy. Once you find a brand to your cat's liking, stick with it. You may first need to experiment with a few different types of litter, so start with the smallest packages available. Deodorized litter may sound

LOCATION, LOCATION, LOCATION

Where you put the litter box is as important as what you put in it and involves thinking like a cat. Accept that your never-ending job of scooping poop is vital to your cat's happiness, then both you and your pet can focus on more important things, such as playtime.

◆ Place the litter box in an accessible but private and quiet location; an out-of-the-way spot is a must if there is a child or dog in the house. The bathroom is a good option if you can ensure that the door is always left open. Beware of the seemingly ideal laundry room; the noise of washing machines can make your cat run for cover. Never, ever, let anyone or anything disturb your cat when he is doing his business; this can result in an aversion to the box and you can imagine what that means.

◆ Fill the box with the appropriate quantity of litter. Rather than cutting down on odor, using too much litter causes urine to spread out and will make the problem worse. Also most cats don't like wading through hip-deep litter. With too little, absorbency is restricted and this also leads to potential odor problems. In general, a two-inch layer is about right.

◆ Check the box at least twice a day. Keep a slotted scoop nearby to remove solid waste or clumps of wet litter; for non-clumping litter, have a large spoon to remove urine-soaked particles. Add a bit more fresh litter as necessary and empty, wash, and disinfect the box regularly.

THE FANCY LITTER BOX

 A sifting type of litter box allows you to remove all the clumps without ever having to poke around with a scoop. A common design has a grate under the litter that can be easily replaced or a set of interlocking pans—the top one is used as a sieve, then placed on the bottom; the two that remain overlap in such a way as to contain the litter.

Roll-over boxes let you sift the litter into the cover by simply turning the box over. Waste and clumps are caught in a grill and the top becomes the new bottom. Another model removes waste when you tip the unit one way, then drops it in a removable drawer when you tip the unit back upright.

For the lover of high-tech gizmos there is the fully automated litter box. It senses when a cat has left the box and about ten minutes later a mechanical rake sweeps the box clean of clumps, depositing them into a disposable container. It can be noisy, though, and that disturbs some cats.

There is even a litter-free type that has large stone granules and collects urine on disposable, absorbent pads.

Some litter boxes are designed to look like pieces of furniture. This model provides privacy and when the cat jumps up onto the grate in order to get out, any granules caught in its paws fall back into the box. No more tracking litter all over the house.

appealing, but don't think it absolves you of your scooping duties. Furthermore, some cats are actually put off by the "clean" smell. Signs of discontent include excessive scratching or vocalizing around the litter-box location. Ignore this and your cat will find a definitive way to tell you he doesn't like your litter selection: The box will be clean, the floor dirty.

CHOOSING A LITTER BOX

Litter-box choices range from simple plastic containers that resemble dishpans to covered boxes and a variety of more sophisticated models, as described above. Whatever variation you choose, the box must be big enough to allow your cat to carry out typical feline elimination behavior: sniffing the area, digging a hole, and turning around several times before getting down to business. Kittens require a box with sides low enough for them to get in and out easily. Once they can climb or jump, a model with higher sides provides privacy and helps keep the litter inside the box.

Covered boxes prevent stains on walls from cats that stand up to urinate and scattering of litter by cats that scratch excessively in the box. They also keep the contents out of reach of dogs and small children. The covered boxes do have drawbacks. They trap the litter dust that can cause health problems and if you neglect maintenance duties because you don't smell or see the contents, the box's advantage becomes a disadvantage. Your cat, with his finely honed sense of smell, has to deal with a stinky neglected litter box and may end up eliminating elsewhere.

CLEANING UP

How do you avoid that dreaded housebound cat smell? Simple: Clear out waste frequently and keep the box itself clean. Scoop out the waste at least twice a day, tie it up in a plastic bag, and throw it away; if it's flushable, you can simply drop it into the toilet. Completely empty and clean the box about once a week. Scrub the pan and the scoop with detergent to clean and a small amount of bleach to disinfect, then rinse thoroughly. Let the box dry fully before refilling it with litter. A plastic liner makes your cleanup easier, but works best in a box with a rim or cover to hold it in place. Cats that really enjoy scratching in the box may tear the plastic, thereby defeating the purpose. A secondary benefit of these chores is that they give you the chance to keep tabs on your cat's health. If you notice changes in feces, blood in the urine, or any unusual elimination habits, call the vet for advice.

LOOKING AT LITTER

TYPE	DESCRIPTION	CHARACTERISTICS
Citrus peel	Processed orange or grapefruit peels	Natural; lightweight; highly absorbent; flushable in small amounts. Acids in peels neutralize urine odor. Safe for recently declawed cats.
Clay (conventional)	Rocky granules	Common; very inexpensive; available in wide range of formulas varying in degree of dustiness; not flushable. Unless urine-soaked litter removed, must be completely replaced every few days.
Clay (clumping)	Sandy texture; ranges from very fine to large grains	Common; longer-lasting than conventional clay; relatively inexpensive; comes in wide range of formulas varying in dustiness and solidity of clumps; most brands not flushable. Unless contains odor-reducing additive (e.g. baking powder), clumps must be removed to cut smell.
Corncobs	Ground corncobs formed into pellets	Natural; highly absorbent; forms clumps; flushable in small amounts. Neutralizes urine odor.
Grass	Pelletized winter wheat grass	Natural; highly absorbent; flushable in small amounts.
Nut shells	Granules made from powdered and reconstituted peanut shells	Natural; lightweight; forms clumps; flushable in small amounts.
Paper	De-inked, recycled newspaper; pelletized or granular texture	Eco-friendly; low-dust; some types form clumps; flushable in small amounts. Safe for recently declawed cats.
Wheat	Fine-textured ground wheat	Natural; low-dust; forms solid clumps; flushable in small amounts. Neutralizes urine odor.
Wood	Wood chips, pellets, or sawdust and shavings	Natural; flushable in small amounts. Neutralizes urine odor. Some types safe for recently declawed cats.

FELINE BEAUTY
· PARLOR ·

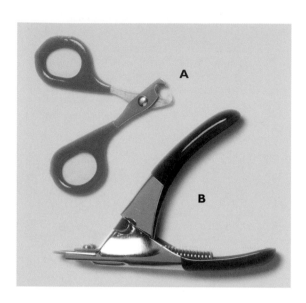

Scissor- **(A)** or guillotine-type **(B)** clippers cut your cat's claws at the proper angle without crushing them. Keep the blades sharp to ensure clean cuts.

If you are assuming that cats take care of all their grooming needs themselves, think again. Your role in your cat's grooming is a little more complicated than simply running a brush through his fur. While keeping the coat clean, shiny, and untangled is a large part of the job, your cat's toilette is not complete until his claws are trimmed, his eyes and ears cleaned, and his teeth brushed. Your duties may even extend to bathing your pet in some instances: for longhair cats, on occasion, and for older cats no longer flexible enough to completely groom themselves. Not only does all this maintenance keep your cat beautiful, but some of it also serves as preventive medicine. The more hair you remove by brushing, for instance, the less your cat will ingest when he grooms himself, reducing the number of hairballs he throws up and averting a potentially deadly blockage of the intestines by clumps of hair.

Clipping your cat's claws reduces the likelihood of damage to the furniture and helps protect your skin from playful scratches. It's safer to trim less rather than more of the nail, to avoid cutting through the quick—the thicker section of the nail that is supplied with blood *(inset)*.

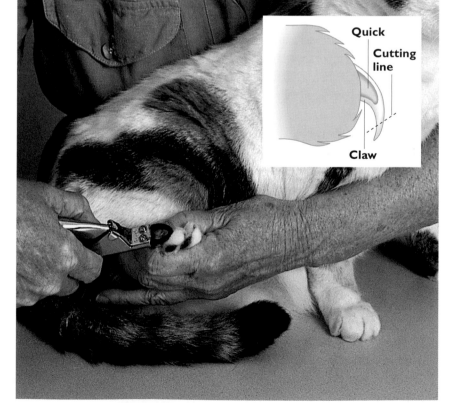

Set up a grooming routine at a regular time and in a quiet room; for skittish pets, divide the procedure into short, cat-acceptable sessions. Have all the grooming tools and supplies you may need within easy reach.

TRIMMING CLAWS

Trimming claws needn't strike terror in the heart of you or your cat. Even an adult cat that is unaccustomed to nail clipping can grow to accept the procedure, although it's best to start when the cat is young and everything is novel. Kittens' tiny needlelike claws should be trimmed once a week; by the time a cat is about eight months old, you can reduce the trimming to once every two to four weeks for the rest of the cat's life.

Place your cat on a table or hold him on your lap, or kneel down and clamp him between your legs. Grip a paw firmly and gently press on the pad to expose the claw. Don't forget to also trim the dew claws that are further up along the paw. If you have a polydactyl cat, one with extra toes similar to thumbs, the claws in the folds between the paws and the "thumbs" also need trimming.

Using special clippers (*opposite*), trim off the clear, curved part of the claw in one rapid motion, cutting straight across and making sure to stay at least one-tenth of an inch away from the thicker part containing the vein, or "quick." When in doubt, cut off less claw and do the job more often. If you do accidentally cut the vein, stay calm. The claw will bleed, but your demeanor will affect your cat's reaction. Ideally, have clotting powder, a styptic pencil, cornstarch, or soft bar-soap on hand before you begin and apply it to the end of the claw. Or, you can press a gauze pad, clean cloth, or tissue over the damaged nail for several minutes until the bleeding stops.

Some cats (even first-time adults) will allow you to cut all their claws right away. For less cooperative cats, start by simply handling their paws more and more, pressing lightly on the paw pads to extend the claws. Once this is accepted, try clipping one or two claws, stopping and letting your cat go whenever he starts to resist; eventually, you will cut them all. A team effort may be necessary to contain a writhing cat, with one person firmly grasping the loose skin at the scruff of the neck or holding the cat wrapped in a towel with just one paw at a time free, leaving the second person to handle the task of clipping.

CLEANING EARS AND EYES

Check inside the ears every week and if you see a waxy residue, wipe it off with a cotton ball moistened with a small amount of feline ear cleaner or baby oil. (Never use a swab on a stick; if your cat moves suddenly, as he is wont to do, you may injure his ear canal or eardrum.) Hold the ear flap gently and dab carefully with the cotton ball. If your cat fidgets during cleaning, restrain him as you would when cutting his claws.

Be very gentle when cleaning your cat's ears; they are sensitive. A mild ear cleaner, specifically for cats and available at pet-supply stores and vet clinics, will help you with this task. Only wipe what you can reach with a cotton ball; don't stick anything down inside the ear. Dark residue may be a sign of ear mites (*page 147*).

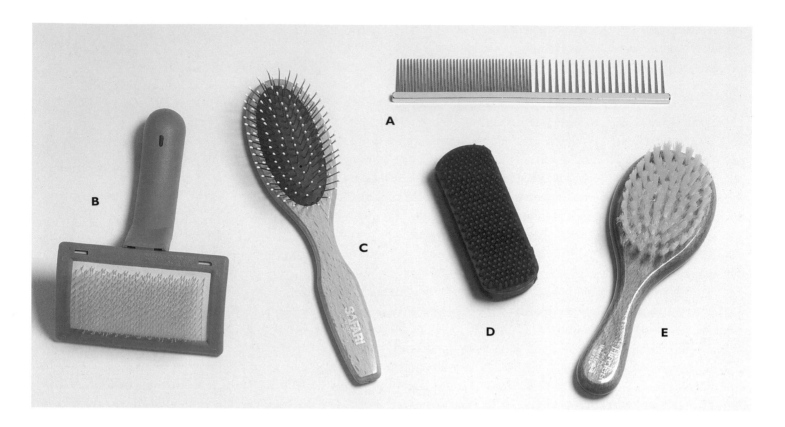

(A) A metal comb picks up stray hairs after a thorough brushing. Use a medium- or wide-toothed comb for longhair cats, a fine-toothed comb or even a very fine-toothed flea comb for shorthair cats.

(B) The slicker brush removes light tangles and mats from longhair cats. It can also be used to brush cats with short or semi-long hair once any mats have been removed.

(C) A wire-pin brush is meant for longhair cats.

(D) A rubber brush is ideal for shorthair cats.

(E) A bristle brush with long, widely spaced bristles is good for longhair cats. For shorthair cats, bristles should be short and closely spaced. Silky hair calls for soft bristles, while stiff bristles are good for coarse hair.

Clean around the eyes with a cotton ball or a soft, clean cloth dampened with warm water. Certain breeds will require more attention in this area. Flat-faced cats such as Persians, for example, tend to tear more than other breeds and the discharge may build up if you aren't vigilant. Apply a tearstain remover specifically for cats if the face is getting discolored.

BRUSHING

Although cats are tidy creatures by nature and groom themselves, they still need regular brushing. In addition to removing loose hair that would otherwise be swallowed or left on furniture, brushing promotes good circulation, stimulates the skin, and keeps the coat shiny. It's also a way to bond with your cat, as well as to check for any body changes that may signal a visit to the vet.

The procedure is much the same for shorthair and longhair cats, but the tools will differ, depending on the length and texture of your cat's fur. A selection of basic brushes and combs is shown above. You may have to experiment a bit before you hit on the ideal ones for your cat.

Be sure to check a longhair cat for mats before you start brushing and very gently untangle any you find using your fingers or a wide-toothed comb. Soak more tenacious knots with detangling liquid or spray. If a mat won't come apart, you can, if you're very careful, snip it out with blunt-tipped scissors. Your cat's skin is very sensitive, as well as being loose, and it's fairly easy to make an accidental nick. Protect your cat by placing a fine-toothed comb between the mat and his skin. The alternative is to have mats removed by a professional groomer; if your cat is badly matted, this is the only option. You may also want to trim the furry trousers of a longhair cat to prevent them from trapping waste from the litter box. Some owners of longhair cats who find feces in the house mistakenly think that their cats are defecating outside the box, when in fact the stool has hitched a ride out of the box on the cat's hairy hindquarters.

Begin grooming by passing the brush along the cat's head and back. By following the same line you would if you were petting him, chances are the cat will relax, lulled by the pleasant sensation. Then, brush down the length of each side. As you go, stop often to clean the brush of collected hair. Next, brush down from below the chin along the throat and chest. To brush the inside of your cat's leg, hold him against your chest and reach over the outside of the leg. Your cat may object when you get to such areas as the rear thighs, the region where the legs join the body, and the belly. Be gentle and reassuring, but persevere without overdoing it. If the cat is getting anxious, stop and continue later; otherwise, you risk turning grooming into a hateful experience. Do the tail last, one small section at a time, carefully combing in the direction that the hair grows. Then, repeat the sequence with a fine-toothed comb, taking particular care on sensitive areas, to pick up any remaining loose hairs.

Eyes squeezed in contentment, this cat loves the feel of the rubber brush. Although shorthair cats are easier to groom than longhairs and generally don't have a problem with mats, they, too, should be brushed regularly.

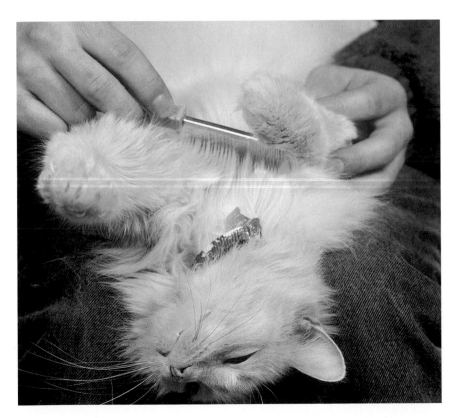

While not all cats will be as relaxed during their grooming, this longhair obviously enjoys his owner's efforts. If the coat is neglected, mats can become so bad that even walking pulls on the fur and causes pain. At this point, a professional groomer is needed. Your cat may come home looking like he's stepped in from the wild, with a so-called "lion" cut, in which everything but his "mane," legs, and tip of the tail is shaved. Generally, the fur takes at least three months to grow back to its original length, giving you the chance to start brushing regularly before it is long enough to get tangled again.

BATHING A CAT

An older or injured cat may not be able to keep itself adequately clean and may need to be bathed. Some cats become very agitated during the process, however, so it's up to you to make bathing as stress-free as possible for all participants. You'll probably want a helper so one of you can hold the cat while the other does the shampooing. Both of you will probably get quite wet, so have lots of towels at the ready. It's also possible that you may get scratched, so take a few moments to trim the claws first.

Placing something in the sink or tub that your cat can grip with his claws—a window screen, rubber mat, or several thick towels—may help him feel slightly more in control and less inclined to struggle. Never dump your cat into a sink full of water; total immersion is not the idea here. Instead, fill the sink with just enough warm water to rinse him easily. Hold your cat firmly, with one hand grasping his front legs, and place him in the water. Pour water over him with a small container and use a washcloth to wet more delicate areas such as the face and ears. Standard shampoos formulated for cats should be rubbed in thoroughly, then fully rinsed. Any traces of shampoo left on the cat's coat can cause irritation, so don't rush through this stage. If you are washing the cat with a flea shampoo, follow the directions for the product to the letter.

After properly rinsing your cat, wrap him in a thick towel and hold him close to absorb the excess water. Continue drying by carefully squeezing the

Not many cats are big fans of water. Most put up quite a fuss at bath time, so go through the procedure as calmly as possible. If you are using a spray hose, test the water temperature first and use a gentle flow. Placing the nozzle directly on the body will make the jet less frightening to the cat.

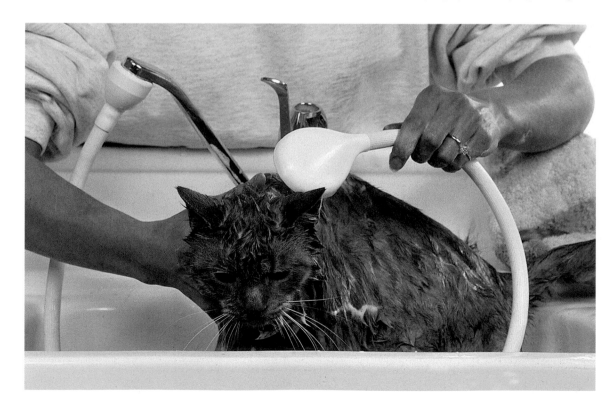

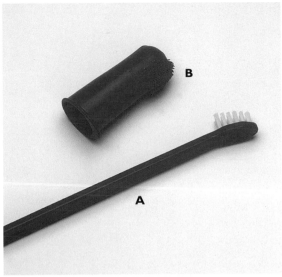

Brushing your cat's teeth regularly will not only save you the expense of having the procedure done by your vet, but also saves your cat from having to be anesthetized, which poses serious risks for cats with underlying health problems such as heart and kidney disease. Patience is key to conditioning your cat to toothbrushing. Keep sessions short and be very gentle and encouraging. A cat toothbrush (A) is designed specifically for small feline mouths; a finger brush (B) offers more control. A folded square of gauze can substitute for either.

towel against his body and pulling it away again. You can gently rub short-hair cats with a towel, but this may cause matting in cats with longer coats. A small hair dryer can be useful (unless your cat is frightened by the noise of the motor). Keep the hair dryer on its lowest setting and never point it in your cat's face. Once he is dry, brush him thoroughly and compliment him effusively on how wonderful he looks.

DENTAL CARE

As part of a regular checkup, your vet will look for signs of plaque and tartar buildup on your cat's teeth. Left unchecked, periodontal disease can actually contribute to heart, liver, or kidney disease. If a significant problem has begun to develop, a thorough cleaning, requiring the cat to be anesthetized, will have to be scheduled.

To avoid the bother and expense of such cleaning, which is typically required every few years, brush your cat's teeth at least every other day. This is not as difficult, or crazy, as it might sound, as long as you introduce the procedure very slowly. For the first few days, sit quietly with your cat and gently stroke the outside of his cheeks. Then, let him lick a small quantity of cat dentifrice—never human toothpaste—off your finger. Next, place a small quantity of the paste on a cat-sized toothbrush or gauze square. Gently push back the cat's top lip with your thumb and brush one or two teeth and the neighboring gums in a circular motion, pressing very lightly. Over several days, gradually brush a larger number of teeth. After each short session, reward your cat with a treat, preferably one for tartar control.

COMMON HEALTH
· PROBLEMS ·

Grooming time is the perfect opportunity to give your cat a weekly mini-checkup. Look for fleas or flea dirt, for black waxy residue in his ears, and for runny eyes. Feel his whole body for any unusual lump or skin problem. A dull, dry coat or a bald patch tells you that your cat isn't in top health. Once a month, extend this into a more thorough physical exam: Check the teeth for yellow or brown tartar deposits, and press on the gum; once released, it should quickly pinken. Carefully pull down each lower eyelid; what you see should be pink. Both pupils should be the same size; shine light on them and they should both narrow. Note your findings in your cat's medical journal and call your vet about anything out of the ordinary.

Despite your best efforts at keeping your cat healthy and safe, chances are that he will become ill at some time or other in his life. But since he can't tell you about any physical changes he's undergoing or if he's feeling ill or is in pain, you'll need to pick up on any physical symptoms or subtle (sometimes not so subtle) changes in his behavior. The earlier any warning signs are detected and brought to your vet's attention, the sooner treatment can begin, possibly preventing a much more serious and potentially expensive problem. Your vet will certainly look for any physical signs of problems and ask you about behavioral indicators during the annual checkup, but keeping an eye out for changes between vet visits can make a big difference to your cat's health.

In order to note any deviations from the norm, however, you need to know what the norm is for your cat. Such things as activity level, sleeping habits, and temperament are easy to identify. They define the cat you live with. But you should also observe posture, gait, and general appearance. Weigh him once a month and pay attention to his eating, drinking, and elimination habits (including amount and consistency of waste). Changes in these areas are very good indications that something is awry. Start a simple feline medical journal for all this baseline information. Also record vaccinations and medications that the cat is given and any other veterinary procedures that the cat undergoes.

Call your vet to discuss any subtle changes to your cat's behavior or body described in the chart at right. If necessary, get to the clinic within the time frame suggested. Serious injuries or acute disorders may require immediate veterinary care; knowing some basic first aid *(page 168)* can mean getting the cat to the clinic alive.

BEHAVIORAL SIGNS

Cats do not announce their health problems to the world at large, not because they are stoic or don't feel pain, but because in the wild any outward sign of weakness is a fatal invitation to predators and competitors. Even the most ferocious of wild cats will retire and hide when injured or ill so that healing can happen undisturbed. Small changes in your cat's habits may be your only clue to his discomfort.

Although cats are solitary, most interact with their owner in the course of the day and stick to their familiar routines. A cat that chooses to be alone

HEALTH PROBLEMS AT A GLANCE

Sign	Possible causes or conditions	What to do
Abdominal pain or hardness	Bladder infection or blockage; severe constipation; pregnancy; intestinal problem	Consult vet immediately.
Change in eating or drinking habits	Stress; variety of disorders	Consult vet; if cat hasn't eaten for twenty-four hours, see vet as soon as possible.
Coughing	Allergy; upper respiratory system infection; lung parasites	Consult vet within twenty-four hours.
Constipation	Change in diet; dehydration; intestinal blockage	Add water or fiber (bran, pumpkin) to food or try hairball remedy. If symptoms persist, consult vet.
Dark residue or foul odor in ears; shaking of head or scratching ear	Ear mites; ear infection	Consult vet within twenty-four hours.
Diarrhea	Stress; change in diet; food allergy; intestinal infection or parasites; inflammatory bowel disease	If symptoms persist for more than a few days, consult vet. If combined with vomiting, see vet as soon as possible.
Difficulty breathing; wheezing	Asthma; allergy; respiratory system infection; lung parasites	Consult vet immediately.
Difficulty urinating; blood in urine	Urinary tract infection or blockage	Consult vet immediately.
Excessive scratching or licking	Fleas; skin disorder; allergy; wound	Check for and eliminate fleas (page 152); otherwise consult vet within twenty-four hours.
Excessive thirst and urination	Diabetes; kidney disorder	Consult vet within twenty-four hours.
Foul breath	Dirty teeth; gum infection; abscess	Brush teeth (page 145) and feed dry food; if symptoms severe or persist, consult vet.
Inflamed eyes or eyelids	Eye infection; allergy; injury	Consult vet within twenty-four hours.
Loss of appetite (anorexia)	Stress; gastrointestinal or other disorder	If cat hasn't eaten for twenty-four hours, see vet as soon as possible.
Loss of balance or coordination	Injury; blood loss; brain or spinal trauma; poisoning	Consult vet immediately.
Pale gums and mucous membranes	Anemia	Consult vet immediately.
Sneezing; runny nose or eyes	Upper respiratory system infection; allergy	If symptoms persist for more than a few days or cat stops eating, consult vet as soon as possible.
Vomiting	Food allergy; stress; hairball; many other disorders possible	Consult vet within twenty-four hours. If combined with diarrhea, see vet as soon as possible.
Weight loss	Many disorders possible	Consult vet within twenty-four hours.

Knowing how to take your cat's temperature is a great help when he is under the weather. This can tell you whether to rush him to the vet or just monitor his condition closely. Using a rectal thermometer, shake the mercury below 99°F (37.2°C) and lubricate the bulb with petroleum jelly. Slowly and gently push the thermometer about an inch into the rectum and leave it for at least one minute, preferably two or three. If your cat is uncooperative, have someone restrain him while you hold the thermometer.

for more than twenty-four hours is probably experiencing some trouble. A normally playful cat that loses all interest in toys or a listless cat that refuses to move at all may be in distress. Don't be fooled by your cat's purring. This doesn't always indicate contentment; when combined with a bad mood and extreme defensiveness, this rumbling may signal that he is in pain.

TIME TO CALL THE VET

If your cat displays any behavioral anomalies, give him an extra careful physical exam and pay closer attention to his routine, referring to your previous notes. Not even the most secretive cat can hide physical signs of injury or illness completely. Some signs may be obvious—a wound, a lump, or difficulty breathing—but others can be more vague. Your cat may just not seem "right" to you. If your touch makes him growl or snap, the area you touched may be tender. Watch him as he moves, looking especially for any sign of weakness in his limbs or problems with his paws. Check his balance and head position, and ensure that he responds to sight and sound. Examine his skin for blood, pus, or other discharge, large cuts, abscesses or blisters, or a persistent scab, crust, or foul smell. If your cat is injured in a fight, immediate vet care will help prevent serious infection and abscesses.

Taking your cat's temperature, as shown at left, when he is showing any aberrant signs will arm you with useful information when you call your vet—and will also tell you when to call. A cat's temperature should be between 101 and 102.5 degrees Fahrenheit (38.3 and 39.1°C). A slight increase over that may signal nothing more than a reaction to hot weather, anxiety, or activity. But if the thermometer reads 105 degrees (40.5°C), take your cat to the vet that day; if it's 106 degrees (41.1°C) or higher, go to the vet immediately. Temperatures below 100 degrees (37.7°C) can also signal something serious. See your vet the same day if you get a reading of 99 degrees (37.2°C); go immediately if it's 98 degrees (36.6°C) or less.

By feeding your cat regularly and emptying the litter box twice daily, you'll become familiar with his appetite and elimination habits, allowing you to notice any early warning signals. Look for any radical increases or decreases in your cat's appetite for food or thirst for water. His bowel movements should be regular, his stools firm and consistent. If you ever see blood, worms, or things that look like grains of rice in the feces, take a stool sample from the litter box (don't worry if there is litter on it), place it in a clean plastic bag, and take it to your vet for testing. If you can't drop it off while it is still fresh (ideally within four hours, minimally within the same day), double-bag the sample and keep it refrigerated. Increased urination, usually paired with a noticeable increase in thirst, is a classic sign of several disorders, such as kidney failure or diabetes. Constipation can also be cause for concern. If your cat strains unproductively or sits in a hunched position in the litter box, he may need your help. Try adding water to his food or switching to a diet higher in fiber. If this doesn't work, he may have a serious disorder or an intestinal blockage that must be evaluated by a vet. Your cat's urine should be a clear yellow color and he should have no trouble or pain when urinating. Cloudy or bloody urine, pain or vocalization when urinating, or straining without producing any (or only very little) urine can indicate a urinary blockage or bladder infection, which can be very serious; get your cat to the vet without delay.

Vomiting and diarrhea are common and may be caused by a simple gastric upset or be a sign of something more serious. Vomiting can result from eating too much too fast, food allergies, or hairballs; diarrhea can be caused by stress, eating spoiled food, spicy table scraps, or milk, or any dietary change. Constant vomiting, projectile vomiting, blood in the vomit, or unproductive retching (dry heaves) may indicate a serious stomach problem, such as ulcers or a foreign object in the digestive tract. Persistent

ZOONOSES

 Vigilant maintenance and prevention are the key factors in the health of your cat—and that of your family. There are more than two hundred known zoonoses (animal diseases transmittable to humans), about thirty of which can be found in household pets. Sick and elderly people, whose immune systems are already compromised, are at greatest risk. But overall, zoonotic diseases are rather rare; the more common ones are relatively harmless and easily treated in healthy humans.

Outdoor cats have a much greater risk of contracting viral, bacterial, and parasitic infections than those kept indoors. Bacteria in the cat's mouth and under its claws can lead to such diseases as cat scratch disease and pasteurella. Transmitted through feline scratches and bites, these bacteria can infect the human victim's blood or skin and can lead to a variety of health problems if left untreated. However, most healthy adults suffer no effects whatsoever as long as the affected area is immediately cleaned and disinfected. And even if a nodule develops near the

wound site or the lymph nodes closest to the affected region swell, the disease is self-healing in most people.

A variety of internal and external parasites such as fleas and intestinal worms as well as ringworm (a fungus) can be passed from cats to humans. Although serious infection in humans is uncommon, parasites can damage tissues, attack vital organs, and lead to infections that can cause blindness or permanent nerve damage. As excrement is a very likely vehicle for parasites, keep children away from the litter box; and if you have a backyard sandbox, cover it when it is not in use.

Some of the more dangerous, but even rarer, viral diseases humans can catch from cats include feline plague and rabies, which outdoor cats can contract by preying on infected rodents, rabbits. or squirrels. Fortunately, rabies shots are mandatory for cats in most states.

Pregnant women are routinely tested for toxoplasmosis, an animal-borne parasitic infection that can cause birth defects in humans. The risk of contracting toxoplasmo-

sis from a cat is actually much lower than from eating improperly cooked meat or from handling raw meat without proper hand-washing afterward. Nevertheless, it's important to get the cat's feces out of the litter box quickly since the parasite's eggs become infectious a day after the feces are passed. A pregnant woman should avoid cleaning out the litter box, if possible, or wear rubber gloves and also wash her hands well. The risks should be discussed with a vet and the cat's stool should be tested.

Consult both your physician and your vet for information on the common zoonotic diseases in your area. To keep your cat from getting sick, stick to his vaccination schedule, have any wounds treated immediately, and have his stools tested regularly for parasites. To protect yourself from cat-borne illnesses, wash your hands often and wear rubber gloves when changing the litter. Keep your cat's claws trimmed short to prevent deep, penetrating punctures and avoid the kind of rough play, especially by children, that may prompt a cat to bite or scratch.

To "pill" your cat, hold his head from behind; with your thumb and middle finger at the corners of his mouth, press gently to open it. Tilt his head back and using a finger to pull down his lower jaw, place or drop the pill in the back of his mouth. If the pill lands on his tongue, try to push it gently down with a finger. Hold his mouth closed until he swallows. A "pill gun" will help save your fingers from bites: Available at pet-supply stores and vet clinics, this syringelike device lets you deposit a pill right in the cat's throat past the back of the tongue.

Above, right: Administering ear medication is easy, but can be messy. A cat will usually shake its head as soon as it is released, spraying liquid all over. Gently pull back your cat's ear flap and drop the medication into the ear canal. Then, very quickly close the flap and massage the base of the ear. You should hear or feel the liquid sloshing around, spreading throughout the ear canal. Hold the flap closed for a few seconds to keep in as much medication as possible.

diarrhea may indicate a number of serious disorders. And if your cat suddenly is failing to use his litter box, have him checked by your vet before you become angry with him. This change may indicate that he has a gastrointestinal or urinary tract problem.

Sneezing or coughing, often accompanied by runny eyes, usually means a common cold or flu-type illness. These symptoms generally clear up within a few days, but if they persist or at any time they are complicated by puslike discharges, drooling, listlessness, or especially loss of appetite, see your vet. Your cat may stop eating and drinking, becoming seriously dehydrated, simply because he has a blocked nose and can't smell his food.

Labored breathing and constant panting are also cause for concern. Your cat should breathe at a rate of between twenty and forty breaths per minute; his breathing should be nearly inaudible. Difficult breathing, rapid breathing, and wheezing, whistling, or persistent coughing can be signs of asthma. Take your cat to the vet immediately if his breathing is labored.

Anemia, detected by pale gums and tongue and lack of energy and appetite, is usually a sign of some other disorder. If you observe these signs in your cat, an immediate trip to the vet is warranted. Heart disease also affects cats, but rarely takes the form of a sudden heart attack, as suffered by humans. Cats can die quite suddenly from an arrhythmia, however, which is a disruption in the heart's normal rhythm. Nonfatal arrhythmias exist as well, as do heart murmurs. Both are usually caused by an underlying heart disease and are easily detected by vets during checkups. Further tests such as x-rays, ultrasounds, or electrocardiograms can then be done to find the source of the problem. Unfortunately, most other heart conditions usually go unnoticed since the animals generally show no outward sign of the problem until it is in an advanced state. Once symptoms of listlessness, lack of stamina, and panting for no apparent reason start to show, the disease is likely very severe and difficult to treat.

GOOD MEDICINE

Luckily, most conditions that could affect your cat's health can be effectively treated or controlled by medication prescribed by your vet. Getting that medicine into your cat, though, can be a challenge. Ask your vet to give the first dose so you can see how it's done by a pro. At home, the trick is to appear confident. If your cat senses any hesitation on your part, the game is over. Pills should be swallowed whole *(opposite)* unless your vet tells you that they can be crushed into the cat's food. But even that solution can be a problem: Your cat's highly tuned senses may alert him to the addition and he may refuse to eat the food.

Before administering ear medication *(opposite),* use a cotton ball to remove any residue from inside the ear. Apply eye ointment *(right)* in small amounts at a time, so that as the cat blinks the ointment spreads evenly over the eye instead of ending up as a glob on the eyelid. Avoid touching the eye with the tube or eyedropper; this can cause irritation or even injury. Dole out liquid medication *(below)* in very small portions and make sure your cat swallows it before giving more. Never skimp on medication or stop administering it because your cat looks better. Use it exactly according to your vet's instructions and for the specified number of days.

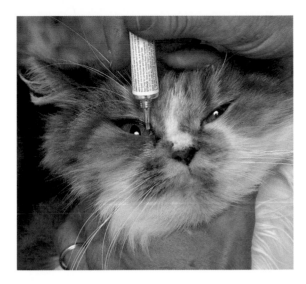

To apply eye medication, hold your cat's head and gently stretch open his eyelid. Apply the ointment or liquid from behind, with your hand on the top of his head, so he doesn't become anxious by seeing the tip of the tube or bottle.

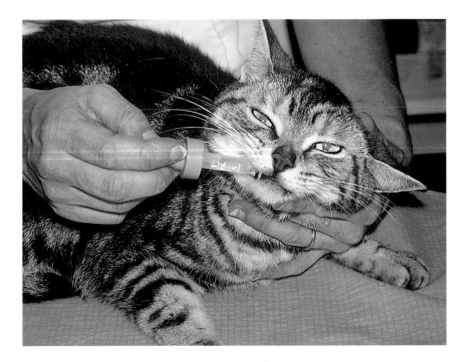

To get your cat to take liquid medication, squirt it as far back into his mouth as possible using a syringe or dropper. Hold his head up until he swallows so he does not spit or drool it out. If he is uncooperative, hold his head and open his mouth the same way you would to give a pill (opposite).

FIGHTING
·FLEAS·

There are few things cats like better than a good scratch, but if your cat is digging at himself incessantly or suddenly twisting around to attack himself, you could be dealing with fleas. Skin and coat problems, such as reddish areas, sores, dryness or crusting, or loss of fur in patches are other signs of infestation. Fleas are more than mere nuisances: They're parasites and may carry disease or other parasites, cause anemia in young or infirm cats, or provoke allergic reactions. All-out warfare is required to eliminate them.

Horrible creatures that they are, fleas are nothing if not survivors. They've been around for at least a hundred million years and plaguing cats for much of that time. Use any opportunity—grooming, petting, playing—to check your cat for signs of infestation: the fleas themselves or flea "dirt" (tiny black specks that turn red when wet). Fleas tend to gather where your cat can't groom effectively: on his neck and around his ears, near the tail, and in folds where fur is thickest. And for every adult flea you can see, you may be dealing with hundreds of eggs. Eggs fall off your cat and, safely ensconced in your carpet or the cat's bed, develop into larvae, then pupae before emerging as adult fleas in a cycle that typically takes three weeks to a month, but can last as long as several months. The key to shutting down the flea circus in your home is to treat both your cat and the environment, including any other pets, for as long as it takes to eradicate all fleas at all life stages. The moment you spot evidence of fleas on your cat, isolate him in an uncarpeted area (such as the bathroom) with all his essentials until you can treat him. This way, if any eggs fall off your cat, they'll be in a room that's easy to clean. Next, tackle the rest of your home, and plan to repeat this housecleaning weekly until all the varmints are eradicated.

DECIMATING THE ENEMY

Unless you decide to take the low-tech route of the flea comb in your war against fleas, your best ally is your vet. A vet can recommend (and usually supply) the best product for your cat, probably one of the new topical or systemic ones. The arrival of these flea fighters, only available through vets, was a boon for pet owners. Depending on the type, the treatment is either applied to the cat's back, added to food, or injected by the vet. Several of these products kill live fleas immediately and continue to dispatch new fleas for several weeks. Others cause the fleas to lay defective eggs.

The other weapons in the war on fleas are sprays, mousses, dips, shampoos, and powders. All of these kill fleas on contact, but most do not prevent reinfestation. Also, many cats hate being sprayed or bathed, making it difficult to treat them thoroughly. Powders can also be drying to skin and irritating to the respiratory system. Flea collars are usually ineffective and some may cause dermatitis. Make sure any product you use is specifically for cats (not dogs or the environment) and follow the instructions carefully. Never mix products; even safe ingredients can become hazardous when

FLEA-CONTROL PRODUCTS

Some products affect only adult fleas, others only the eggs and larvae. If only adults are killed, there will be a reinfestation when the eggs hatch. If only eggs and larvae are dealt with, the adults will still annoy your cat, and will lay more eggs. When figuring out your flea-control strategy, keep in mind that you must attack all the life stages of the flea both on your cat and throughout the house. Start with the least toxic flea-control formulations and use only these for very young, old, or infirm cats. Run your plan of action by your vet to ensure that the chemicals in any different products won't end up simply doing battle with themselves.

Product/category	How/where is it applied?	Is it toxic?	How does it work?
Flea comb	Groom cat; drop fleas into soapy water	No	Removes adult fleas and eggs
d-Limonene	Spray on cat, environment	No	Poisons adult fleas and larvae
Imidacloprid	Liquid applied to fur on cat's back	No	Poisons adult fleas and larvae
Lufenuron	Orally (liquid added to food) or by injection	No	Interferes with development of eggs and larvae
Insect-growth regulators	Apply to cat, environment	Nontoxic to somewhat toxic	Interferes with development of eggs and larvae
Diatomaceous earth	Sprinkle in environment	Somewhat	Dehydrates adult fleas
Borax	Sprinkle in environment	Somewhat	Dehydrates adult fleas, eggs, and larvae
Fipronil	Liquid applied to fur on cat's back	Somewhat	Poisons adult fleas
Pyrethrins	Spray on cat, environment	Yes	Poisons adult fleas and larvae
Carbamates	Spray on cat, environment	Very	Poisons adult fleas and larvae
Organophosphates	Spray on cat, environment	Very	Poisons adult fleas and larvae

combined. For a few hours after treatment, watch your cat for reactions. At the first sign of anything unusual, such as a rash, shaking, vomiting, lethargy, diarrhea, or drooling, rush your cat (and the product) to the vet.

WAGING WAR ON THE HOME FRONT

You'll have to go on a cleaning rampage. Before starting, cut up a flea collar and put the pieces inside your vacuum cleaner. Vacuum thoroughly, including spaces between and under couch cushions, under furniture, and in closets. Seal the vacuum bag in a plastic bag and get rid of it promptly. To deal the death blow to larvae in carpets, use a special flea powder or sprinkle on table salt or borax. Keep your cat out of the room and vacuum the carpet the next day. Throw bedding, seat covers, and any other washables your pet touches into the washer at least once a week with the hottest water possible and some flea shampoo that works against both adult fleas and eggs. The shampoo can also be used to wash floors. Buy sprays to treat crevices.

If necessary, call in the flea bombs or foggers, which are effective for three to six months. Your family and all pets must evacuate while the chemicals are being released into the air. Residue has to be cleaned meticulously.

PREGNANCY &
·BIRTH·

Cats are among the most attentive mothers in the animal kingdom, and newborn kittens, such as the one above, require TLC. Born blind, nearly deaf, and too weak to walk, kittens are totally reliant on a mother's care to survive the first few weeks of life.

Unless your female outdoor cat is spayed, inevitably she will become pregnant. Even if you try to keep her indoors while she is in heat, an escape of only a few hours is more than enough time for her to find a male or for males to find her. Signs of pregnancy begin about three weeks after conception, when your cat's nipples change from pale to deep pink and begin to swell and stiffen as the teats prepare for lactation. A cat will not change noticeably in size until the four- or five-week mark, when her belly will begin to swell.

IN THE "FAMILY WAY"—FELINE STYLE

Pregnancy normally lasts between nine and ten weeks (sixty-four to sixty-nine days). Like any pregnant mom, your cat will need more protein and energy. Ask your vet for specially formulated food. As the kittens grow, her internal organs will become cramped, so serve her smaller but more frequent meals. Watch her weight: An increase in weight of 20 to 25 percent is normal, but excessive weight gain can interfere with labor. Cats can, and should, remain active throughout pregnancy in order to keep fit and prevent obesity. But toward the end, you can expect your lady-in-waiting to become more sedate.

Some cats, especially first-time mothers, may be a bit bewildered or agitated by the physical changes and discomfort they experience. If your cat seems very nervous and excitable or becomes aggressive or more vocal, consult your vet; medication may help. And some cats miscarry. If your cat hemorrhages or has a foul-smelling discharge, have a vet check her.

To prevent birthing in an inconvenient or unsafe place, prepare a disposable birthing box *(opposite)*. Accustom your cat to the box early so that she will choose to give birth in it, lining it with her usual bedding and encouraging her to sleep in it for a week before the babies are due. Keep closet doors shut and block access to as many other places as possible. As delivery approaches, confine her to the house, even better to one room, and prevent vigorous activity. She may become irritable, so keep other animals away. Prep a longhair cat by carefully trimming (not shaving) the fur around her nipples and genitals. Clean cloths, towels, a pair of scissors, a baby's nose-suction bulb, dental floss or sturdy thread (to tie off the kittens' umbilical cords), petroleum jelly or other lubricant, and disinfectants (rubbing alcohol and povidone-iodine) should be kept close at hand.

These ten-day-old lion cubs will depend on their mother to provide food, warmth, and security for at least a year.

KITTEN TIME

Just before she enters labor, the expectant mother will probably be anxious and restless, and might appear to be searching for something. She will probably lose her appetite; in any case, feed her sparingly or give her only water. When she settles into her birthing area, she will shred the nesting materials and lick at her abdomen and genital areas. As she enters the first stage of labor she will fuss over the nest, kneading it into shape. Colostrum (first milk) may leak from her nipples and there may be a blood-tinged discharge from her genitals. As contractions begin to move the kittens down the birth canal, her breathing and pulse will elevate, and her body temperature will drop. Wash your hands now and disinfect the scissors by soaking them in rubbing alcohol for a few minutes.

In the second stage, forceful, straining contractions begin. The cat may lie on her side or chest, or she may squat. The first kitten should emerge within thirty minutes and subsequent kittens should be born at intervals of fifteen to thirty minutes. There may be fluid if the amniotic sac ruptures on the way out. If the sac is intact, the mother will tear it herself, sever the umbilical cord, clean and groom the kitten, and perhaps nurse it while waiting to give birth to the next one. The kittens are born blind, nearly deaf, and helpless: Their mother's care is essential. If she is doing a good job by herself, has groomed and is nursing the kittens, don't interfere. Anxious mothers, especially first-timers, have been known to abandon their kittens in favor of attention from their owners, so keep her calm and reassured. What the mother and her newborns need most right now is a warm, dark, quiet, and secluded nest—and no external stress. Visually examine the kittens for defects and to make sure they are healthy, but without being intrusive; a worried mother will want to move her nest to a safer location. Then, leave the family alone for a few days, keeping other animals away as well.

A BIRTHING BOX

Provide your cat with a clean, safe environment in which to give birth and nurse her kittens.

◆ Use a clean, sturdy cardboard box at least two feet by three feet in area and one foot tall. Cut an opening in one side for the mother to use. It should be about five inches from the floor so the kittens can't get out of the box until they have developed some strength and coordination. Make the hole big enough so that you can see and reach inside in case you need to extract a kitten.

◆ Keep the top on the box or cover it with a flat piece of cardboard or a large cloth to help retain heat and keep the interior dark and secure.

◆ Fill the bottom of the box with shredded newspaper (and keep extra newspaper on hand for refilling it) and line it with a clean cloth.

◆ Place the box in a warm, quiet place that is free of drafts.

FOSTERING AN ORPHAN KITTEN

 The best mother for a rejected or orphaned kitten is another cat that will nurture and reprimand the little one in the feline way. Raised by humans who hesitate to correct it, a kitten tends to be spoiled, which sometimes results in behavior problems later on.

A nursing cat will usually accept an extra kitten or two if they are about the same age as her own, but if you cannot find a candidate, you're it. Welcome to surrogate cat-motherhood! And be prepared to become very good friends with your vet over the next few weeks.

Keep the kitten's nest cozy by draping a heating pad over the side and adjusting it until the temperature inside the box is about 90°F (32°C). Alternatively, you can shine a reading lamp down on the box until the same temperature is reached.

Feed kitten formula using a bottle with a small pet nipple or an eyedropper or syringe. Never force-feed a kitten by squirting formula into its mouth. It may inhale some into its lungs and end up with pneumonia. Follow your vet's advice or the instructions that come with the formula for the correct amount and the feeding schedule, which usually depends on the kitten's weight. Shortly after each feeding, stimulate defecation by massaging the baby's body in imitation of its absent mother's grooming. Gently rub the anal area with a moistened swab or cotton ball.

Stools usually have the consistency of toothpaste; if they are any looser, you should ask your vet for advice. If the kitten isn't passing waste at least once a day, call your vet. If the kitten hasn't found the litter box on its own by about four weeks of age, place it in the litter box so it makes the connection between defecation and the box. Make sure the sides of the litter box are low enough for little legs to manage.

At about three weeks of age, the kitten should be able to drink out of a shallow dish and begin to eat solid food. Start by letting the kitten "play" with its food and water.

Kittens must eat a small amount every few hours. While kitten formula is the ideal, puppy formula or double-strength baby formula will do in a pinch.

What if nature doesn't take a smooth course? Get ready, you will have to pitch in as midwife and you should be prepared to contact your vet at any time. If after a minute following the birth of a kitten the mother hasn't ruptured the amniotic sac, cut it yourself. If she hasn't severed the umbilical cord within a few minutes, tie it off with dental floss or strong thread about an inch or a little more from the kitten's abdomen. Then, cut the cord between the knot and the placenta. Dip the end of the cord in povidone-iodine to prevent infection. If the kitten is not breathing or is squirming very weakly, wrap it in a towel and use a baby's nose-suction bulb to suck the mucus out of its nose and mouth. Then, to get breathing started, give the kitten a gentle massage, covering it with a towel. Contact your vet if you have trouble with any of this or if there are any other complications. These may include: the first stage of labor (where the mother is acting restless, licking her chest and genitals, and frequently visiting the nesting area) continuing for six hours with no change; no kitten emerging or a green, black, or bloody discharge after two hours of strong contractions; continued straining with no results more than an hour after delivering a kitten; or if a placenta is not delivered for every kitten. After birthing, get veterinary help if the mother cat is bleeding; if she has a colored, white, or foul-smelling discharge; if she seems restless or feverish; or if she doesn't want to eat or to let her kittens suckle immediately.

WHAT'S NEXT?

Now that the drama's over, things should settle down into a routine. Have a vet see the kittens at two to five days of age to rule out congenital abnormalities. Most mothers will take care of their kittens' needs and there won't be call for you to intervene. To socialize the kittens, start gently handling them daily once their eyes are open, or around five to ten days of age. The mother usually weans the babies by about seven weeks and you can start to supplement her milk with kitten food after the three-week mark. At eight weeks, the kittens should visit the vet again for a thorough exam and to begin their series of vaccines. Keep the feline family together for eight to twelve weeks before you send the kittens off to their new homes.

Prospective owners should be knowledgeable and nurturing, never adopting a kitten on a whim, solely for their children, or as a present for someone else. Go through the guidelines of responsible pet ownership (page 82) with them and feel free to refuse anyone you feel will not offer the kitten a good home. Asking for payment to offset your vet costs will help rule out people who aren't serious. Sound them out about whether they will get the kitten sterilized; if not, you are ultimately responsible for adding to the cat overpopulation problem. There is no guarantee, however, that even an apparently ideal adopter will keep the kitten for its entire life, and give it nothing but the best care. You owe it to each kitten to be willing to take it back at any point in its life if things don't work out, and keep it yourself or find it another home.

DOING THE RIGHT THING

There are already too many kittens and cats without homes. You'll have your work cut out for you finding good homes for your litter, and your new mother could become pregnant again even before her kittens are weaned. Ask your vet how soon you can have her spayed, and absolutely do not let her outside until then. If you also have an unneutered male cat, keep them separated and run, don't walk, to the vet to get *him* neutered. Every year millions of perfectly fine but unwanted cats are euthanized. Many were adopted as kittens, only to be abandoned as adults, no longer so adorable and declared to be too much trouble or expense. And those that escape euthanasia and remain strays are malnourished and susceptible to contagious diseases, some of them fatal. Don't contribute to this tragic problem.

The only thing sadder than a stray cat is a stray kitten. Because stray cat mothers usually hide their kittens, humans may not get to handle the babies during the all-important socialization period that starts at two weeks and goes to about eight weeks of age. These kittens usually grow up to be very fearful of humans.

CARING FOR
·AGING CATS·

Cats show their age less than humans do. This thirteen-year-old may look as youthful as an adolescent, but its age is the equivalent of sixty-eight human years. Despite the aging body of your senior feline, your care and attention can keep him happy and healthy for many more years of affection and companionship.

Wild cats rarely live longer than ten years. Since their declining bodies and senses cannot cope with hunting and younger competitors, they succumb to malnutrition, disease, or injury. In this regard, civilization has its benefits. Although domestic strays live out much the same story as their wild cousins and rarely live beyond a few years, well-cared-for indoor domestic cats can live well into their teens, even into their twenties.

THE GOLDEN YEARS

A domestic cat is considered "senior" at about seven or eight years of age, when body tissues begin to lose their ability to regenerate, the effectiveness of the major body systems decreases, and metabolism slows down. Even though the aging process is impossible to stop, it can be slowed by good nutrition, daily exercise, and prompt attention to medical problems. Cats also become more susceptible to stress as they age, so the security, both physical and emotional, of their environment is vital. Your senior will need more attention and affection to help him cope with any change, such as the birth of a child or moving to a new house. Even trips to the vet become more traumatic for an older cat. You can mitigate the stress somewhat by keeping his familiar bedding and a favorite toy in the carrier.

Your cat will probably be anxious about his deteriorating abilities, especially because they were so sharp to begin with. If he was rambunctious, a decline in his agility is likely to cause stress. Most cats do tend to slow down as they age, and engage in play less often and less energetically. But don't leave your cat to sit in some warm, cozy spot just because he is old. He needs moderate play and activity to keep his muscle tone, help prevent obesity, and get his blood flowing. A stubborn reluctance to exercise may be due to stiff muscles or arthritic joints. If so, jumping and climbing may be out. Some creaky seniors find it impossible even to jump up to a favorite chair. Make sure that all your cat's amenities—food dishes, litter box, favorite perch or bed—are easily accessible to him.

Your cat may also have difficulty reaching his entire body for grooming, so brush him every day to remove loose hair. Hairballs can cause serious digestive problems in an older cat. This extra grooming provides you with a good opportunity to check for abnormal lumps, growths, or lesions. Anything of this nature should be examined by your vet. And if he isn't using his scratching post as often as he used to, you'll need to trim his claws more frequently, too. Don't forget to care for teeth and gums. Gently scrub his teeth a few times per week *(page 145)* and have them cleaned by your vet as necessary. A cat with painful gums, usually the result of plaque buildup, will go off his food, especially dry food.

You know your senior is getting deaf when he appears inattentive or fails to respond to either his name or the usual sounds associated with feeding or playing. Have a vet check for infection or a tumor in the ear canal, but if the hearing loss is due to aging, there isn't much you can do except to keep him away from any dangers he can't hear, such as those he might encounter outdoors. Be understanding if he increases the volume of his cries; he probably can't hear himself. Signs of vision problems include pupils that don't respond to light, inability to follow objects such as toys, and bumping into things. Sudden blindness may be caused by a detached retina due to hypertension. Prompt treatment is essential and may return some vision. Even blind cats can manage well, as long as everything stays in its familiar place. The center of the eyes may seem to cloud slightly, owing to increased density in the lenses, or the irises may look "worn out," but these things may not

Older cats may no longer be able to jump up to their favorite spots. Spare them from injury—and humiliation—by providing a ramp with a carpeted surface for secure footing or by placing a stool or low table next to a destination as a mid-station.

WHY ADOPT AN OLDER CAT?

Often perceived as boring and lazy, older cats are often overlooked for adoption. Some things improve with age, though, and there are advantages to adopting a mature cat.

A senior cat usually does not have the same behavior problems of a young one; it is older and wiser, and more used to living with people. And since the cat's personality is well developed, you can more easily choose one suited to you. Older cats are less impelled, and less able, to climb curtains and rather than chase imaginary mice at four in the morning will probably snuggle quietly in bed with you. It is true that older cats sleep more than kittens, yet the lure of a toy will still awaken their feline play instincts.

In a home with small children, an older cat will be more tolerant of a toddler's hugs. An older cat is also a more suitable companion for an elderly person. The boisterous energy of a rowdy kitten or even a young adult can be too much for an older person to handle, whereas a sedate, affectionate lap cat is likely more appropriate.

Many adult cats find themselves in an animal shelter when their owners move, change their living arrangements, are ill, die, or even more sadly, simply tire of them. Kittens in the shelter are far more likely to be adopted, leaving older cats to be euthanized. If you want to save a cat, consider giving an older one a chance to enjoy the rest of its years as your companion.

significantly interfere with vision. A whitish, opaque clouding of the lens may indicate a cataract, which is often treated successfully by surgery. A loss of the sense of smell interferes with perception of the world: a cat knows its people and places by their smells. This is another reason to keep an older cat indoors, or outside only on a harness and leash, even if it was a street-smart outdoor cat in its youth.

As your cat's senses of smell and taste dull, his regular fare may taste bland, and the cat who always wolfed down his food may become a finicky eater. Try warming the food to enhance its aroma or flavor it with a small amount of a high-protein, strong-smelling food, such as cheese or cooked fish, as long as there are no medical problems such as kidney disease. Weight loss can signal a potentially serious problem. In older cats, diet, hairballs, or disorders in other systems often cause gastrointestinal dysfunctions such as vomiting, diarrhea, constipation, or loss of appetite, but persistent weight loss may be the sign of a serious problem. Weigh your cat regularly, keeping a record of the date and figure.

Another common problem for older cats is overfeeding. As your cat becomes physically less active, he still needs good nutrition, but requires fewer calories. Your best bet here is a food specially formulated for senior cats; if he has any health problems, he may need a specialized diet recommended by your vet. This isn't the time to spoil your cat with food: Obesity depresses the immune system and contributes to a number of serious disorders, including arthritis, diabetes, and liver disease.

GERIATRIC PROBLEMS

Cats, too, can become senile, acting erratically or forgetting the location of the litter box. Try to be patient and understanding. Add extra litter boxes, especially near your cat's favorite sleeping spots. Continued incontinence, though, may be the sign of a medical problem; ask the vet to check your cat.

As a cat ages, its immune system becomes less efficient at fending off diseases and parasites. Tissues are less able to repair themselves and will degenerate somewhat, compromising normal body functions and taxing the cat's ability to deal with stress and sickness. A deficiency in one system often overburdens another, leading to potentially serious complications from what would be a minor illness in a younger cat. Although any aging cat will slow down and become less active, a very low energy level, lack of stamina, or labored breathing can be signs of heart disease and must be checked by a vet.

Cancer often shows up as a lump, bump, persistent sore, scab, or other abnormality. Watch for any of these signs; your vet will also check for this sort of thing during visits. Radiation, chemotherapy, or surgery can be effective on some tumors, but discuss these options with your vet. The stress of the treatment may be worse for your cat than a peaceful end.

Symptoms of kidney or liver disease usually do not appear until the disorder is already severe. This is why vets often recommend regular blood tests. With early warning, a change of diet often controls the disease. Signs of kidney failure include excessive thirst and urination or a complete loss of appetite. Liver disease may cause jaundice, where pale body tissues such as skin and the whites of the eyes turn yellowish. Other signs of both conditions are vomiting, diarrhea, poor appetite, and weight loss.

Cats with diabetes tend to drink and urinate excessively and though they eat more, they lose weight. Diabetes can be controlled by replacing the missing insulin and sometimes resolves on its own. Your vet will help you decide on the best treatment.

Hyperthyroidism, an enlargement of the thyroid gland in the neck, leads to an increased production of two hormones that help control your cat's metabolism. Signs of this condition are loss of weight despite an insatiable appetite, excessive eating and drinking (and the resulting increase in defecation and urination, sometimes outside the litter box), hyperactivity, poor coat condition, and diarrhea. It may be treated by surgery, controlled with drugs, or cured with radioactive-iodine therapy.

A HUMANE END

Often you and your vet may have to face the biggest decision of all: when to end your cat's life. This is a time to calmly and rationally consider quality of life. Discuss and examine all options with your vet. If there is no treatment for your cat's ills, no way to keep him comfortable, and living is painful, then euthanasia is the humane choice. Keeping your cat alive and suffering because you cannot deal with his death isn't humane. When he can't enjoy even the most basic of life's pleasures such as eating, ask yourself: Is it time?

Once you have made the decision, you may wish to spend a little bit of extra time with your cat to say goodbye. Try to stay calm before the euthanasia procedure so your cat doesn't pick up your anxiety. Consider bringing a friend or relative with you for support. You may wish to remain in the room with your cat during the final moments, so that your comforting voice is the last thing he hears. Euthanasia is now performed most often by injection of an overdose of anaesthetic: He will fall unconscious within seconds, and die, very peacefully, within a minute.

Although euthanasia is a quick and painless death for your cat, it can be a heartbreaking experience for you and your family. Grief over the loss of any loved one is legitimate and can be profound. Give yourself time to mourn, and do what you feel is appropriate. Some people choose to hold a memorial service or funeral at a pet cemetery. Others make a charitable donation in their pet's name or keep the ashes on the mantle. Try not to dwell on your loss or your cat's absence, but celebrate the good life he had, and the pleasure that you derived from him.

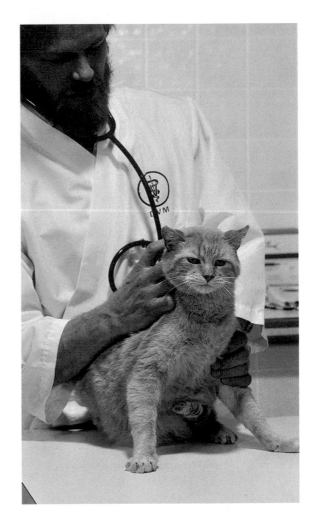

Regular checkups are most important for an aging cat and the older it gets, the more frequent visits should become—perhaps every six months. Many of the disorders associated with aging are very difficult, if not impossible, to detect on your own. Although it may be stressful for your cat, a careful examination by a veterinarian can catch early, subtle signs of a disorder and provide a treatment or a diet to help keep your cat healthy.

VISITING A
·VETERINARIAN·

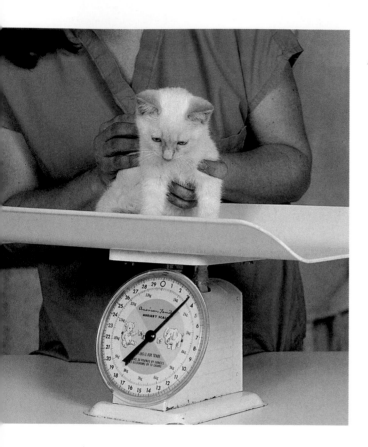

Keeping track of basic information such as weight and size will help your vet get an idea of your cat's general health, as well as provide clues if something is wrong.

An ounce of prevention is worth a pound of cure, and a quick, inexpensive checkup is surely preferable to a lengthy, expensive treatment. Annual vet visits can save your cat from the pain and trauma of serious illness, even save his life. While you can do much to keep your cat healthy at home, some of the signs of ill health can be subtle, especially since cats tend to keep their pains and afflictions to themselves. There may be early signals of a problem that only a professional would find. Other problems develop very slowly, and small, gradual changes often go unnoticed by those living with the cat every day.

During the checkup, your vet will ask you about your cat's general health. Mention any problems or changes in your cat's behavior and habits, no matter how insignificant they may seem to you. Has he become lethargic? Have any of his eating or litter-box habits changed? Has he exhibited unusual aggressiveness, shyness, or other odd behavior? Take along your cat's medical diary, including vaccination records, incidents of illness or injury, and notes on any medical treatments (along with any side-effects) so that your vet has complete information.

The vet will give your cat a thorough physical, including a head-to-tail visual and tactile examination. Point out anything you have noticed while playing, grooming, or examining your cat yourself: bumps or lumps, skin or fur problems, or anything else out of the ordinary. Don't be shy; your cat relies on you to be his spokesperson since he can't speak up for himself. A checkup is also a good time to have your cat's teeth looked at and to schedule a cleaning by the vet if necessary. Tartar buildup can lead to gum infections, which can, in turn, cause other illnesses.

VACCINATIONS

Vaccinations are an important part of the visit, especially for cats living in multi-cat households, and even more so for outdoor cats. Some cat diseases are highly contagious to other cats and can be fatal. There are effective vaccinations for eight common diseases. The American Association of Feline Practitioners (AAFP) and the Academy of Feline Medicine (AFM) have recommended that all cats be vaccinated against four core infectious diseases: rabies, feline panleukopenia, feline herpesvirus, and feline calcivirus. The vaccine for the latter three is available as one product, the FRCP vaccine. These core vaccinations are recommended because of the prevalence and seriousness of the diseases, and the dangers they pose to cats and, in the case of rabies, to humans, too. Once a cat has been diagnosed with rabies, it must be euthanized. Vaccinations for rabies are required by law in most areas of the United States.

Many veterinarians include chlamydia among the core diseases. Others group it with the so-called noncore diseases: feline leukemia virus (FeLV), feline infectious peritonitis (FIP), and microsporum canis (ringworm). Inoculation with these noncore vaccines is recommended only for cats that are at risk for the diseases. Risk factors include age, exposure to other cats and animals, and geographic location. Ask your vet to give your cat only those vaccines he really needs and ask for vaccines in single-dose vials. Some vaccines are available intranasally, as drops for the nose or eyes, rather than as injections.

Booster shots are required for all these vaccinations, sometimes within a few weeks of the first shot and always after one year, every one to three years thereafter for rabies and FRCP. FeLV and FIP boosters should be administered every year. Cats at higher than usual risk may benefit from more frequent vaccination. Although both the AAFP and the AFM recommend a three-year rabies shot for all cats, some areas may require more frequent boosters for this disease. Discuss your cat's risk factors with your vet to develop a vaccination protocol that is both appropriate for your cat and complies with the law in your area.

SIDE EFFECTS

For the vast majority of cats, vaccines are safe and effective, but some cats experience an adverse reaction to vaccinations. Stay at the clinic with your cat for a short time after any shot, then confine him to home for a few hours. Allergic reactions to vaccines usually appear within fifteen minutes and can include hives, facial swelling, foaming at the mouth, difficulty breathing, vomiting, and diarrhea. If your cat has a reaction after you get home, take him back to the vet immediately. The next time he gets shots, your vet can try to prevent a recurrence through the use of antihistamines or steroids. For a day or so after vaccination, your cat may be sensitive in the spots where the shots were given, so be careful how you pick him up.

A lump may develop at the vaccine injection site; if it persists for several weeks or gets larger, consult your vet. In some cases, about one in ten thousand, a cat may develop a malignant tumor at the injection site. Discuss with your vet the pros and cons for your cat of inoculation versus the chance of developing a tumor.

Your cat's risk factors may change. An indoor cat can start going outdoors or you may move to an entirely different geographic location. Inform your vet of any such changes at each annual checkup so your cat's vaccination program can be adjusted appropriately.

ALTERNATIVE VET CARE

As alternative therapies such as acupuncture, aromatherapy, and homeopathy have gained in popularity with people, the same ideas and techniques have been applied to veterinary care.

Veterinary versions of acupuncture, chiropractics, and hydrotherapy can be effective in treating old injuries, arthritis, paralysis, and other painful or chronic disorders. If drugs, insecticides, and other harsh products do not fit into your lifestyle, a vet practicing homeopathic medicine may offer you a more natural alternative in the treatment of degenerative diseases.

Alternative therapies may be far removed from mainstream veterinary medicine, but some, such as acupuncture, can offer effective temporary relief from afflictions such as joint pain.

THE CASE FOR
·STERILIZATION·

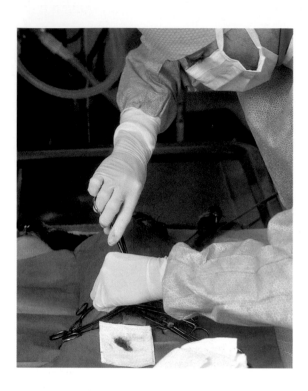

Spaying, shown above, and neutering are operations performed under general anesthesia. Ask your vet about possible side-effects of anesthetic, medication, or procedures used and what facilities are available in case of an emergency during surgery. Also get detailed instructions on care and feeding procedures when your cat comes home.

M ost veterinarians, animal-welfare organizations, and even animal-rights advocates strongly recommend sterilizing all pets to prevent reproduction, ideally before they are sexually mature. It is probably the one subject on which there is such widespread agreement. In addition to controlling the cat population and reducing the number of unwanted, homeless felines, sterilizing also benefits the individual cat.

Even if your pet never leaves your house, sterilization is better for your cat's health. Sterilized cats tend to live longer, healthier lives than their sexually active counterparts. Obviously, diseases of the removed organs are completely prevented, and the risks for a host of related diseases, including such things as mammarian cancer, are reduced. Contrary to popular belief, "fixed" cats do not become overweight, lazy, or depressed. These conditions are due to overfeeding and lack of exercise.

More importantly, this operation will help preserve your sanity on a day-to-day basis. Have you ever tried to sleep while a female cat in heat paces incessantly around the house, yowling in apparent distress? Or have you ever smelled the pungent urine of an intact male? Even in the litter box the odor is enough to make your eyes water, and if he begins spraying urine around the house to mark his territory the situation can become unbearable. Sadly, through no fault of their own, many unfixed males are dumped off at animal shelters because of this very problem. If their owners had had them neutered before the cats hit puberty, they likely would have never started to spray. Some do stop after neutering, but for others the habit is too ingrained. While their urine doesn't smell any worse than that of a female once they are neutered, it still will be deposited around your house. In fact, both females (which may also spray) and males should be sterilized by six months of age, although the surgery can be performed any time after. Some vets, particularly those in animal shelters who do not want to let a cat that has not been sterilized out their doors, will operate on kittens as young as six to eight weeks of age.

There are some other benefits: Cats not focused on finding a mate generally transfer their attention, and affection, to their owners. Sterilized outdoor cats won't roam far and wide looking for mates, and so are less likely to get lost. Neutered males stay out of the violent competitions for females that often lead to wounds and abscesses. Indoor cats, particularly males, will also show less aggression with other cats.

THE PROCEDURE

 Sterilization—spaying of females and neutering of males—involves the removal of the reproductive organs of the cat. But although it's a very common procedure now and relatively minor as surgery goes (especially the neutering of males), any operation is a major event for a cat and it will require a few days of extra care and recuperation afterward.

Your cat will be monitored by clinic staff on reviving and recovering from the general anesthetic. As the anaesthetic wears off, the cat will be disoriented and uncoordinated, and will probably be uncomfortable, perhaps in some pain. Ask your vet to prescribe pain medication. Never medicate your cat yourself, especially with common analgesics such as acetaminophen or ibuprofen, which are highly toxic to cats. Males usually leave the clinic the same day; females typically are kept overnight and observed for pain, swelling, fever, and vomiting.

The biggest risk is from infection. Once home, keep the site of the incisions clean and dry. Also check for fever, inflammation, swelling, or oozing, all signs that warrant a call to your vet. Provide clean bedding and, since the dust of regular litter can cause infection, use a dust-free type, such as that made of paper, and change it often.

A male cat's incisions are often not sutured, and must be kept clean and left to close on their own. A female usually takes only a day or two to return to her normal self, but jumping or playing may open her sutures. If necessary, isolate her in a quiet room until the wound has had time to close fully. Excessive licking or any pulling at the stitches can irritate the wound; buy an Elizabethan collar *(page 172)* or borrow one from your vet to protect the surgical site if your cat is irritating it.

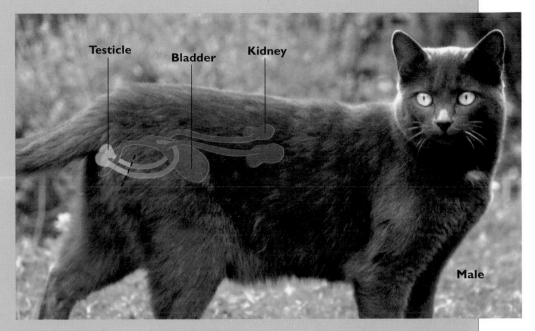

Testicle Bladder Kidney

Male

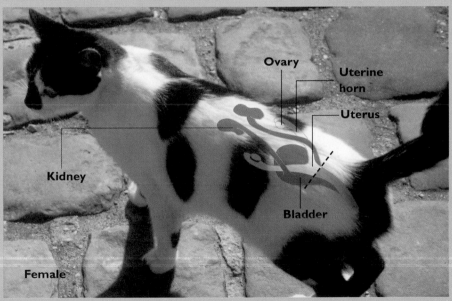

Ovary Uterine horn

Uterus

Kidney

Bladder

Female

For males, neutering removes the testicles through incisions in the scrotum. Spaying is the removal of the uterus, uterine horns, and ovaries of a female through an incision in her abdomen. While vasectomies and tubal ligations provide birth control, they are rarely recommended since they don't put a stop to urine spraying or the female heat cycle, nor do they prevent the health problems that standard sterilization does.

THE CASE AGAINST
·DECLAWING·

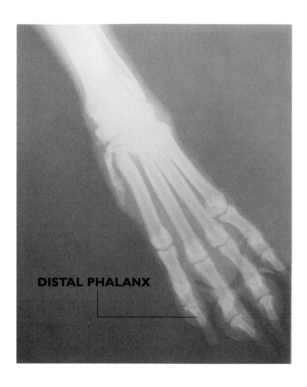

This x-ray shows the intact paw of a cat before declawing. The vet amputates the distal phalanx of each digit (each toe at the first joint), where the claw arises.

DISTAL PHALANX

The thing we love so much about cats is their nature: tame, but so close to the wild. Your cat, slinking along the sofa back, is nothing if not a miniature mountain lion. Understanding *why* cats scratch, knowing that it isn't "bad" behavior but part and parcel of the feline nature, may make this habit easier to live with. Keep in mind that once you decide to share your home with an animal, there may be a certain amount of household damage. In exchange, you receive years of wonderful companionship.

Scratching is one of the definitive feline behaviors. As cats scratch, they release scent from their paws, which serves as a way of marking territory. This routine also provides a feline fitness session, working back, shoulder, and leg muscles, supplying a good, long stretch, and shedding the dead outer layer of the claws. Scratching behavior is so innate that even declawed cats will go through the motions.

Declawing is a painful procedure that has long-term physical and emotional effects, but there are some simple alternatives. Clip your cat's nails regularly *(page 140)*. Blunt claws are less likely to shred upholstery than the sharp hooks you're snipping off, and trimming once a week will keep the claw from growing into a hook. Invest some time in encouraging your cat to use a scratching post *(page 121)* instead of furniture. Or, try one of the many products designed to save furniture *(opposite)*.

WHY NOT DECLAW?

In declawing, or onychectomy, the last bone of each toe, the one containing the claw, is surgically removed. All the cat's toes are amputated up to the first joint. Without their final toe joints, their tiptoe gait and agility are compromised. Without their claws, their ability to cross narrow surfaces is reduced since they can't grip without them. Declawed cats must never be allowed outdoors on their own. They can't use their talons to fend off aggressors and can't easily scamper up a tree to escape danger. Some cats can still climb trees using just their rear claws, but they can't back down. Your cat may also lose some of his muscle tone from being unable to climb and do the stretching workout. If the back claws are also removed (which is completely unnecessary since they don't do the same damage as the front claws), the cat's ability to jump can also be affected.

When a feline loses its claws, which are its first line of defense, it may bite to protect itself. Bites can be more dangerous than scratches. If your

Immediately after a declawing operation, this cat lies next to the grisly evidence of bone, claw, and fur. This operation is an unnecessary and often painful amputation of healthy digits. The paws stay bandaged for two to three days, but post-operative pain can last a week or longer. And the older the cat, the worse the pain.

cat is scratching people, clip his claws so scratches are less likely to draw blood, but, more importantly, teach your youngsters to respect the cat. If he is scratching or biting them, they may be mishandling him.

While there is no statistical evidence to show that a cat suffers psychological damage after losing its claws, there are reports of cats becoming a bit lethargic after declawing. Cats can also experience extreme pain, difficulty walking, swollen or bleeding paws, and loss of appetite. And unless the litter is changed for a type easier on the cat's sore paws, such as paper litter, for week or so after the surgery, the cat may develop an aversion to the litter box because of the pain associated with digging in it.

If alternatives to declawing are not appealing and you still want a cat, adopt one that has already been declawed. If you can't solve the scratching problem with an existing cat, there is another surgical option that is preferable to declawing, especially for adult cats. Flexor tendonectomy is easier on the cat, and has a shorter recovery period and less chance of complications. The tendons that allow the cat to extend its claws *(page 20)* are cut, so that the claws are permanently retracted. Since the claws are still there, they must be trimmed regularly or they will become ingrown.

Declawing should only be undertaken as a last resort, once you have tried everything else and your cat risks losing his home or faces euthanasia if no one else will adopt him. However, it is very hard on cats over the age of one year (younger for heavy cats). Make sure the vet will provide pain medication after the surgery or find a vet who uses a laser. Laser surgery, which uses light rather than a blade to cut, vaporizes the nerve endings as the distal phalanx is excised, making for a much less painful recovery.

HUMANE ALTERNATIVES

 Before declawing, try one or all of the products specifically designed to prevent damage from scratching. A lot of these items are available through mail order, so check cat magazines and surf the internet for sources.

Vinyl nail caps are glued over the cat's claws and last from four to six weeks. Initially, the cat may groom them excessively and you may have to refasten them several times. Don't worry; they're safe, even if swallowed. Your cat will eventually get used to them.

Instead of merely placing a scratching post against the arm of your couch, buy the type of post with an arm that slides underneath to hold it firmly in place. Or, you can try the rigid, clear-plastic shields that protect both sides of the couch arms.

Strips of double-sided adhesive tape applied directly to furniture discourage scratching for the simple reason that the stickiness feels unpleasant to your cat's paws. Once the cat learns that upholstery doesn't feel right but the scratching post does, you can remove the tape.

EMERGENCY
· CARE ·

You may need to restrain your cat to provide first aid or diagnose a problem. Even a normally placid cat may become defensively aggressive or panicked if injured or in great pain. The classic, firm scruff-hold shown above prevents the cat from biting you; ideally, you should grip the front paws at the same time and have a second person check or treat the cat. Do not scruff a badly injured cat; gently wrap it in a towel instead.

Accidents happen. No matter how careful you are and what precautions you take, even your indoor cat can fall seriously ill or become badly injured. Knowing what to do in an emergency may make the difference between life or death for your cat. But keep in mind that the first aid techniques described here are only stopgap measures. The ultimate goal is to get your cat to a vet as quickly as possible. Even if your vet has twenty-four-hour emergency service, you should also know the location of the nearest walk-in emergency clinic. Post these numbers, as well as that of an animal poison-control center, near your phone. You might consider taking a course in cardiopulmonary resuscitation (CPR) for cats, or your vet may be able to show you how to do it. Only attempt CPR if you know how.

Take the time to gather the necessary first aid supplies before a calamity happens, keeping them together in a readily accessible place. Know exactly where to find anything you might need that doesn't fit into the kit (such as a board to serve as a stretcher). You can buy a first-aid kit designed specifically for pets or put one together yourself *(page 199)*.

WHEN THE UNTHINKABLE HAPPENS

Whether your cat has a sudden critical disorder or has suffered some sort of trauma, the most important thing you can do is to stay calm. You can't help your cat if you aren't thinking straight. Pause for a few seconds, take a few deep breaths, and approach the situation calmly to provide needed care. Make sure that the scene is safe. If not, move as soon as possible to a less dangerous area—to the sidewalk, for instance, if your cat has been hit by a car. Then, try to determine the nature of the problems and prioritize them. If several things are wrong, deal first with the more serious problems, then worry about the secondary ones. Be firm, so that you can examine the cat thoroughly, but gentle, so that you do not exacerbate injuries. If the cat is uncooperative, it may need to be restrained *(left)*; try to enlist the help of another person.

Check the cat's vital signs: breathing, pulse, and temperature. Be sure to write down your readings; even an excellent memory is unreliable in a crisis. You should already know your cat's normal vitals, so you can note any differences. A cat should breathe at a rate of about twenty to forty breaths per minute, although on hot days or after exercise breathing can be a lot faster. Watch your cat's chest for in-and-out movement and hold a piece of

EMERGENCY CARE AT A GLANCE

Problem	First aid required
Bleeding (cut, scratch)	Apply pressure to wound until bleeding stops *(page 171)*, then bandage. If bleeding does not stop or if foreign object lodged in body, seek veterinary care immediately. If cat bitten by animal of unknown rabies status, seek emergency veterinary attention.
Blocked urination/blood in urine	Seek veterinary care immediately.
Burn, chemical	Flush with large amounts of water. Seek veterinary care immediately.
Burn, thermal	Apply cold water or cold compress, then disinfectant. Seek immediate veterinary attention to check lungs for damage from smoke.
Choking	Remove obstruction *(page 173)*, being careful of bites. If not breathing, apply artificial respiration only if you know how. Otherwise, if unconscious or not breathing, seek veterinary care immediately.
Convulsions	Restrain gently with towel or light blanket. If longer than five minutes or repeated, seek veterinary care immediately. Otherwise, call vet for advice.
Electrocution/electrical burn	Turn off power or remove from source of electricity without making direct contact—use broomstick. Seek emergency veterinary attention.
Fracture	Immobilize *(page 171)* and get veterinary care immediately. If bleeding, apply gentle pressure *(page 171)*.
Frostbite (pale, cool skin)	Rewarm affected area with heat of your hand, by applying warm compresses, or by immersing in warm water (102° to 104°F, or 38.8° to 40°C). Seek emergency veterinary care if any pain, swelling, discharge, or discoloration or if skin does not return to normal after twenty minutes. Otherwise, get to vet within twenty-four hours.
Hypothermia (decreased alertness, weak pulse, shallow breathing)	Rewarm by wrapping in warm blanket and applying towel-covered hot-water bottle filled with warm water. Get to vet as soon as possible.
Insect bite/sting	Pull out insect stinger, if any. If signs of allergic reaction, seek emergency veterinary attention.
Poisoning (salivation, excessive vomiting, grogginess, unconsciousness, convulsions)	Call poison control center or vet, having product container on hand if possible. If conscious, induce vomiting by administering syrup of ipecac in dose recommended only if you are instructed. Monitor for shock *(page 170)*; if convulsing, provide gentle restraint. Seek emergency veterinary attention, bringing product container or sample of toxin with you.
Shock (lethargy, rapid breathing, weak pulse, low body temperature)	Keep warm *(page 170)*; seek emergency veterinary attention.
Major trauma (fall, car accident)	Monitor for shock *(page 170)*, keep warm, immobilize *(page 171)*, and stop bleeding *(page 171)*. Seek emergency veterinary attention.

THE SYMPTOMS OF SHOCK

Shock is the name given to a condition where the cardiovascular system is no longer efficiently delivering oxygen to body tissues. Although shock is a survival mechanism, slowing the metabolism in order to delay the effects of injuries or illness, it can sometimes lead to death, especially when accompanied by severe injuries.

Outward, observable signs include: inactivity or uncharacteristic quietness; rapid, shallow breathing; a rapid heart rate, accompanied by a rapid and/or weak pulse or no pulse at all; poor capillary refill time (measure this by pressing the cat's gums until they are white; when you let go, they should turn pink again within two seconds); and lowering of body temperature.

Shock almost always indicates a severe underlying problem, such as internal injuries, poisoning, or serious illness. Keep your cat warm by wrapping him in a blanket and rush him to the vet for emergency treatment.

paper or a mirror in front of the mouth and nostrils to check for breathing. Measure the cat's pulse *(below)*: It should be identical to the heart rate, normally between 130 (resting cat) and 200 (agitated cat) beats per minute. To gauge your cat's temperature, rather than using a thermometer (bad idea if he is injured and too time-consuming), just judge how his ears, nose, and extremities feel; are they warmer or cooler than usual? A low temperature may indicate shock *(left)*.

If your cat is ill or has minor physical injuries, transport him to the vet in his carrier. If he has severe injuries, the less handling and movement the better; gently immobilize him on a homemade stretcher *(opposite, top)*.

TRAUMA

Any wound, no matter how insignificant it may seem, should be treated as potentially serious. Even minor cuts and scratches can become infected or form abscesses; tiny puncture wounds may have resulted from bites or stings that introduce infection or venom. Clean minor wounds with mild soap and water, then swab them with an antiseptic solution. A bandage may be more trouble than it is worth for minor nicks. Have any unidentified bite or sting wound checked by a veterinarian.

Control heavy bleeding by applying pressure *(opposite, bottom)*. When the bleeding has stopped, bandage the wound: Wrap the bandage around the wound and around the entire injured area of the body—the whole tail or limb, or the entire torso or head. Do not bandage tightly. The idea is to secure the cloth without cutting off circulation. If there is a foreign object lodged in a wound, do not try to remove it; in fact, bandage around it without disturbing it at all. A tourniquet should only be used as a last resort

The most convenient place to feel a cat's pulse is inside its hind leg where the femoral artery is close to the surface. (Use your fingers, not your thumb, which has a pulse of its own). Press firmly enough to feel the pulse, but gently enough to allow free blood flow.

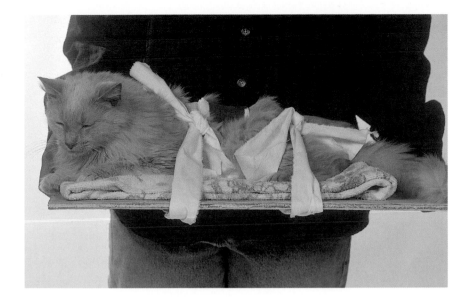

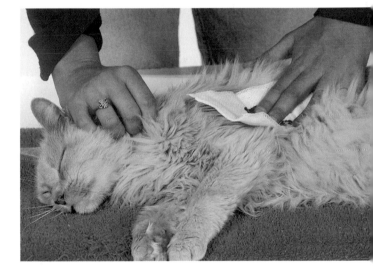

A severely injured cat may need to be immobilized in order to prevent movement that could cause further injury. Make a stretcher with a piece of plywood, padding it with a small blanket or folded towel. Place the cat on the board, preferably on its side; on its stomach will do as long as the cat is comfortable. Gently but firmly lash the cat to the stretcher with strips of cloth, being careful not to aggravate injuries or interfere with its breathing.

if a limb or tail is too badly damaged for the bleeding to stop. Blood loss is a major cause of shock, so monitor breathing, pulse, and general condition on the way to the vet.

A limp or swelling and signs of pain in a specific area may indicate a contusion (bruise), strain, sprain, or fracture. Contusions and strains are rarely serious taken by themselves, although if the pain continues for more than a few days a trip to the vet is warranted. Sprains, the stretching or tearing of ligaments, and fractures, the cracking or breaking of bones, are more serious. Usually the ligaments or bones need to be set and immobilized in a splint or cast by your vet. It may be difficult for you to differentiate between the various possibilities, so it's better to be safe than sorry. After any kind of trauma, have a vet examine your cat for any associated internal injuries.

A dangling or twisted limb or a bone protruding out of the skin is a sign of a serious fracture. Be careful; fractures with jagged edges may cause further internal injuries. Get your cat to the veterinarian as quickly as possible, but attempt to limit his movement for the trip. You can immobilize him on a stretcher (above), which is particularly important if you suspect injury to the torso; or, place him in some kind of container. A cat carrier is the ideal receptacle (especially the type that opens from the top), but a cardboard box or laundry basket can also serve. But be careful when restraining your cat in either of these ways, mainly to avoid causing him pain, but also because an injured cat has a tendency to bite.

Any trauma serious enough to cause a deep wound or broken bone has probably caused many other less obvious injuries as well. Falls and car accidents commonly cause multiple injuries, including cuts, fractures, and injuries to internal organs. After you apply first aid to your cat, immobilize him on a stretcher and get him to a vet immediately.

Most bleeding can be stopped within a few minutes by applying pressure. First place a gauze pad on the wound, then a piece of absorbent cloth. Press carefully and firmly on the wound. If the cloth gets soaked through, do not remove it; instead, place another piece on top of the first. If a foreign object is lodged in the cat's body or if a shard of bone has broken through the skin, place the gauze and cloth around it, being very gentle. If gauze is unavailable, paper towel fresh from its plastic wrapper is fairly sterile and an acceptable substitute.

A cat's tongue is rough enough to severely irritate a wound and a cat is deft enough with its teeth to remove bandages and sutures. **An Elizabethan collar may make your pet look like a satellite dish, but it will also keep his face and body apart until you can get him to the vet to get the area properly treated. Back home, the collar will allow any antiseptic, ointment, or sutures to do their job out of tongue's reach and will also keep him from scratching at irritations on his head. If you don't have one on hand, construct a temporary one out of cardboard. Roll the cardboard into a cone around his neck, about as tight as a collar, and tape or staple the ends together. Or, fasten it to his collar like the store-bought model shown above.**

If an injured cat resists being placed on a stretcher or in any sort of carrier, simply wrap it loosely in a clean towel and transport it as is. Fighting the attempt at immobilization is likely to cause additional injury.

EYE INJURIES

If your cat has something in his eye, hold his head steady and his eye open, and try to wash it out with tepid water or eye wash. Or, you can remove a foreign particle with a cotton swab. If you can't get it out or if it penetrates the eye or lid, get the cat to a vet promptly. If your cat is blinking, squinting, avoiding bright light, or his eyes are tearing excessively, he may have an irritation or injury to the eye surface. If you cannot see any injury, try an eye wash to cleanse any possible irritant. If you see an injury or if there is no visible injury but the problem persists, take your cat to the vet.

After a traumatic incident, different-sized pupils usually indicate a serious eye or brain trauma. Your cat will need immediate veterinary care to save the eye or, if there is bleeding or swelling in the brain, to save his life.

DIFFICULTY BREATHING

If your cat cannot breathe, he may have an obstruction: Clear his airway (*opposite*). If something is lodged too far down and your cat's mucous membranes are blue, you can try a cat Heimlich maneuver. Press sharply just below his rib cage in and up, in the direction of his head. But be careful not to press too hard or you risk breaking your cat's ribs.

If there is no obstruction, but your cat is wheezing, coughing, or not breathing at all, he needs emergency medical care.

BURNS

Don't underestimate the seriousness of a burn. Cats' skin doesn't blister like human skin. Instead, in a deep burn, the skin will appear reddened and the fur in the affected area may fall out. Apply cold water or a cold compress to the area for twenty minutes, then wash gently with disinfectant. Have all burns, even those that appear minor, checked by a vet. Avoid burn ointments since they are difficult to remove if other treatment is called for.

A cat that likes to chew may gnaw through a live electrical wire, causing electrocution and burns. Electrical burns, usually in and around the mouth, are pale yellow, bloodless, and cold. This kind of burn usually causes serious damage to skin and can result in a buildup of fluid in the lungs. Take your cat to a vet as soon as possible.

If your cat has been burned by chemicals, don't treat him until you have put on gloves, or you risk burning yourself. Remove and dispose of his collar or harness, which may have soaked up some of the chemical. Flush the area with large amounts of cool water and get to a vet immediately, bringing the package or a sample of the chemical with you.

WEATHER-RELATED CONDITIONS

Heat stress can be a problem in warm weather, especially for chubby, older, or longhair cats *(above)*. You don't need to worry about hypothermia and frostbite unless your cat goes out in the winter. Signs of hypothermia are decreased alertness, weak pulse, slowed heart rate, and shallow breathing. Wrap the cat in a blanket. Until you can get your cat to the vet, slowly rewarm him by wrapping a hot-water bottle filled with warm water (or a warm chemical-gel heating bag) in a towel and applying it to his body. Frostbite, commonly found on foot pads, the ears, or the tail, is indicated by pale, cool skin and numbness. Rewarm the frostbitten area with the heat of your hand, by applying a warm compress, or by immersing in warm water (102 to 104 degrees Fahrenheit, or 38.8 to 40 Centigrade). Get your cat to the vet immediately if he is in pain; if there is swelling, discharge, or considerable discoloration; or if the skin remains pale, cold, and hard after twenty minutes of rewarming. Otherwise, have a vet check the cat within a day.

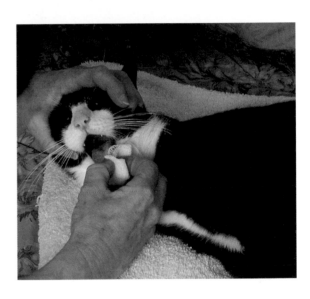

NERVOUS SYSTEM DISORDERS

Convulsions, or "grand-mal" seizures, may be caused by neurological disorders, brain injury, toxins and venoms, or heat stress. A cat experiencing a grand mal seizure, in which all the muscles go into spasm, usually first appears restless or anxious for a minute or two and may seek affection. Next, the cat loses consciousness, may convulse or drool for a few seconds to a few minutes, and may become incontinent. If the cat is convulsing, provide gentle restraint. Although your cat may appear to be quite normal when he regains consciousness, call your vet for advice; often the veterinarian will suggest keeping him confined for a day or two under close observation. Seizures lasting more than a few minutes or several seizures in succession constitute an emergency; get to the vet quickly.

To check for obstructions in the airway, hold the cat's head firmly with one hand and pull open its mouth with the other. If the cat resists, wedge its mouth open by applying gentle pressure through the cheeks between its back teeth. If you see an obstruction, remove it with your fingers or with tweezers. Be careful; the cat may bite. If possible, make this a two-person, four-handed operation.

· 6 ·

CAT
BREEDS

· · · ·

"A cat must either have
beauty or breeding,
or it must have a profession."

·

MARGARET BENSEN

PUREBRED
·BASICS·

How many breeds of cats could you identify? Chances are you would recognize at least a few of the following: Persian, Maine coon, Siamese, Abyssinian, exotic, Oriental, Scottish fold, American shorthair, Birman, or Burmese. These are the ten most popular breeds, as compiled by the Cat Fanciers' Association (CFA), the world's largest breed registry. There are about forty other cat breeds, however, some of which are quite new or rare and not yet officially recognized by many feline associations. The "Top Ten" breeds, along with a selection of these others, are profiled beginning on page 182.

Considering our long and successful relationship with the domestic feline, the phenomenon of the purebred cat is a surprisingly recent one. Cats have graced us with their presence since the time of the ancient Egyptians, possibly much earlier. But it took the rise in popularity of cat shows in late nineteenth-century England to kick-start the selective coupling of the domestic cat into separate breeds. All but a few domestic cat breeds are less than one hundred years old and most of them appeared on the scene far more recently. Compare this to the dog world, where rudimentary selective breeding started several thousand years ago.

An example of a hybrid, or man-made domestic breed, this Bengal cat is as close to the wild as you want to get. The breed is a mix of the domestic cat and the Asian leopard cat, a stunningly spotted or striped wild cat roughly the size of a domestic cat. But the wild blood must be diffused through the breeding of Bengals with other Bengals for four generations before the cats are considered fully domestic and appropriate as pets. Initial babies are still quite wild, and males in the second and third generations are often sterile. But by the fourth generation, these hybrids have the look, without the wild character, of the leopard cat.

Overleaf: Blue-point Siamese

TO BREED OR NOT TO BREED

Humankind has been dabbling in the science of heredity, or genetics, in both the canine and equine world for centuries to encourage specific physical traits for practical purposes: dogs for guarding herd animals or the homestead; horses for speed or for pulling heavy loads. But the small build of felines excluded them from anything beyond mousing. So when breeders turned their attention to the cat, it was for esthetic, not practical, reasons.

The cat fancy movement (groups dedicated to the selective breeding, proper care, and showing of cats) started up in the late 1800s. At this time, the great majority of the feline population, the ubiquitous mixed-breed household cat, was the result of natural selection. But what could the early breeders work with? To spice up the mix, enter the variety of "natural," or historic, types occupying geographically isolated pockets of the world. Cats used for crossbreeding—Turkish Angora, Persian, Siamese, British shorthair, Russian blue, and Abyssinian—had achieved distinctiveness without human intervention hundreds, in some cases thousands, of years ago (although some have since been refined by modern breeders).

The Somali (left) and the Abyssinian (below) are actually longhair and shorthair varieties of the same type of cat, but have been accorded individual breed status. Some other breeds are similarly classified, such as the exotics, which are shorthair Persians. In other cases, no new breed status is accorded and cats of different hair length are simply separated into subcategories or divisions—Oriental shorthairs and longhairs, for instance. The Cymric, which once had its own breed status in some registries, has been reclassified as a longhair Manx by the Cat Fanciers' Association.

THE MIXED-BREED CAT

The most popular of all cats has no pedigree. The mixed-breed, or random-bred, cat—known as the domestic shorthair—that makes up an estimated 95 percent of the world's domestic cat population is the result of natural selection and random, not selective, breeding. The cats come in all shapes and sizes, with a great variety of color, pattern, and length of hair. The bushier varieties, or "domestic longhairs," are usually just grouped in with the catchall label of domestic shorthairs.

The overall appearance of mixed-breed cats can be traced to one of the natural types: cobby, foreign, or in-between. Mixed breeds bearing a strong resemblance to pure-bred cats are fairly common. Longhair random-breed cats, while less common because of the recessive gene that creates long hair, often resemble the pedigreed Maine coon or Angora. The temperament of mixed-breed cats is less predictable than that of purebreds, though, and probably influenced more by environment than by genetics.

Aside from being a wonderful addition to your household, mixed-breed cats can compete in the Household Pet category of most cat shows. Often used to create new breeds by crossing them with existing purebreds, the mixed-breed cat has the honor of being the inspiration for breeds such as the American shorthair.

When people started to "work" with these natural breeds, others arose, either through hybridization or opportunistic use of spontaneous mutations. The vast majority of breeds are hybrids, created by crossing already established breeds with each other. For instance, the popular exotic combines the sturdy build and broad face of the Persian with the more manageable coat of the American shorthair and other shorthair breeds. The other way that new breed characteristics sprout is through haphazard mutations. These genetic changes result in traits such as taillessness or stub tails, abnormally short legs, bent or curled ears, curly hair, or even hairlessness. While some mutations are crippling or deadly and others merely controversial, some are desirable, and these traits were deliberately isolated and bred for repetition by cat breeders. Some feline mutations, such as the tailless-ness of the Manx from the Isle of Mann and the shortened appendage of the Japanese bobtail, flourished without human intervention, but within the vacuum of geographic isolation.

STANDARD PRACTICES

To be considered an authentic purebred, a cat must be registered with a cat association and come with a pedigree that attests to its parentage and traces its lineage. Purebred cats are judged and defined according to a precise set of esthetic ideals called breed standards. Drawn up by breed registries, these standards govern the "conformation"—size and shape of the body, head, tail, face, ear, eye, nose, muzzle, chin, neck, leg, and paw—as well as coat density, texture, and specific colors or patterns. Failure to con-

TABBY TYPES

 "Tabby" is not a breed, but a description of one of four coat patterns found in a rainbow of colors on numerous purebreds and the domestic shorthair. The four tabby varieties are mackerel, classic, spotted, and ticked.

The mackerel pattern is made up of narrow parallel stripes. A classic tabby cat has wide stripes and blotches that combine to form dense swirls and sometimes bulls'-eyes on the sides. The spotted pattern is actually made up of stripes that are broken into spots or "buttons."

The background of the mackerel, classic, and spotted patterns is comprised of "ticked," or banded, hairs. Each ticked hair contains stripes of light and dark color. These three tabby types also have rings on the legs and tail, bars on the face, and an "M" mark on the forehead.

The fourth variety, the ticked tabby, has an "agouti" coat made up of banded hairs, except on the belly and chest. These cats have facial bars and an "M" mark on the forehead, and also may have lines on their legs and tail.

Classic tabby (Manx)

Mackerel tabby (mixed breed)

Ticked tabby (Singapura)

Spotted tabby (ocicat)

The munchkin's short legs, a form of dwarfism, make it one of the more controversial new breeds.

form to any one part of the standard may disqualify a cat from competitive showing. But whether or not a cat is show quality is only relevant if you plan to enter your cat in competitions; what's considered a "flaw" is superficial and of no concern if you just want a pet.

With seven different registries in North America alone and several others in Europe, standards and even breed acceptance can vary dramatically from group to group. Although approximately fifty cat breeds are officially recognized by at least one registry, fewer than thirty are acknowledged by all of them. Philosophical differences among and even within the different organizations account for much of the inconsistent nature of modern cat appreciation. Purists favor strict guidelines in defining existing breeds and in accepting new ones, while others encourage experimentation and are quicker to accept new breeds. However, getting a new breed recognized can be difficult, even by the more liberal registries, and can take years. The regulations for acceptance vary, but each new breed must be distinct from existing breeds, exhibit good health, and lack genetic defects. Breeds usually go through steps of provisional acceptance until they are accorded full breed status.

PROFILING BREEDS

Bred for beauty rather than function, the different cat breeds vary far less dramatically than say, a Chihuahua from a Great Dane. Nor has selective breeding in felines created the same wide range of personalities as is found in canine breeds. But some variations exist, most of which are tied to the different body types of the natural breeds. The larger, thick-coated cobby types, such as the Persian, hailing from the colder climes of Asia, displayed a reserved and placid temperament, while their foreign-bodied counterparts from warmer areas, such as the Siamese, tended toward liveliness. The body type in-between these two ends of the feline spectrum, best exemplified by the American shorthair, occupies a temperamental middle ground. Like the mixed-breed cat they resemble physically, in general these cats are neither particularly aloof nor especially demanding of affection and attention.

Unfortunately, poor selective breeding can exaggerate some of these natural personality types. Problem personalities and behaviors such as neurotic overgrooming have emerged from what some critics call the excessive inbreeding of some cats.

The only cat ever specifically bred for a personality or behavior is the ragdoll, although this may mark the beginning of a new trend in cat breeding. Also known as the American ragdoll, this cross between a Birman and a nonpedigreed longhair goes completely limp when handled, thus its name. Critics of the breed suggest that this distinctly uncatlike behavior may imperil the cat, though, and some ragdoll breeders are now

attempting to produce a cat that is very relaxed and easy to handle, but without the limpness.

When cats are bred for extreme physical features, especially in the search for new breeds, physiological and health problems, as well as controversy, are bound to result. The dwarfism that causes short legs and sometimes restricts jumping ability in munchkins is considered too great a departure from the normal feline anatomy by some registries. The lack of hair in the sphynx deprives it of the ability to control its body temperature; due to fear of health problems, this breed is accepted by only one registry. Even established breeds such as the Persian have drawn fire for producing radical facial features that may result in breathing difficulties and constantly runny eyes.

Despite these controversies, most cat breeders and the registries that work to organize the thousands of shows around the world every year do more than simply promote purebred cats. They also raise the feline profile, which has a positive effect on the well-being of all cats.

This "tigron" is the result of a highly unnatural coupling between a male tiger and a female lion. (A male lion and a female tiger would produce a "liger.") In the wild, different species of cats almost never mate, even in densely populated areas, although it has been known to happen in zoos. Sometimes this controversial breeding was even encouraged to attract crowds to see the hybrid offspring. Tigrons and ligers, usually infertile, feature physical characteristics of both parents, but one is often dominant over the other. No major zoos in North America will permit this interspecies breeding to happen today since they prefer to work with species survival plans in order to maintain pure species of endangered animals.

·PERSIAN·

Their sometimes grumpy expression belying a sweet personality, Persians are by far the most popular of pedigreed cats in the United States, capturing the top prizes at cat shows as well as the hearts of cat lovers. Arriving on the European scene in the early seventeenth century from Persia (now Iran), the early Persians and Turkish Angoras were bred indiscriminately under a single category of "longhair." Since preference was given to the longer coat of the Persian, the Angora gradually disappeared as it was amalgamated into the Persian. (In the 1960s pure Angoras were rediscovered in Turkey and brought to the U.S., where they regained breed status.)

Thick, shiny, and exceptionally soft, with hair up to eight inches in length, its coat is the Persian's most outstanding and recognizable feature. In fact, it is still called the longhair in Britain, where each of the fifty or so color and pattern variations is considered its own distinct breed. Breeders and judges on both sides of the Atlantic agree that the ideal Persian possesses a medium to large cobby-type body set low on short, stocky legs and large, tufted paws. A pair of small, round-tipped ears sit low on the cat's broad, round head, and its large, bright eyes are set far apart. Overall, the body, head, and face of the Persian suggest both nobility and sturdiness.

Persian noses and faces should be flat. However, a controversy exists over which face shape best represents the Persian ideal. Some breeders and show judges, mostly in the United States, favor a flatter face than others. The ultra-flat profile at times results in problematically narrow nostrils and tear ducts, and tooth malocclusion. Breeding for large heads has caused a dramatic rise in the number of Caesarean deliveries of Persian litters. Many breeders, especially those in Britain, prefer the more traditional, less extreme "doll-face" Persian.

More the interested observer than curious explorer, the Persian has a quiet, easygoing, and sometimes playful nature that makes it an exceptional housemate. However, its delicate coat requires an extremely attentive owner. Daily grooming is essential in preventing coat matting and hairball formation. Late sexual maturity and small litters make the Persian an extremely expensive cat. But owners who enjoy its striking beauty and charming company say it's worth every penny.

Cameo smoke Persian

·MAINE COON·

Sturdy, handsome, and blessed with a warm and loving personality: It's no wonder the Maine coon enjoys great popularity. The ancestors of this longhair beauty originated in Europe and, in fact, its robust physique and constitution and long, shaggy coat suggest a not-too-distant relation to the Norwegian forest cat. Maine coons are said to have arrived in America in the early eighteenth century, working their way across the ocean aboard sailing vessels, where they protected food supplies from rodents. A perfect example of "survival of the fittest," the Maine coon evolved to its current large and rugged state thanks in part to the New England climate. Harsh northern winters, combined with this feline's history as a working cat, have produced an exceptionally muscular build and a thick, weather-resistant coat. A skilled hunter, the Maine coon has large, tufted paws that are ideal for walking on snow.

The Maine coon is a particularly late blooming breed, usually taking up to three or four years to reach full maturity. And while twenty pounds would be considered seriously overweight in most cats, perfectly fit male Maine coons commonly tip the scales there. Both sexes should be well proportioned: long, big-boned, and broad across the chest. Despite its imposing size, this gentle giant is an affectionate and extremely devoted companion to both humans and other animals. The cat is particularly famous for its warm greetings and happy trill. Mischievous and stoic at the same time, the Maine coon can sit and contemplate the world outside a window for hours on end, then turn and wreak havoc inside the home. New owners are cautioned to keep their bathroom doors shut since this cat's great fascination with water will often result in wet and messy forays into the bathtub and toilet bowl.

THE MAINE COON AT A GLANCE

Conformation: Medium to large body; medium wedge-shaped head should be in proportion to body. Legs medium in length and set wide; large, round, and well-tufted paws. Tail long; wide at base, and tapered. Large, tapered ears set high and well apart. Medium-long nose. Eyes large and set wide; slanted toward outer base of ear. Face seems slightly concave when viewed in profile.

Common colors: Numerous colors and patterns under five classes: solid, tabby, tabby and white, particolor, and "other." Only chocolate, lavender, and pointed, or Himalayan, excluded. Eyes gold, copper, or green; blue or odd-eyed allowed in white cats.

Coat type: Long, glossy, and shaggy. Heavy, yet silky. Shorter on shoulders and longer on stomach.

Grooming requirements: Moderate; fur quite resistant to matting and knotting. Brush and comb three times per week. Bathe occasionally.

Temperament: Gentle, loving, and calm. Intelligent, patient, and good with children. Known for making soft trilling sounds.

Smoke patched tabby with white Maine coon

·SIAMESE·

Blue-point Siamese

Piercing blue eyes, the hallmark of this graceful beast, peer out from a dark mask. But aside from their dramatic eyes, the Siamese are easily identified by their long, svelte bodies and limbs and characteristic color allocation. But this coloration takes a while to kick in. Siamese kittens are solid white at birth and the "points," or darker areas, only develop on a little one's extremities—face, ears, legs, and tail—as it matures.

Although a dark brown face is most common, there are actually four traditional Siamese colors, including seal point (a fawn body with nearly black points), chocolate point (an ivory body with milk-chocolate points), blue point (a grayish body with dark gray points), and lilac point (a white body with pinkish gray points). Other colors exist, such as red point or lynx point (known as tabby point in England), and depending on the cat association in question, either are considered a division of Siamese or are classified as another breed entirely, namely the colorpoint shorthair.

The fine-boned Siamese of today, with its large-eared, wedge-shaped head and lithe, albeit muscular, body is a far cry from the original creature that originated several centuries ago in Siam (now Thailand). Legend has it that in ancient times these prized cats served as guards for palaces and temples, and that royalty offered them as gifts, paving the way for their eventual worldwide distribution. The crossed eyes and kinked tail of these prototypical Siamese have been eradicated through careful breeding and are now considered faults in show cats. Some new breeds have arisen by mating Siamese with other breeds: the ocicat (with Abyssinians), the Himalayan (with Persians), the snowshoe (with bicolor American shorthairs), and the Tonkinese (with Burmese).

The very vocal Siamese is affectionate and full of personality. An attention seeker, it frequently pads around after its favorite person or retrieves tossed toys and is quite amenable to being walked on a leash. While smart and curious, the flip side of its intelligent nature is a tendency to demand human companionship. The short, sleek coat of the Siamese requires little grooming to maintain the trademark glossiness.

· ABYSSINIAN ·

As anyone who owns one can tell you, Abyssinians get around. Not only do they constantly circle your feet and race through the house, but as a breed they have a far-flung geographical history. There are several theories on the place of origin of this beautiful, bright, and wild-looking creature. The cat worshiped and mummified by the ancient Egyptians more than four thousand years ago is said to be physically and genetically similar to the modern Abyssinian. The lithe and lanky feline named for and thought to have inhabited ancient Abyssinia (now Ethiopia) also bears a strong resemblance to the African wild cat, the ancestor of all domestic felines. More recent genetic evidence points to southeast Asia as the Abyssinian's point of origin. But while scientists have been busy sorting out its convoluted background, cat lovers have wasted no time in making the Abyssinian one of the most coveted and loved cat breeds in the world.

The Abyssinian, or Aby, is prized for its distinctive, gloriously resilient agouti coat. When cloaked in its historical ruddy brown, it resembles nothing more than the camouflaged coat of the mountain lion. Lean and muscular, the regal Aby's ideal body is a combination of power and grace. Its large ears and expressive eyes speak of alertness and great intelligence. Generally a healthy cat, the Abyssinian is nevertheless unusually susceptible to gum disease.

The Aby's keen mind often endears it to cat fanciers. As quick-witted as it is fleet of foot, this breed can be a handful around the house. If you're looking for a lap cat, look elsewhere. But if a smart, energetic, and friendly companion is what you seek, look no further than this active feline. Adept jumpers and climbers, they are noted for somehow managing to open doors that guard goodies such as catnip. Mealtime often forces Aby owners to be as alert as the cats themselves: Pay attention or your chicken dinner may become cat food in a flash! The Aby is a devoted friend that will follow you around, providing constant companionship and eliciting laughter at its incessant hijinks. Don't bother pinning down your Aby for hugs and kisses, though; the struggle won't be worth the trouble. But on its own terms, this cat will shower you with love, usually with forehead rubs and shoulder-perch purrs. Not a vocal cat, an Aby will nevertheless let you know one way or the other what it wants, whether it is affection or food or both.

THE ABYSSINIAN AT A GLANCE

Conformation: Lithe and graceful, but muscular. Medium-length body. Modified wedge-shaped head with large, sometimes tufted ears. Large almond-shaped eyes. Long and tapering tail.

Common colors: Ruddy, red, blue, and fawn; lilac, cream, and silver still under assessment. Brilliant eyes of gold, copper, hazel, or green.

Coat type: Dense, medium-length, fine-textured, and springy. Hairs long enough for two to three bands of ticking.

Grooming requirements: Brush weekly. Pay special attention to dental hygiene.

Temperament: Energetic, athletic, and highly intelligent. Affectionate, loyal, and very playful.

Ruddy Abyssinian

·EXOTIC·

THE EXOTIC AT A GLANCE

Conformation: Rounded, medium-sized body; broad across chest. Short, thick neck and legs. Short, but proportionate tail. Massive, round head and flat face. Small, round-tipped ears. Large, round eyes set in level position.

Common colors: More than fifty varieties in all colors and patterns, including pointed. Multiple eye colors, most often copper. For showing, eye color must conform to coat color.

Coat type: Soft, dense, and full of life. Medium in length. Up to two inches long; should stand out from body because of heavy undercoat.

Grooming requirements: Weekly combing and occasional bathing to prevent matting. Daily combing to promote new hair growth. Regular wiping of eyes to prevent staining of coat.

Temperament: Lively and alert. Playful (likes hunting games), loving, and intelligent.

B orn in the late 1950s through an attempt by some American shorthair breeders to improve the coat quality and body conformation of their cats, the exotic is basically a shorthair version of the Persian. Thanks to the Persian's immense popularity, many judges and cat fanciers turned a blind eye to this blatant bending of the rules, and for a brief period the American shorthair category became a confused jumble of body and coat types. In 1967, to protect the integrity of the original American shorthair and to recognize the popularity of the successful cross, the newly dubbed exotic was officially recognized as its own distinct breed.

Physically, the exotic, or exotic shorthair as it is also known, is identical to the Persian except for its much shorter coat. Its cobby body is set on short, thick legs and its head is round and massive, with the Persian's sweet expression and broad, flat face. Unfortunately, exotics may suffer from the same respiratory and dental problems as Persians do.

The exotic's plush but only medium-length coat has earned it the unflattering nickname of "lazy person's Persian" in some circles. Although it does not require the constant care of the Persian's, the exotic's coat is by no means a maintenance-free one. A weekly combing and occasional bath will keep it glossy and mat-free. Many cat lovers prefer the exotic's plush coat to the Persian's since it allows for a better appreciation of the impressive cobby body.

All comparisons with the Persian end when discussing the exotic's personality. Bright, playful, and livelier than its longhair relation, the exotic is extremely friendly. Potential exotic owners should expect to be followed from room to room by this curious creature. The exotic enjoys up-close hugs and kisses and is even willing to share its affection with perfect strangers. As much as it enjoys nuzzling, lap-sitting, and being groomed, the exotic also loves to play chase. After its last ounce of energy is spent, expect a long, serious nap.

Red mackerel tabby exotic

·ORIENTAL·

The Oriental is basically a Siamese as if seen in dim light. Built on the stunning splendor of the Siamese, but without the color pointing and obligatory blue eyes, the popular Oriental has all the physical and temperamental charms of its famous cousin. It was developed to display a stunning array of color and pattern combinations—some three hundred in all.

In the 1950s and 1960s, American and British breeders wanting to capitalize on the tremendous popularity of Siamese cats began crossing them with both pedigreed and mixed-breed shorthair cats of many colors (and patterns). Before long, every color and pattern possibility in the domestic cat's gene pool began cropping up in this designer Siamese hybrid. First named the foreign shorthair in Britain, it was dubbed the Oriental shorthair on its introduction to the United States in the 1970s to acknowledge its Far East origins. By 1976 the Oriental shorthair had achieved official championship status in the Cat Fanciers Association. With its tremendously varied genetic background, it was no surprise to breeders when longhair varieties began cropping up. In the mid-1990s, the Oriental longhair joined with the shorthair variety to form two divisions of a single breed: the Oriental.

Classically foreign in type, the Oriental is a lithe but muscular cat with a proportionate, triangular or wedge-shaped head. Its long legs, neck, and tail may make it appear delicate, but the Oriental is surprisingly strong and agile. It's playful, good-tempered, and inquisitive. Somewhat capricious, unpredictable, and often demanding and vocal, the Oriental nevertheless makes for a bright, loyal, and entertaining companion. Like all thin-coated breeds, it prefers a warm lap to cushions, and its coat will leave little hair on your furniture. If you would like to treat your cat to a taste of fresh air but don't want to risk the dangers of leaving it to tackle the great outdoors alone, choose an Oriental. It quickly becomes used to a harness and it responds favorably to being on a leash. Orientals generally live long, healthy lives, although some suffer from forms of inherited heart disease.

THE ORIENTAL AT A GLANCE

Conformation: Long, slender, tubular body. Slim legs and oval-shaped feet. Wedge-shaped head with large and pointed ears. Almond-shaped, medium-sized eyes.

Common colors: Huge variety of colors and patterns in both shorthair and longhair varieties. Green eyes; eyes of solid colors may be blue, green, or copper.

Coat type: Long or short hair; fine, glossy coat that lies close to body.

Grooming requirements: Minimal shedding. Weekly brushing with rubber brush.

Temperament: Active and athletic. Loyal, inquisitive, and highly intelligent.

Red spotted tabby Oriental

SCOTTISH
·FOLD·

THE SCOTTISH FOLD AT A GLANCE

Conformation: Medium-sized, round, and well-padded body. Round head with firm chin and jaw. Large cheeks; jowly appearance in males. Small ears folded forward and downward. Eyes large, round, and well separated.

Common colors: Wide variety of colors and patterns, except hybridizations resulting in chocolate, lavender, or Himalayan pattern. Eye color corresponds to coat color.

Coat type: Dense, resilient coat; longhair and shorthair varieties.

Grooming requirements: Occasional combing for shorthairs. Daily brushing for longhairs.

Temperament: Calm, quiet, and undemanding. Playful; enjoys human contact.

If unique and striking characteristics were the sole basis on which ribbons were handed out at cat shows, the Scottish fold would probably win every competition, ears down. But don't applaud clever breeders for the bonny fold's trademark ears; thank Mother Nature. A spontaneous genetic mutation was responsible for this feline's unique appearance.

The success story of this owl-like breed began with the discriminating eye of a Scottish cat-loving shepherd by the name of William Ross. In 1961 Ross spotted a white kitten with folded ears named Susie playing in his neighbor's yard and was so captivated by her pixieish looks that he convinced her owners to give him one of her offspring. Two years later, they gave Ross a snow-white female with folded ears that in turn produced a folded-eared white male named Snowball. This began the rapid rise of the Scottish fold, which culminated with the granting of championship status by the Cat Fanciers' Association in 1978.

As fast as the fold's ascension in the breed world may have been, it was not without controversy. The incomplete dominant gene responsible for the weakened cartilage that caused the ears of half of these kittens to permanently fold forward was also at first accused of producing deafness and such skeletal abnormalities as heavy boning and short, stiff tails. Breeders soon saw their way around these health problems, though, by using fewer white cats to eliminate deafness and by never directly mating two folded-eared cats together. Apart from normal, prick-eared folds, acceptable crosses included the sturdily built British and American shorthairs, in an attempt to retain the original fold's rugged barnyard frame. Although some critics unfairly dismiss it as nothing more than a shorthair with freakish ears, the Scottish fold has developed a look all its own, complete with a well-padded body, dense coat, sweet, wide-set eyes, and well-rounded whisker pads. The shorthair and longhair varieties are recognized as two divisions of the Scottish fold breed. Calm, playful, and good with children, both make wonderful companions.

When choosing a kitten from a breeder, give it a quick, gentle body-and-tail inspection. Avoid cats that display short, stiff tails, splayed toes, short, overly thick legs, or poor mobility.

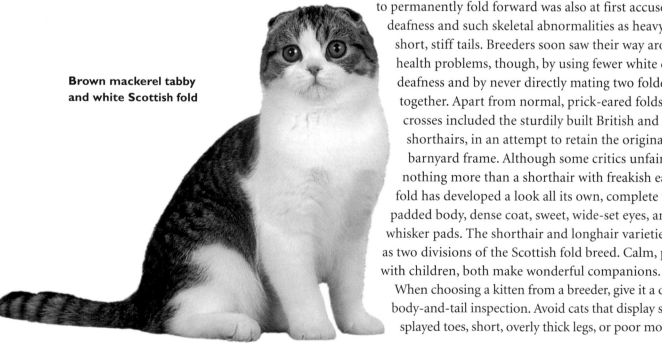

Brown mackerel tabby and white Scottish fold

AMERICAN
·SHORTHAIR·

The American shorthair is really just a landed immigrant. Ancestors of the so-called "all-American cat" are said to have accompanied the pilgrims to the New World on the *Mayflower* and other ships like her from western Europe in the early seventeenth century. Once settled, the cats earned their keep by household pest control. Now retired as a full-time hunter of rodents, the American shorthair is widely loved for its charming personality and its quintessential "catness." The robust good looks of this feline earn it high praise from cat lovers who prefer mixed-breed cats to their blue-blood cousins.

Originally known as the "domestic" shorthair, the American shorthair was considered no great shakes in the world of cat fancy for the longest of times. Although it was recognized by the Cat Fanciers' Association (CFA) as one of the first five pedigreed cat breeds when the group was founded in 1906, it looked far too much like an ordinary house cat to be accorded much respect from the upper echelons of cat fancy. When cat shows ran short of cages, the lowly American shorthairs were often the first to be evicted from theirs. That attitude began to change after an American shorthair silver tabby won the U.S. Cat of the Year award in 1965.

In 1966 CFA members voted to change the name from the domestic shorthair to the American shorthair in honor of the cat's heritage and hardy constitution. Since then, the breed has consistently ranked in the top ten at cat shows.

The American shorthair has been crossed with other breeds to create several new ones: with Siamese for the colorpoint shorthair, with Burmese for the Bombay, and with Persian to produce the exotic. Sturdy of body and with short, hard-textured, low-maintenance coats, this breed is used to shore up the lines of other less robust breeds.

But it takes more than a pretty face and a great body to survive four centuries. An extremely healthy breed, the American shorthair lives on average fifteen to twenty years. Loyal and easygoing, it makes an excellent family companion. It likes children and will tolerate other animals, even dogs. Smart and self-reliant without being standoffish, the American shorthair even adapts well to owners who are away from home often.

THE AMERICAN SHORTHAIR AT A GLANCE

Conformation: Powerful body. Neck and legs are well-muscled. Medium-long tail with wide base and blunt end. Large head with full cheeks and gentle expression. Eyes set wide apart, with outer corners slightly higher than inner corners.

Common colors: More than 80 colors and patterns, including classic and mackerel tabby, and solid, smoke, shaded, and parti-colors. Silver tabby is the most popular, followed by the brown tabby. Eyes gold, green or hazel.

Coat type: Short, dense, and hard in texture. Resistant to cold and moisture.

Grooming requirements: Occasional brushing with a rubber brush.

Temperament: Loving; intelligent; calm; very quiet voice. Friendly and highly adaptable.

Silver classic tabby American Shorthair

· BIRMAN ·

THE BIRMAN AT A GLANCE

Conformation: Long, stocky body and large, rounded head. Full cheeks and rounded muzzle. Eyes almost round in shape. Medium to small ears; rounded at top and wide at base. Medium-length tail.

Common colors: Seal point, lilac point, blue point, and chocolate point. Some registries accept a number of other colorpoints. Deep blue eyes.

Coat type: Medium to long; silky with heavy ruff around neck.

Grooming requirements: Heavy shedding, but mat-free. Quick daily combing only.

Temperament: Affectionate, intelligent, and devoted. Playful and active, but extremely gentle.

Seal-point Birman

Also known as "the sacred cat of Burma," the Birman comes complete with a legend as beautiful and dramatic as its appearance. According to an oft-repeated tale, the statue of a beautiful, blue-eyed goddess once kept watch over a group of priests who shared their temple in western Burma (now Myanmar) with a hundred white cats. Every evening, a white-haired priest named Mun-Ha prayed before the statue, accompanied by a cat named Sinh. But one night, his prayers were interrupted as he was mortally wounded by a band of raiders from Siam. As Mun-Ha lay dying, Sinh stood and faced the statue with his paws on his master's head. As he stared at the statue of the goddess, Sinh is said to have miraculously taken on her golden hue and sapphire eyes. Only his paws, touching his fallen master's snowy head, remained a pristine white, as pure as the priest's soul. The next morning, the rest of the temple's cats were identically transformed. From that day forth, these cats and their offspring were considered holy.

The sacred cat's early western development took place in France, where it was first recognized for showing in 1925. The destruction of World War II is said to have nearly eliminated the breed, but by the mid-1950s, it was fully revived. A few years later, the first of these cats began arriving in the United States. Around that time, the sacred cat's name was changed first to Burman, then to Birman (from Birmanie, French for Burma).

Crossings between Siamese and longhairs are most likely responsible for the Birman's long, silky, colorpoint coat and long, neither svelte nor cobby, body. Always born pure white like the Siamese, the Birman develops color, traditionally seal point, only at around three or four months of age, but maintains its legendary white-gloved paws.

Although it may have the Siamese's famous coloring, the Birman's personality is miles away from that of its demanding cousin. Gentle and calm, Birmans are devoted to their human companions and are good with children, too. But don't be fooled by the soft fur and even softer voice. Playful and bright, they are especially quick at learning and responding to their names, and they are by no means averse to mischief.

·BURMESE·

Few breeds can boast of origins as well documented as the Burmese's. Its ancestors, native to southeast Asia and known as "copper cats" for their short, brown coats, are believed to have inhabited Buddhist temples as far back as the fifteenth century. But all modern Burmese can be traced back to a small, brown, and slightly pointed female named Wong Mau, given to Dr. Joseph Thompson of San Francisco by a sailor from Rangoon, Burma (now Myanmar), in 1930. Captivated by Wong Mau's compact body, but mostly by her stunning coat, Thompson set out to start a new breed by mating her with a seal-point Siamese. Three types emerged from Wong Mau's first litter: a Siamese pointed, a dark body with dark points like their mother, and a dark sable-brown type with only minimal pointing that is considered to be the first true Burmese.

To distinguish the Burmese from the Siamese, breeders have worked at producing a rounder, more solid-looking cat. Today's American Burmese are often referred to as "bricks wrapped in silk" for their hard, compact bodies and soft, glossy coats. "Extreme" versions of the cat, bred for a shorter nose and much broader muzzle, are sometimes born with a very serious skull defect.

Intelligent and high-spirited, the Burmese craves and demands its owner's undivided attention. Unhappy if left alone for too long, it requires companionship in the form of humans, other cats, or even dogs. If work or travel keeps you away from home a lot, do not take on a Burmese. But if you have the time, your devotion will be returned tenfold through its sweet expressions, innocent eyes, and constant purring.

Blue Burmese

THE BURMESE AT A GLANCE

Conformation: Medium-sized foreign body; compact and muscular, surprisingly heavy for its size. Round head and full, broad face with round, well-separated eyes. Medium, round-tipped ears tilted slightly forward. Straight, medium-length tail.

Common colors: Sable, champagne, blue, and platinum (known as lilac and lavender in other breeds), shading to lighter color on underparts. Dark mask on most champagne-colored cats. Yellow to gold eyes.

Coat type: Glossy, satinlike texture. Short and fine; lies close to body.

Grooming requirements: Can be groomed by petting, but weekly combing will remove dead hair. Occasional rubbing with damp chamois will enhance shine of coat.

Temperament: Playful and curious, sometimes to a fault. Very athletic climber and jumper. Intelligent and affectionate attention-seeker. Sociable; should not be left alone for more than a few hours. Not very vocal unless encouraged.

AMERICAN CURL

Conformation: Medium-sized, semi-foreign body; moderately muscled. Head is modified wedge, with distinguishing curled-back ears. Walnut-shaped eyes.

Common colors: All colors and patterns accepted. Eye color harmonizes with coat.

Coat type: Both shorthair and longhair have silky fur with little undercoat.

Grooming requirements: Minimal brushing for both shorthair and longhair.

Temperament: Highly curious and active; kittenlike even as adults. Undemanding, easygoing, and affectionate; very sociable. Not very vocal.

Blue patched tabby and white American curl

Silver mackerel tabby American wirehair

AMERICAN WIREHAIR

Conformation: Very similar to American shorthair, with which it is crossed. Medium to large, sturdy, and muscular body; legs medium in length and muscular. Round head with prominent cheekbones. Medium-sized, slightly rounded ears. Big, round eyes set far apart and slightly slanted.

Common colors: Bicolor; classic and mackerel tabby; tabby and white; shaded; smoke; and solid. Any color except lavender or chocolate; no pointed patterns. Variety of eye colors.

Coat type: Coarse, dense, medium-length coat. Rough, resilient texture; down, guard, and awn hairs all wiry (crimped, hooked, or bent).

Grooming requirements: Little to no brushing. Bathe every month, applying shampoo designed for harsh coats.

Temperament: Outgoing. Extremely friendly and affectionate, yet independent. Athletic, playful, and amusing.

BALINESE

Conformation: Medium-sized, long, and lithe but muscular body; long, slim legs (like Siamese—Balinese originally called longhair Siamese). Tapering, wedge-shaped head. Strikingly large ears. Almond-shaped eyes that angle upward.

Common colors: Seal point, blue point, lilac point, and chocolate point. Some associations accept red point, tortie point, and lynx point; others call these variations "Javanese." Eyes deep, vivid blue.

Coat type: Medium-length, close-lying fur; may be longer on belly, tail, and neck. Fine, silky single coat; no undercoat means less tendency to mat.

Grooming requirements: Little shedding; occasional brushing and combing.

Temperament: Intelligent, active, very sociable, and affectionate. Dislikes being left alone for long periods of time; may be mischievous if bored. Vocal, but not as loud as Siamese.

Lilac-point Balinese

Black
Bombay

BOMBAY

Conformation: Medium-sized and muscular body; surprisingly heavy (Burmese and American shorthair crossbreed.) Round head with short, broad muzzle. Ears wide at base with rounded ends. Rounded, widely separated eyes.

Common colors: Black only color accepted for showing. Cats with sable coloring (dark brown, lighter underneath) can only be shown in some associations. Eyes copper or deep gold.

Coat type: Very short and satiny; naturally glossy. Lies close to body.

Grooming requirements: Occasional brushing with rubber brush or palm of hand. Minimal seasonal change in coat.

Temperament: Calm and sweet-natured; highly sociable attention-seeker. Smart, curious, and playful, but not too active. Loves warmth. Likes to be dominant cat. Voice neither loud nor grating, but very distinctive.

BRITISH SHORTHAIR

Conformation: Stocky, powerful body (medium to large in size) with short to medium legs; short neck and thick tail. Round head with big, rounded whisker pads. Ears medium-sized with rounded tips. Round eyes.

Common colors: Solid blue, black, cream, or white; bicolor; calico; tortoiseshell; black or blue smoke; brown, red, silver, blue, or cream tabby (mackerel, classic, or spotted pattern); and white and tabby. Eyes usually copper or yellow.

Coat type: Short, plush, dense coat.

Grooming requirements: Daily brushing during spring and fall shedding period; minimal brushing otherwise.

Temperament: Affectionate without being overly demonstrative. Calm, quiet, and good-natured. Responsive: likes involvement in household goings-on; adapts easily to new situations.

Cream spotted
tabby British
shorthair

Blue
chartreux

CHARTREUX

Conformation: Medium-sized, husky cat; bearlike appearance. Fine-boned legs and small feet. Round, broad head with medium-sized ears set high on head. Small, tapered muzzle; small whisker pads. Round, moderately wide-set eyes.

Common colors: Soft, blue-gray tones ranging from deep slate-gray to pale ash. Silver-tipped hairs. Ideal eye color brilliant orange, but can range from copper to gold.

Coat type: Resilient undercoat and water-resistant top coat. Plush, woolly texture; stands slightly apart from the body. Medium-short hair.

Grooming requirements: Minimal shedding; occasional brushing with rubber brush, especially during shedding season.

Temperament: Tranquil, attentive, and affectionate; devoted to owner. Hardy, intelligent, and agile; enjoys hunting games, interactive toys, and even playing with dogs. Surprisingly quiet voice; tends to chirp and trill rather than meow.

CORNISH REX

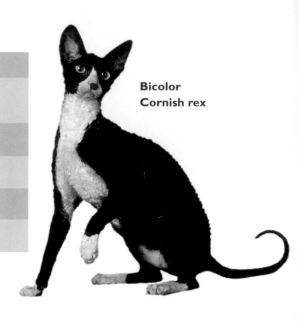

Bicolor Cornish rex

Conformation: Small to medium in size. Dainty, but solid and muscular body; long, powerful springlike legs. Oval face with pronounced cheekbones; large ears set high on head. Oval eyes with upward slant.

Common colors: All colors and patterns accepted by most cat associations; popular colors include particolor, shaded, smoke, solid, and tabby. Eye color harmonizes with coat color.

Coat type: Short, dense coat with no guard hairs. Awn and down hairs give soft and silky coat that lies close to body in tight marcel wave; size and depth of wave may vary.

Grooming requirements: Minimal grooming: Every few days, stroke coat with rubber brush; once a month, wipe with damp chamois to remove dead hairs.

Temperament: Inquisitive, active, and acrobatic; excellent manual dexterity. Requires space to play. Gregarious and people-oriented; enjoys a lot of social interaction.

Silver Egyptian mau

EGYPTIAN MAU

Conformation: Medium-long, muscular, graceful body with longer hind legs and small feet. Head slightly rounded wedge; ears large, somewhat pointed, and may be topped with tuft of fur. Big, almond-shaped eyes angled slightly toward ears.

Common colors: Spotted tabby pattern. Dark spots on background of silver, bronze, pewter, black, or smoke. Stripes on legs and rings on tail. "M" on forehead; scarab beetle mark on head and pair of "mascara" lines on each cheek. Vivid green eyes.

Coat type: Medium-length, lustrous coat. Hairs in smoke-colored coats soft and silky; denser in other colors.

Grooming requirements: Minimal shedding. Brush daily; comb with fine-toothed comb weekly.

Temperament: Expressive and vocal cat; melodious voice. Fearless and very playful; particularly enjoys hunting games. Very loyal.

JAPANESE BOBTAIL

Conformation: Medium-sized, slim, long body with good muscle tone. Unique short tail; curved or kinked and extending no more than three inches from body. Triangular head with high cheekbones; big, alert ears. Large, oval eyes; widely spaced and slanted up toward ears.

Common colors: Traditional color white, black, and red, known as Mi-ke. Also bicolor (especially vans: white with most patches of color on head, legs, and tail; fewer on body), tabby, tortie, and tabby or tortie and white. Variety of eye colors; should go with coat color.

Coat type: No noticeable undercoat. Shorthair variety medium-length, silky fur. Longhair medium-long to long silky hairs; longer mane and trousers.

Grooming requirements: Little shedding; longhair typically mat-free. Minimal brushing for both shorthair and longhair.

Temperament: Athletic, playful, and rambunctious. Affectionate; requires attention. Gets along well with other pets. Quite vocal; soft voice likened to singing.

Bicolor van Japanese bobtail

Red classic tabby Manx

MANX

Conformation: Sturdy, muscular, and medium-sized. Short body with arched back and overall round appearance; short front legs and longer, strong back legs. Typically without tail ("rumpy"), but may have tail knob ("riser"), short tail ("stumpy"), or even long tail ("longy"). Round head and round whisker pads; medium-sized ears. Big, round eyes.

Common colors: Tabby, calico, and tortoiseshell popular; most cat associations accept all colors and patterns except pointed. Variety of eye colors.

Coat type: Short hair; glossy double coat: thick, cottony undercoat and longer, harder hairs in outer coat. Longhair variety (previously called Cymric) has heavy, medium-length double coat; silky with stiffer guard hairs.

Grooming requirements: Little brushing for shorthair; twice weekly for longhair.

Temperament: Active, playful, and people-friendly; very loyal and often becomes strongly attached to one person in family.

NORWEGIAN FOREST CAT

Conformation: Large, solidly muscled body of medium length. Substantial legs; longer hind legs. Wide, triangular-shaped head on thick neck. Medium-sized ears set as much on side as on top of head; usually longer fur on tips of ears. Eyes large and almond-shaped; slightly angled toward outer ear base.

Common colors: Brown mackerel or classic tabby, often with white, most common; any color or pattern acceptable, except for Siamese markings and chocolate or lilac colors. Eyes shades of green, hazel, and gold; white cats may be blue- or odd-eyed.

Coat type: Longhair. Silky, water-resistant, double coat with dense, woolly undercoat. Front-bib ruff and back-of-neck ruff frame head like a mane. May have tail, ear, and toe tufts. Bicolors and solid colors have softer coats than tabbies.

Grooming requirements: Very little brushing; coat usually mat-free. Molting in spring.

Temperament: Affectionate and people-friendly; craves company and attention. Charming and loving; quickly becomes attached to members of household. Playful; likes to climb.

Brown mackerel tabby Norwegian forest cat

Chocolate ocicat

OCICAT

Conformation: Medium to large cat. Solid and muscular, yet long-bodied and lithe. Long, muscular legs; thin tail. Head modified wedge with wide muzzle; large ears and large, almond-shaped eyes.

Common colors: Dark spots and tabby stripes on lighter background; agouti hairs and "M" on forehead. Colors include tawny, chocolate, cinnamon, fawn, blue, lavender, black-silver, chocolate-silver, cinnamon-silver, blue-silver, lavender-silver, and fawn-silver. Eyes any color but blue.

Coat type: Close-lying, glossy coat.

Grooming requirements: Minimal grooming: Every few days, run hand to remove loose hairs; once a month, groom with rubber brush and fine-toothed comb.

Temperament: Curious, highly active, and intelligent; fairly easy to train. Very sociable, faithful, undemanding, and good with children. Should not be regularly left alone for long stretches of time. Can be quite vocal.

RAGDOLL

Conformation: Large, powerful, heavily-boned cat; full, broad chest same width across shoulders and hips. Medium-length legs; large, tufted paws. Long, fluffy tail. Head modified wedge; large, oval eyes.

Common colors: Colorpoint comes in Siamese colors: seal, blue, chocolate, or lilac with well-defined points contrasting with body color. Mitted ragdolls pointed, but front paws have white gloves; back legs and paws white. Bicolor has white, inverted "V" mask on face and white legs, feet, and ruff. Eyes sapphire blue—the bluer the better.

Coat type: Medium-long to long plush and silky coat; longest around neck and outer edges of face. Minimal undercoat.

Grooming requirements: Coat does not mat easily, but must still be brushed daily, especially at end of winter. Little shedding.

Temperament: Tranquil, intelligent, affectionate, and loving; quickly becomes attached to owners. Playful, but not overactive. Very tolerant; gets along well with children, dogs, and other animals. Gentle voice. Known for going limp when picked up.

Bicolor ragdoll

Blue Russian blue

RUSSIAN BLUE

Conformation: Fine-boned body; long, lithe, and graceful, yet muscular. Head medium-wedge in shape, set on thin neck. Wide-set eyes. Tail long and in proportion; long, fine-boned legs.

Common colors: Even, bright blue color. Guard hairs silver-tipped, which gives lustrous and silvery shine. Some countries recognize black and white, but blue more common. Must be free of tabby markings. Intensely green eyes.

Coat type: Distinctive coat resembling seal fur: short, dense, and plush. Soft and silky to touch.

Grooming requirements: Weekly grooming; occasionally smooth fur with damp chamois.

Temperament: Loyal and devoted; becomes very attached to human family, while staying aloof with strangers. Affectionate, gentle, and quiet; intelligent and playful without being insistent. Gets along well with children; other pets once accustomed to them. Secure; adjusts well to being left alone.

SINGAPURA

Conformation: Small, but muscular; typically weighs four (female) to six (male) pounds. Muscular body and limbs; thin tail. Rounded head with large ears and huge, almond-shaped eyes.

Common colors: Sepia agouti hairs (dark brown ticking on ivory base). Pale color on muzzle, chin, chest, and underside; top side of tail dark. Some stripes on inner legs. Delicate "M" marking on forehead; beginnings of lines radiating down from inner corner of eyes similar to those of cheetah. Eyes yellow, green, or hazel.

Coat type: Very short, fine hairs, lying close to body.

Grooming requirements: Weekly brushing with rubber brush.

Temperament: Extremely intelligent and curious. Agile; quite active and ever-playful, yet very cuddly and peaceful. Loving, loyal, and highly sociable; gets involved in family activities. Adaptable; gets along well with other pets.

Sepia agouti Singapura

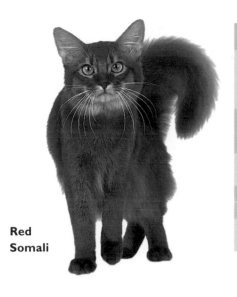

Red Somali

SOMALI

Conformation: Lithe, graceful, and medium-long torso with well-developed muscles. Rounded ribcage and arched back. Head softly rounded wedge with rounded muzzle and large, pointed ears. Eyes large and almond-shaped. Legs proportionate to rest of body; feet small and oval. Full, slightly tapering tail.

Common colors: Blue, fawn, red, or ruddy. Agouti coat, but due to length of hairs, ticking less distinguishable than on shorthair ancestor, Abyssinian. Some tabby lines on face, including "M" on forehead; dark line runs length of spine, resulting in darkly-tipped tail. Gold or green eyes.

Coat type: Plush, fine double coat of medium length. Longer hairs in ruff around neck and breeches; very full tail.

Grooming requirements: Minimal shedding. Weekly brushing to remove dead hair, especially in winter months.

Temperament: Very active, intelligent, and intensely curious. Not very vocal. Affectionate; thrives on interaction with people, but can amuse itself. Adapts well to new situations.

TONKINESE

Conformation: Body type between cobby and foreign; mixture of Burmese and Siamese. Medium-sized torso with well-developed muscles; surprisingly heavy. Slim legs and small oval paws. Head modified wedge with slightly blunt muzzle. Almond-shaped eyes.

Common colors: Natural mink (medium brown with darker brown points), champagne mink (buff-cream with brown points), blue mink (soft blue with slate-gray points), and platinum mink (silvery gray with frosty gray points). Contrast between body and points should be weaker than in Siamese. Aqua-colored eyes.

Coat type: Lustrous, fine and silky; short and close-lying.

Grooming requirements: Weekly grooming with rubber brush.

Temperament: Active and athletic; amusing, playful, and intelligent. Fairly vocal; mild voice. Very friendly; seeks attention. Can usually be leash-trained.

Natural mink Tonkinese

Odd-eyed white Turkish Angora

TURKISH ANGORA

Conformation: Long, slender, and muscular torso; fine-boned and medium-sized body. Wedge-shaped head with pointy muzzle. Large, tufted ears set close together on top of head. Large, almond-shaped eyes, slanting slightly upward. Legs long and fine boned; hind legs longer than front legs. Plumelike tail tapers to narrow end.

Common colors: The most popular color is white. Other variations are solid black or blue; tabby in a variety of colors; particolors; smoke; bicolor and combinations with white. Eyes may be green, gold, copper, blue, or odd-eyed.

Coat type: Medium-long, silky single coat; longer at ruff.

Grooming requirements: Coat tends not to mat; still requires regular brushing.

Temperament: Affectionate, entertaining, and gentle. Intensely inquisitive. Loves to be around humans and participate in activities; likes to show off agility.

CAT OWNER'S

RESOURCE
GUIDE

◆ ◆ ◆

IN CASE OF
·EMERGENCY·

For a medical emergency, prepare a first-aid kit *(box, right)* ahead of time so you can stabilize your cat until you can get him to a vet *(page 168)*. In the event of an environmental emergency, such as a serious storm, flood, or hurricane, have an evacuation plan in place for your cat. Emergency management authorities generally consider pets a low priority. If you have to be evacuated by emergency personnel, they may refuse to allow you to bring your pet, and most emergency shelters set up to house people cannot accept animals. If you have an early warning, confine your cat to one room so he'll be easy to find when you have to get him out. Or, if possible, move your cat out of the area to stay with a friend or relative or at a vet or boarding facility before the storm arrives. Find out if any humane societies are boarding animals for the duration of the disaster.

In preparation for a quick escape, have the following ready in an easily accessible place: cat carrier, large enough to fit two bowls and lined with a familiar blanket; at least one week's supply of food and water in closeable containers; can opener and spoon, if necessary; cat treats; unbreakable bowls; litter, small pan, and scoop; and a few toys. You'll also need some plastic bags, paper towels, and dish soap. Be ready to put your hands on your cat's medical and vaccination records: Most animal shelters will not take a pet without proof of up-to-date vaccinations. And, of course, bring along any medications your cat is taking.

Make sure your cat is properly identified *(page 206)*. Even if he has been microchipped, add a collar with an ID tag. (Key tags make good temporary IDs.) Include the phone number where the cat will be staying, your number, and a contact number outside the area in case the phone lines go down. A harness and leash will allow you to let your cat out of the carrier safely. And recent photos of your cat will help in the event he gets lost.

FELINE FIRST-AID KIT

In an emergency, having the proper supplies can save your cat's life. Most of following items are available in drugstores.

- ◆ Scissors
- ◆ Tweezers
- ◆ Claw clippers
- ◆ Penlight flashlight
- ◆ Magnifying glass (type with light recommended)
- ◆ Examination gloves
- ◆ Rectal thermometer and lubricant
- ◆ Isopropyl rubbing alcohol (70%)
- ◆ Hydrogen peroxide (3%)
- ◆ Povidone-iodine
- ◆ Antibiotic ointment (neomycin, polymixin B, or bacitracin)
- ◆ Assorted sizes of sterile non-stick pads

You can simply expand a human first-aid kit to serve both you and your cat. Replace any items you use.

- ◆ Gauze squares
- ◆ Cotton balls and roll
- ◆ Adhesive tape
- ◆ Roller gauze (self-adhering)
- ◆ Elastic bandage
- ◆ Eyedropper
- ◆ Syringe (needle removed)
- ◆ Syrup of ipecac (Caution: Only to be given on instructions by vet or poison control center and only in dosage specified.)
- ◆ Eye wash
- ◆ Styptic powder or pencil
- ◆ Elizabethan collar (available at pet-supply stores and many vet clinics)

HOUSEHOLD
· POISONS ·

Many toxic products are labeled with warnings. But the toxicity of other products may not be immediately apparent, and your cat doesn't necessarily have to eat or drink something to ingest it; when grooming, your cat will swallow anything on his paws or body. Furthermore, some toxins can be absorbed directly through the skin or gums and still cause serious problems. If you don't know that a product is safe, treat it as a potential poison. Store it in a tightly sealed container in a securely closed cabinet, preferably out of reach of your cat.

Signs of poisoning in your cat include: drooling; vomiting; diarrhea; difficult or rapid breathing; changes in drinking or eating habits; lethargy; and neurological symptoms such as convulsions, loss of coordination, disorientation, or coma. If your cat exhibits these symptoms, try to determine exactly what substance he ingested. Call your veterinarian immediately, with the product container on hand, and take it along with you to the vet.

The following list includes common household items that must be kept out of the reach of a curious cat's paw or tongue.

POISONOUS PRODUCTS
- acetaminophen
- acetone
- ant/bug traps and baits
- anti-flea foggers
- antifreeze
- antihistamines
- anti-rust agents
- antiseptics
- aspirin (ASA)
- automobile batteries
- automotive coolant
- bath oil
- bleach
- boric acid
- brake fluid
- carburetor cleaner
- chocolate (especially dark or bitter types)
- cleaning products
- cockroach poison or bait
- dandruff shampoo
- de-icers (to melt snow)
- deodorants
- deodorizers
- detergents
- diet pills
- disinfectants
- drain cleaners
- dry-cleaning fluid
- dyes
- fertilizers
- fire-extinguisher foam
- fireworks
- flea spray, powder, or shampoo
- fuels
- fungicides
- furniture polish
- gasoline
- hair coloring
- heart pills
- herbicides
- ibuprofen
- insecticides
- insect repellents
- kerosene
- lamp oil
- laxatives
- lead
- lead-based ceramics and paint
- lighter fluid
- liniments
- lye
- matches
- medications
- metal polish
- mineral spirits
- mothballs
- moth repellents
- motor oil
- nail polish
- nail polish remover
- pain relievers
- paint
- paint remover
- pastels (art crayons)
- perfume
- permanent-wave lotion
- photographic developers
- pine-based cleaners
- pine-oil products
- plant food
- rat/rodent poisons
- road salt
- rubbing alcohol
- rust remover
- shoe dye
- shoe polish
- sleeping pills
- snail or slug bait
- soaps
- solder
- solvents
- stain removers
- swimming-pool products
- suntan lotion with cocoa butter
- turpentine
- weed killers
- windshield-washer fluid
- wood preservatives
- zinc-based paint

PLANTS
·TO AVOID·

While cats in the wild may instinctively avoid toxic plants, your pet cat may not be as savvy. Make the choices simple for your mischievous friend: Don't include any of the harmful plants listed below in your house or in your garden.

TOXIC PLANTS

- alfalfa
- aloe vera
- amaryllis (especially the bulb)
- apple-leaf croton
- arrowhead vine
- asparagus fern
- autumn crocus
- avocado
- azalea
- baby's breath
- belladonna
- bird of paradise
- blackberry
- black nightshade
- branching ivy
- buckeye
- buddhist pine
- bull nettles
- buttercups
- cactus (spines)
- caladium
- calla lily
- castor bean

- ceriman
- cherry (including the pit)
- chinaberry
- Chinese evergreen
- chokecherry
- Christmas rose
- chrysanthemum
- cineraria
- clematis
- climbing nightshade
- cordatum
- cornstalk plant
- crocus
- croton
- crown-of-thorns
- Cuban laurel
- cycads
- cyclamen
- daffodil (especially the bulb)
- dieffenbachia
- dracaena palm
- dragon tree
- dumb cane
- Easter lily
- elaine
- elephant's ear
- emerald feather
- eucalyptus
- fiddle-leaf fig
- Florida beauty
- foxglove
- fruit-salad plant
- geraniun
- giant dumb cane

- gold-dust dracaena
- hemlock
- holly
- honeysuckle
- hurricane plant
- hyacinth
- hydrangea
- iris
- ivy
- Jack-in-the-pulpit
- Janet Craig dracaena
- Japanese show lily
- Jerusalem cherry
- kalanchoe
- larkspur
- lily of the valley
- Madagascar dragon tree
- marble queen
- marijuana
- Mexican breadfruit
- miniature croton
- mistletoe
- morning glory
- mother-in-law's tongue
- mushrooms
- narcissus
- nephthytis
- nightshade
- oleander
- onion
- oriental lily
- peace lily
- peach (including the pit)
- pencil cactus
- periwinkle

- philodendron
- plumosa fern
- poinsettia
- poison ivy
- poison oak
- potato (especially the eyes and green parts)
- pothos (golden, satin, or silver)
- precatory bean
- primrose
- purple foxglove
- red emerald
- red princess
- rhododendron
- ribbon plant
- rubber plants
- sago palm
- schefflera
- skunk cabbage
- spider plant
- spotted dumb cane
- string of pearls
- striped dracaena
- sweetheart ivy
- Swiss-cheese plant
- taro vine
- tiger lily
- tobacco
- tomato plant
- tulip (especially the bulb)
- weeping fig
- wisteria (especially the bulb)
- yew

CAT-SAFE
· PLANTS ·

You can try to keep your plants safe from your cat by putting a bit of spicy pepper sauce or cat repellent in your mister, or by hanging the plants out of the cat's reach.

If you don't mind the occasional bite mark on your plants or you prefer not to hang plants, make your garden a safe place for your cat to satisfy his hunger by including nontoxic plants that are strong enough to survive playful munching.

Plain grass or sprouting wheat or oats make a fine snack, provide fiber to aid digestion, and supply extra nutrients *(box, right)*.

The plants in the list here pose no danger to your cat.

SAFE PLANTS

- achillea
- African violet
- alyssum
- aster
- basil
- bean sprouts
- begonia
- buddleia
- calendula
- catmint
- catnip
- celosia
- chamomile
- chervil
- chives
- cleome
- coleus
- columbine
- coneflower
- coriander
- cosmos
- cress
- dahlia
- dianthus
- dill
- dorotheanthus
- forget-me-not
- heliotrope
- hollyhock
- hyssop
- impatiens
- jade
- lavender
- lemon balm
- lemon verbena
- lettuce
- lovage
- marum
- miniature rose
- mint
- monarda
- nasturtium
- oat grass
- orchid
- oregano
- pansy
- parsley
- pea (not sweetpea)
- peppermint
- petunia
- phlox
- portulaca
- rose
- rosemary
- sage
- scabiosa
- shasta daisy
- snapdragon
- spearmint
- spider plant
- spinach
- strawflower
- succulents
- sunflower
- tarragon
- thyme
- torenia
- verbascum
- violet
- wheat (not wheat grass)
- zinnia

GROW A CAT GARDEN

To grow grass for your cat indoors—fast-growing lawn grass, oat grass, fescue, or wheat—choose a shallow pot so your pet has easy access. Fill the pot with sterilized packaged potting soil, leaving some space around the edge for watering. Moisten the soil, then sprinkle the grass seeds on it.

Potted grass will grow best in a sunny area, but remember to water it often so the soil doesn't dry out. And since young and unstable roots are no match for a cat, keep the pot out of his reach. If your cat is tenacious and agile, consider buying a mini-greenhouse to protect the seedlings. Soon enough, kitty will be able to enjoy his green treat.

If you let your cat outdoors to munch on grass, make sure the lawn hasn't been sprayed with toxic chemicals.

CLEANING
·CAT STAINS·

Occasional accidents are a fact of life with cats. A quick and thorough cleanup can usually keep stains from becoming permanent. Keep club soda on hand. Its bubbles lift soil to the surface, and its salts help prevent stains. Removing all traces of odor is equally important, so buy a pet-odor neutralizer. These products, available at pet-supply stores, don't just mask the odor of urine or feces, but eradicate it by breaking up the particular combination of odor molecules. If your cat's sensitive nose can detect even a smidgen of the smell, he may continue to eliminate in the same spot. For a similar reason, avoid ammonia-based cleaners since ammonia smells similar to urine.

Remove any solids with a spatula, stiff cardboard, or a paper towel before attacking the stain itself. If the stain is dry, don't dampen it with water; just apply the appropriate cleaner. Always spot-test the cleaner first on a concealed area of the carpet or fabric. If stains remain, use a commercial stain remover designed for pet stains and appropriate for the material. Follow label directions and be sure to test it on a hidden area first. And if even an odor neutralizer can't dispense with the smell, call in a cleaning professional or get rid of the rug or chair.

Cat gyms and condos can be cleaned with products intended for the materials they are made of: wood, carpet, or fabric. But don't be so fastidious that you're removing all your cat's scent markings. Remove hair with masking tape or sticky lint removers, a damp sponge or rubber gloves, or a stiff-bristled hairbrush.

CLEANUP ESSENTIALS

- ◆ Paper towels
- ◆ Spatula or cardboard
- ◆ Club soda
- ◆ Baking soda or salt
- ◆ Hydrogen peroxide (3%)
- ◆ Ammonia
- ◆ Pet-odor neutralizer (available at pet-supply stores)
- ◆ Commercial stain remover designed for pet stains
- ◆ Commercial carpet and upholstery cleaner

STAIN CLEANING METHODS

Stain	Cleaning method
Urine	Blot up liquid with paper towels. Pour club soda on the area, then blot it up with paper towels. Next, apply a pet-odor neutralizer, following the product's directions. If stains remain, use a commercial stain remover designed for pet stains.
Feces	Remove solids, then blot up any moisture with paper towels. Follow with cleaning procedure for urine.
Vomit	As quickly as possible, scoop up solids and apply baking soda or salt. When dry, vacuum up the rest. Follow by pouring club soda on the area, then blotting it up with paper towels. If stains remain, apply a nontoxic commercial carpet and upholstery cleaner or stain remover designed for pet stains.
Overturned plant	Vacuum up soil. For stains, let any remaining moist soil dry first, then vacuum again. Apply club soda and blot with paper towels. Follow with a nontoxic commercial carpet and upholstery cleaner or stain remover.
Other	For difficult-to-remove matter, follow cleaning procedure for urine. If stains remain, mix 1/2 cup of 3% hydrogen peroxide with 1 teaspoon of ammonia and apply solution to stain. Rinse with club soda to remove peroxide and ammonia residue.

KEEPING OUTDOOR CATS
· INDOORS ·

Cats raised from kittenhood indoors are less likely to want to explore an outside world they hardly know exists. However, if you adopt an older cat that was used to running loose outdoors, he may use any opportunity to escape. With time and persistence, outdoor cats can be converted into indoor cats. The winter season, when most cats happily stay indoors, or during a move are great times to convert puss into an indoor cat. Whether your cat has moved with you or is recently adopted, first let him explore his new indoor territory. He will likely go through his daily routine of patrolling for intruders, sniffing for unfamiliar marks, scratching, and settling into a favorite spot for a nap.

The golden rule is to never—ever—let him out. No matter how much he meows and yowls, don't give in. If you do, he will learn that all he has to do to force his will on you is to make enough noise. Instead, try to get him away from the door by distracting him with a food treat followed by a play session. For some time he will probably keep trying to make a mad dash out the door whenever you open it to enter or leave. Be prepared by keeping treats by the door. If he's persistent, drop your keys when you are entering to make a noise. If he does get past you, never mind; keep trying. Never punish him when he comes back, though, as he will then have a bad

association with returning home. Because he probably will defeat your best efforts and get out occasionally, make sure he is properly identified *(page 206)* at all times.

Make your house appealing and provide your confined cat with fun, outdoorlike activities. Interactive play can simulate hunting; scratching posts

will let him mark his domain; a cat tree can be scaled just like the real thing; and from a perch in front of a window, the outer limits of the territory can be monitored. Be patient; a die-hard outdoor cat may take four or five months to get used to the idea that life can be just fine indoors. If all else fails, see your vet for medication to calm him.

CAT-PROOF COMPUTERS

Cats and high-tech machinery don't always make for a safe combination. To allow kitty and computer to exist in harmony, follow these guidelines:

◆ Buy computer hardware that can bear the weight of your cat or, if you have fragile parts, store them under a shelf or in a cabinet when not in use.

◆ Use dust covers when you are not using your equipment.

◆ If the system can be turned on by a cat's paw, unplug it when not in use or plug into a power supply that can be turned off.

◆ If your computer doubles as a fax machine, configure your computer to send faxes to your hard disk so that you don't have to leave the printer on.

◆ Spray cords with a cat repellent, secure them to walls or under the desk, or run them through plastic conduits to avoid electrocution.

◆ Use books to prop up any cantilevered paper trays that might break under a cat's weight.

◆ Make sure CD-ROM trays are closed when not in use.

◆ Do not block the cooling vents when making your area safe for your cat.

◆ Clean cat hair from your keyboard regularly using canned compressed air.

◆ Use a mouse pad with a smooth, washable surface. Clean the mouse ball often.

◆ Save your work frequently so that there is no risk of losing or corrupting files if kitty should take a walk on your keyboard. Quit the application or close the window if you will be away from your desk.

HOMEMADE
· FUN ·

Your cat can have just as much fun with a homemade toy as a store-bought one. And aside from saving money, you can enjoy creating feline playthings using nothing more than recycled goods and a little imagination.

The following suggestions will give you an idea of the sorts of things cats like; also look at toys in the pet store. Keep in mind the same safety concerns as for store-bought items: Avoid anything small enough to be swallowed—beads, buttons, or materials your cat might chew bits off. And bring out toys with strings or elastic cords only when you're there to supervise.

Crumple up a piece of stiff paper and toss it to your cat. The subscription cards found in magazines are a good size and weight. Avoid aluminum-foil balls, as your cat can ingest bits as the ball disintegrates. Some cats love to pounce on or hide under large sheets of newsprint. Cardboard tubes from toilet paper or paper towels can be great fun, especially if another toy is dragged through or left peeping out.

Corks from wine bottles are good for batting around, and easy to carry if your cat likes to retrieve. But if he starts to bite bits off, take away the cork. Other rolling toys include ping-pong balls, empty thread spools, and 35-mm film canisters. Cut the pompom off that old ski tuque, or cheat and buy a bag of them at a craft store.

Get some catnip at a pet store, fill an old sock with cotton and this tempting herb, and knot the end of the sock. Dip other cloth toys or pompoms in the nip to add some zing, and freshen up old catnip toys while you're at it.

Plastic caps from juice or milk containers can be flicked across the floor as pucks for a game of cat hockey. The plastic strips that come around mailed boxes as well as the ones peeled off cans of concentrated juices make a crackly noise that appeals to many cats, and you can use the longer ones for interactive games. And for those joint play sessions, make a wand from a wooden dowel and a piece of string or elastic

cord, attaching any number of things to the other end: a crumpled ball of paper, strips of cloth, a few feathers from a feather duster, a pompom, a catnip toy; or, simply dangle the string.

To pique your cat's curiosity with a rattling toy, thoroughly wash out an empty medicine bottle (the rounder the better) with a childproof cap and fill it with dried beans or peas.

In a darkened room, shine a flashlight beam along the floor and up the walls; but be sure to let your cat "catch" the spot of light from time to time. On a sunny day, bounce light off a shiny object. Dilute some dishwashing liquid and blow bubbles for your cat to chase.

LETTING THE CAT INTO THE BAG

Simple is often best: the good old paper grocery bag crinkles enticingly and makes a great den. Try tossing toys inside. Or, construct a tunnel by cutting the bottoms off several bags and taping them together end to end. A cardboard box not much larger than your cat can also be a source of fun.

A word of caution: Cut handles off paper bags and never use plastic ones.

MISSING
· CATS ·

Unless everyone in your household is extremely careful, your indoor cat may dart out and run off. Even cats that are used to going out and know the neighborhood well occasionally disappear. While most will return on their own, some may get trapped in a shed or garage, go too far afield to find their way back, or be mistaken as a stray and taken in by someone.

Proper identification is essential to getting your cat back. He should always wear a conventional collar and identification tag. Choose a sturdy collar made of elastic or with an elastic insert, or with a "breakaway" feature: a clasp that opens when pulled hard so he won't be strangled if it catches on something like a branch. The collar should be tight enough so it won't slip over kitty's ears unless it's stretched, but loose enough to fit two fingers underneath. If your cat balks at the collar, get him used to wearing it for longer and longer periods of time. Then, never take it off, even when he is safely ensconced indoors.

A range of ID tags are available, from engraved to handwritten. There are also small screw-apart barrels that hold folded paper. Include only essential information on any tag: your address and one or two reliable telephone numbers with answering machines.

The disadvantage of collars for identification is that they can come off. Consider a second, more permanent form: the microchip. Implanted by your vet, the microchip can be scanned by an animal shelter or vet to give the name of the registry where your number is on file. This is not foolproof, though. Some smaller shelters may not have scanners and those that do may not be able to read chips from diverse manufacturers until they are all standardized. So, to be on the safe side, put a collar on your cat as well. You may save him a trip to the shelter by allowing whoever finds him to simply call you directly.

Make sure you always have a few clear, close-up, and recent photos of your cat, showing his face straight on, as well as some of his entire body, especially of any identifying features. Vital for "lost" posters, photos also help identify pets at animal shelters and pounds.

LOST CAT

If your cat doesn't return within a day or so, launch an all-out search. First, check your home very thoroughly. He may be trapped in a closet, in hollow furniture, in a hole where pipes enter the wall—anywhere a cat can fit, which can be a surprisingly small space. Check crawlspaces, under porches, outbuildings, even the roof. Remember that sick or injured cats will often hide in a safe place to recover.

Next, go public. Ask all your neighbors, especially children, if they have seen your cat and to keep an eye out for him. Offer a reward, and advertise. Place a good photo of him in the center of a poster with large, clear lettering saying "Reward," "Lost Cat," and giving your cat's breed, color, and any distinguishing marks, and a reliable phone number or two. Head to the copy center and make copies; color ones are best. Put the posters on every visible surface you can find. Staple them to telephone poles and wooden fences, tape them to mailboxes, stuff them in mail slots, ask local store owners if you can put one in their window or at their cash register. Go far and wide; many cats are found miles from home. Take out a classified ad in your local paper repeating the information on the posters, and check the "Found" ads every day.

Find out the animal-control agency responsible for your area, as well as any other shelters, pounds, humane associations, and vet clinics in your area and visit them daily. If possible, go into the stray-cat department yourself. Look carefully and consult your photos: Your cat may be dirty, hidden in the back of the cage, and too stressed even to recognize your voice. Leave photos of your cat with the staff, but keep visiting since many shelters are understaffed and can't check every new arrival against the "lost" list. Ask each one about any other places you should check. And don't give up! Sometimes cats turn up months after they're lost.

ANIMAL
·SHELTERS·

There are many routes to finding an animal adoption agency in your area. If you don't already know the whereabouts of any of the big animal shelters, look in the phone book or Yellow Pages under headings such as "Humane Societies," "SPCA" (Society for the Prevention of Cruelty to Animals) or "ASPCA" ("CSPCA" in Canada), "Animal Organizations," "Animal Protection," "Animal Rescue," and "Animal Shelters." Many of these organizations also seek temporary foster homes for some of their cats.

Call your municipal or county authorities to find out the location of the animal pound for the district. These are the publicly funded "animal control" agencies responsible for picking up strays. Also look for any pet stores that collaborate with area shelters, offering their animals for adoption.

Aside from these sources, there are many smaller animal shelters and private rescue groups, often run on a shoestring budget by volunteers. Some of these groups may not even have an adoption center as such, but instead house the cats with foster families until permanent homes can be found. These organizations often advertise in the pet section of the classified ads in the local newspapers, or place posters on bulletin boards at pet stores, vet clinics, and grocery stores. They will often set up a booth in a shopping mall or at a com-munity street fair in order to seek out potential adopters. You can also contact breeders to find out if they are involved in a breed rescue group

The internet is a great tool to help you find listings of animal shelters, big and small. It doesn't take much surfing to find a plethora of animal shelters throughout North America. You then simply have to scan through the lists to find shelters in your vicinity. The sites listed here will give you a start; many have links to other relevant sites. Or, if you want to do a search of your own using a search engine, try key words such as "SPCA," or "Animal Shelter." If you don't want to cast such a wide net, narrow your search with a few terms such as "Cat" and "Shelter" and "Humane" and "Rescue," your city, and your state or province.

WEBSITES

www.acmepet.com/feline/civic/ index.html
Find a listing of feline shelters and res-cue groups in North America and around the globe at this address.

www.arkonline.com/
This is an online magazine with many links to animal care and welfare organi-zations. For even more links, go to:
www.arkonline.com/animal_ welfare_orgs.html

www.dogdomain.com/humane.htm
This site lists humane societies and pro-vides links to other animal shelters in the United States, Canada, and other countries.

www.homearts. com/depts/pastime/ shelters/shelters.htm
An animal-shelter search at this address helps you zero in on adoption groups throughout the United States.

www.newpet.com
This site offers practical advice for the prospective pet owner, along with a free U.S. shelter-location service ("Match Making") activated by keying in your zip code.

www.petshelter.org
The sort of things you'll find on this site include an online adoption center, a lost-and-found department, and an extensive shelter directory.

www.worldanimal.net/
This network provides information on animal protection issues and links to many other related sites, as well as a directory of animal welfare groups throughout the world.

CAT FANCY
·ASSOCIATIONS·

The cat fancy is a popular and growing pastime, offering rich rewards for cat lovers around the world. Cat associations are primarily registries, setting standards for accepted breeds and providing a formula for the acceptance of new ones. They also supply an umbrella of show rules under which member clubs can sponsor shows. They often produce newsletters and yearbooks, and some furnish very practical information for all cat owners, not just those with purebred cats, about all facets of cat care, contemporary health concerns, and feline veterinary medicine. The Cat Fanciers' Association has gone one step further in establishing the Robert H. Winn Foundation for research on feline medicine.

Owing to the wide popularity of purebred cats, there are now hundreds of local cat associations worldwide and their popularity is still increasing. The largest registering body is the U.S.-based Cat Fanciers' Association (CFA), with member clubs around the world. The International Cat Association (TICA) is also global in scope.

The different associations reflect a variety of breeding philosophies and practices, as well as different kinds of organization and rules, so there is probably one fitting about every personality, be it human or feline. The CFA is composed of member clubs and is markedly conservative in accepting new breeds or varieties of old ones. TICA is governed by the votes of individual members and is more liberal in welcoming new breeds. Several other smaller associations in North America offer slightly different options to their members. The large groups attempt to maintain uniformity of breed standards and show rules and registration policies that will allow exhibitors to breed and show their cats within a fairly wide area while still maintaining local autonomy. But one thing that everybody involved in these groups has in common is an abundant love of all things feline.

Many associations have categories for showing (and sometimes even registration) of mixed-breed cats as well, so virtually anyone can show others what makes their favorite companion special. If showing doesn't interest you (or your cat, as not all felines enjoy the experience), seeing dozens of breeds close-up can make for an interesting outing. Most of the associations listed here can direct you to a regional director or local club and maintain lists of upcoming shows in your area.

American Association of Cat Enthusiasts
P.O. Box 213
Pine Brook, NJ 07058
(973) 335-6717
www.aaceinc.org/

American Cat Association
8101 Katherine Avenue
Panorama City, CA 91402
(818) 781-5656
www.americancat.com/

American Cat Fanciers' Association
P.O. Box 203
Point Lookout, MO 65726
(417) 334-5430
www.acfacat.com/

Canadian Cat Association
220 Advance Blvd., Suite 101
Brampton, Ont. L6T 4J5
(416) 459-1481
www.cca-afc.com/

The Cat Fanciers' Association
P.O. Box 1005
Manasquan, NJ 08736-0805
(732) 528-9797
www.cfainc.org/

Cat Fanciers Federation
P.O. Box 661
Gratis, OH 45330
(937) 787-9009
www.cffinc.org/

The International Cat Association
P.O. Box 2684
Harlingen, TX 78551
(210) 428-8046
www.tica.org/

CAT FANCIER'S
· GLOSSARY ·

Agouti: A salt-and-pepper pattern made by light and dark banded hairs; seen on ticked tabbies and as background on mackerel, classic, and spotted tabbies.

Awn hairs: The stiffer of the two types of fine hair in a cat's insulating secondary or undercoat.

Bicolor: A coat made up of any color or pattern and white.

Blue: A coat color in many breeds that is any variation of gray, from slate to ash.

Calico: A coat pattern that combines the red and black patches of the tortoiseshell pattern with patches of white.

Cameo: A coat color distinguished by the white base and the red tip on each hair. Divided into shell, shaded, and smoke depending on the extent of the tipping.

Champagne: A creamy light brown coat color.

Chocolate: A rich, "milk chocolate" brown coat color.

Cinnamon: A reddish brown coat color.

Cobby body type: The sturdy, round, and compact body shape best exemplified by the Persian and the exotic.

Conformation: Configuration of the cat's body, from fine to heavy boning; shape of skull; and eye, ear, and tail size, shape, and placement.

Cream: A light buff-red coat color; sometimes called diluted red.

Crossbreed: Offspring of two different breeds or the act of mating two different breeds.

Double coat: A thick coat, the result of guard and awn hairs of equal length.

Down hairs: The shorter and less coarse of the two types of hair in the insulating undercoat.

Fawn: A pale, warm, pinkish beige coat color; sometimes called diluted cinnamon.

Foreign body type: The long, slim, moderately tubular, and elegant body shape best exemplified by the Siamese and the Abyssinian.

Guard hairs: Outer hairs that make up the protective topcoat and provide color and shine. The longest of the three types of hair.

Himalayan: Colorpoint Persian. Sometimes considered a breed; sometimes classified as a variety of Persian.

Lavender: A pale, pinkish gray coat color. Sometimes referred to as the combination of the blue and chocolate dilution systems.

Lilac: A pinkish gray coat color; also called lavender.

Mascara lines: The dark lines of color running from the edges of the eye toward the cheek of a cat.

Odd-eyed: Eyes of two different colors, one of which is usually blue. Occurs most often in white or white-spotted cats.

Particolor: A coat comprised of two colors, such as red and black or blue and cream.

Patched: As in patched tabby. A particolor coat overlaid with a tabby pattern. Also referred to as torbie.

Pedigree: Direct line of ancestry going back several generations or the official document attesting to ancestry.

Pointed pattern: A coat pattern in which the color is darker on the extremities, including the legs, tail, ears, and mask, than on the rest of body, as in the Siamese.

Red: A coat color actually closer to orange.

Ruddy: A brownish red coat color often used to describe black or sepia brown ticked tabbies such as Abyssinians and Somalis.

Sable: A dark brown, almost black, coat color.

Seal: A dark brown coat color; the most common color of pointing in Siamese.

Shaded: A color pattern in which a silvery white cat is heavily tipped in black or red, mostly over its back. Can also occur in black on a golden background.

Shell: Similar to shaded, but with less tipping, giving a more delicate pattern.

Silver: Silver-white color of hairs closest to the body in tipped cats. Divided into smoke, shade, shell, and silver tabby varieties.

Single coat: Minimal down and awn hairs. The guard hairs lie close to the skin in both long and short haired varieties.

Smoke: A coat that appears to be solidly colored until it is parted, revealing that the color extends no more than two-thirds of the way down the shaft of each hair. The remaining hair to the base should be pure white.

Tabby: Coat pattern distinguished by stripes and/or patches of color, including spots or blotches; also includes ticked coats.

Ticking: Two or three alternating bands of distinct light-to-dark coloration on individual hairs.

Tipped: Individual coloration of hairs in which dark tips become progressively lighter toward base. Shading limited to tips.

Torbie: *see* Patched.

Tortie: *see* Tortoiseshell.

Tortoiseshell: An irregularly patched or intermingled pattern of red and black (or blue and cream) usually found only in females; also called tortie.

Undercoat: Layer of insulating fur made up of awn and down hairs. Comprised of only down hairs in some cats.

Van: A bicolor pattern with color limited to extremities and one or two spots on torso.

WHERE THERE'S
·A WILL·

If you don't make plans for your cat before you fall ill or die, he may be taken to the pound and euthanized if he isn't adopted within a certain time period. You can prevent this from happening by finding a caretaker and making provisions for your cat now. Since the legal enforceability of a testamentary provision for a cat varies from state to state, consult a lawyer to have everything put in a valid, binding, legal document.

You cannot bequeath property directly to your cat since animals are incapable of holding legal title to property, but you may leave money or income-generating property to, or to be used by, the care-taker. Choose a trusted person to be your cat's caretaker, one who will use the legacy or trust fund according to your wishes, because some arrangements may not be legally enforceable. Calculate the amount of money needed per year for your cat's possible life span, adding extra for emergencies and the additional vet care needed for an elderly cat. You may also need to calculate appropriate compensation for the caretaker.

If you want to be more certain that your cat's caretaker uses the funds for the care of your pet, or if there is a fair amount of money involved, consider leaving money in trust. Established under your will or under a separate document, a trust involves setting aside specified property to provide for your cat during his lifetime. A trustee would distribute funds to your cat's caretaker at regular intervals, and could make sure your cat is being well-cared for before each payment. The trustee would be paid reasonable fees out of the trust funds. If a close friend or relative acts as trustee without remuneration, any out-of-pocket expenses incurred would be reimbursed out of the trust funds. The trust may terminate when your cat dies; make a provision for the distribution of any money remaining after his death.

WHO WILL CARE FOR YOUR CAT?

◆ List people with whom you would trust your cat, then ask them if they would be willing and able to assume the responsibility. Make sure they like cats in general, and yours in particular, and aren't allergic. Be very clear about what will be expected of them and discuss what expenses, if any, your estate will assume.

◆ The caretaker should be serious about taking full responsibility for your cat, and would not drop him off at the nearest shelter if the situation became too inconvenient. Be sure to have an alternate caretaker in case your first choice predeceases your cat or is unable or refuses to act.

◆ Find out if your local animal shelter, vet, and other animal welfare organizations take in animals after the death of an owner as well as what adoption services they offer. Some places provide tempo-rary or lifetime care in return for a donation, and feline "retire-ment homes" actually do exist. Be sure to specify the type of family that would best suit your cat, should he be adopted. If you don't want your pet euthanized, provide the name of a backup person willing to take him if he falls sick or develops behavioral problems in his new home.

◆ As a backup plan, find someone who can temporarily care for your cat while looking for a permanent home. Provide this person with the names of organizations and people who may be able to find your cat a home.

◆ Make copies of the will or trust to give to anyone named in it (the executor or trustee and the primary and alternate caregivers). Keep the original in a safe place.

· F U R T H E R
· INFORMATION ·

BOOKS

Alderton, David
The Tiger Inside
Howell Book House,
New York, 1998

Alderton, David
Wildcats of the World
Blandford, London, 1993

Bamberger, Michelle
*Help! The Quick Guide to
First Aid for Your Cat*
Howell Book House,
New York, 1995

*The Cat Fanciers' Association
Encyclopedia*
Simon & Shuster,
New York, 1993

Clutton-Brock, Juliet
Eyewitness Books Cat
Dorling Kindersley,
London, 1991

Commings, Karen
Shelter Cats
Howell Book House,
New York, 1998

**Fleming, Bill, and
Petersen-Fleming, Judy**
The Tiger on Your Couch
Morrow and Company,
New York, 1992

Fogle, Bruce
Encyclopedia of the Cat
Dorling Kindersley,
London, 1997

Fogle, Bruce
First Aid for Cats
Pelham Books, London, 1995

Gebhardt, Richard
The Complete Cat Book
Howell Book House,
New York, 1991

Hall-Martin, Anthony
Cats of Africa
Smithsonian Institution
Press,
Washington, DC, 1997

Heath, Sarah
Why Does My Cat...?
Souvenir Press, London, 1993

Johnson, Pam
Cat Love
Storey Communications,
Pownal, VT, 1990

**Kilcommins, Brian and
Wilson, Sarah**
Good Owners, Great Cats
Warner Books,
New York, 1995

Kobalenko, Jerry
Forest Cats of North America
Firefly Books,
Willowdale, Ont., 1997

McCall, Karen and Dutcher, Jim
Cougar; Ghost of the Rockies
Douglas & McIntyre,
Vancouver, B.C., 1992

McGinnis, Terri
The Well Cat Book
Random House,
New York, 1993

Newkirk, Ingrid
*250 Things You Can Do to
Make Your Cat Adore You*
Fireside, New York, 1998

Page, Susie
*The Complete Cat
Owner's Manual*
Broadway Books,
New York, 1997

Pinncy, Chris C.
Guide to Home Pet Grooming
Barron's,
Happauge, NY, 1990

*The Reader's Digest Illustrated
Book of Cats*
Reader's Digest,
Montreal, 1992

Shojai, Amy D.
*The Purina Encyclopedia
of Cat Care*
Ballantine Books,
New York, 1998

Siegal, Mordecai, ed.
The Cornell Book of Cats
Villard,
New York, 1997

Simon, John M.
*What Your Cat is Trying
to Tell You*
St. Martin's Griffin,
New York, 1998

**Spadafori, Gina and
Pion, Paul D.**
Cats for Dummies
IDG Books,
Foster City, CA, 1997

Tabor, Roger
Cat Behavior
Reader's Digest,
Pleasantville, NY, 1997

Tabor, Roger
Understanding Cats
Reader's Digest,
Pleasantville, NY, 1995

Thomas, Elizabeth Marshall
The Tribe of Tiger
Simon & Shuster,
New York, 1994

Wright, John C.
Is Your Cat Crazy?
Macmillan,
New York, 1994

MAGAZINES

Cat Fancy
Fancy Publications,
Mission Viejo, CA

Cats Magazine
Primedia,
Peoria, IL

WEBSITES

Alley Cat Allies
www.alleycat.org

ASPCA
www.aspca.org

Big Cats Online
http://dialspace.dial.pipex.com/
agarman/

Cat Fanciers' Association
www.cfainc.org

Cat Fancy Online
www.animalnetwork.com/cats

Cats Magazine
www.catsmag.com

Cornell Feline Health Center
web.vet.cornell.edu/public/
fhc/FelineHealth.html

Delta Society
www.petsforum.com/delta

Discovery Channel Online
www.discovery.com

Feline Conservation Center
www.cathouse-fcc.org

National Geographic (cats)
www.nationalgeographic.com/cats/

**Natural History Museum of Los
Angeles County**
www.lam.mus.ca.us/cats/
encyclopedia

ACKNOWLEDGMENTS

The editors wish to thank the following:

Linda Cobb, Queen of Clean®, a clean little division of Queen and King Enterprises, Inc., Peoria, AZ;
Ross Dawson, Vet Help Inc., Kitchener, Ontario;
Susan C. Dawson, Esq., Cambridge, MA;

Pam DelaBar, CFA Director at Large and Chairman, Animal Welfare/Disaster Relief, San Antonio, TX;
Oliver Haddrath, Royal Ontario Museum, Toronto, Ontario;
Virginia K.H. Lam, Chait Amyot, Barristers & Solicitors, Montreal, Quebec;
Virginia Parker, La Pocatière, Quebec;

Jerome Pruet, Nilodor, Inc., Bolivar, OH;
Purr-Fect Privy, Lakehurst, NJ.

The following people also assisted in the preparation of this book:
Stacey Berman, Hélène Dion, Lorraine Doré, Dominique Gagné, Angelika Gollnow, Ned Meredith, Maryo Proulx, Emma Roberts.

PICTURE CREDITS

Henry Ausloos/Animals Animals **6–7, 30, 37** (right), **106** (upper), **130–131**

Anthony Bannister/Animals Animals **45** (upper)

David Barron/Animals Animals **108**

Norvia Behling **21, 38** (lower), **41** (c), **41** (d), **44** (left), **47, 49** (left), **66, 71** (left), **74** (right), **75, 98, 99, 106** (lower), **107** (upper), **113, 127** (upper), **133, 140** (right), **145** (left), **150** (both), **151** (both), **168, 170, 173, 174–175, 177** (left), **178, 180, 205**

Norvia Behling/Animals Animals **154**

Darren Bennett/Animals Animals **16–17**

Michael Bisceglie/Animals Animals **157**

J.C. Carton/Bruce Coleman Inc. **111**

Chalk/Folio, Inc. **76**

Chanan Photography **5** (upper), **22, 23** (both), **25** (all), **176, 177** (right), **179** (all), **182–195, 196** (middle and lower), **197** (all)

Walter Chandoha **85** (right)

Robert Chartier **140** (left), **142, 145** (right)

John Chellman/Animals Animals **67**

Ken Cole/Animals Animals **63** (lower)

Margot Conte/Animals Animals **87**

Kelly Culpepper/Transparencies **94**

Bruce Davidson/Animals Animals **42**

Richard Day/Daybreak Imagery **37** (middle), **70**

Richard & Susan Day/Animals Animals **104**

Rick Edwards/Animals Animals **62–63**

David Falconer/Folio, Inc. **10–11**

Michael P. Gadomski/Animals Animals **40** (lower)

Phyllis Greenberg/Animals Animals **5** (lower)

Hamman/Heldring/Animals Animals **69**

Leo Keeler/Animals Animals **40** (upper)

Rolf Kopfle/KOPFL/Bruce Coleman Inc. **89** (left)

Gerard Lacz/Animals Animals **31**

Zig Leszczynski/Animals Animals **181**

London Scientific Films, Oxford Scientific Films/Animals Animals **38** (middle)

Robert Maier/Animals Animals **29, 35, 53, 89** (right)

Joe McDonald **26–27, 34, 51**

Joe McDonald/Animals Animals **48, 61** (upper), **78** (left),

Scott McKiernan/ZUMA Press, Inc. **68, 84, 105, 163**

Patti Murray/Animals Animals **60**

Mark Newman/Folio, Inc. **44** (right)

Charles Palek/Animals Animals **78** (right)

Robert Pearcy/Animals Animals **37** (left), **101, 196** (upper)

Courtesy of Purr-Fect Privy **138** (both)

Fritz Prenzel/Animals Animals **43**

Hans Reinhard/Bruce Coleman Inc. **19, 102, 103**

Leonard L.T. Rhodes/Animals Animals **77**

Jon Riley/Folio, Inc. **50**

Norbert Rosing/Animals Animals **18, 45** (bottom), **73 , 122**

Len Rue/Animals Animals **117**

Ulrike Schanz/Animals Animals **41** (b), **165** (upper)

A & M Shah/Animals Animals **8–9, 26, 52, 109, 155**

David L. Shirk/Animals Animals **41** (a)

Art Stein/ZUMA Press, Inc. **93** (left)

Renee Stockdale **28, 36, 38** (upper), **64, 72, 74**(left), **80–81, 82, 85** (left), **86, 90, 91, 92, 93** (right), **95, 96, 97** (both), **107** (lower), **110, 114, 115, 116, 118, 119, 120, 121, 124, 125, 126, 127** (middle and lower), **128, 129, 134, 135, 136, 141, 143** (both), **144, 146, 148, 156, 158, 159, 161, 162, 164, 166, 167, 171** (both), **172**

Renee Stockdale/Animals Animals **49** (right), **123, 152**

Lynn Stone/Animals Animals **24, 46, 61** (lower)

Mark Stouffer/Animals Animals **62** (left)

Norman Owen Tomalin/Bruce Coleman Inc. **55**

Karen Tweedy-Holmes/Animals Animals **165** (lower)

M.C. Valada/Folio, Inc. **132**

Peter Weimann/Animals Animals **33, 54, 58**

Robert Winslow/Animals Animals **12–13**

Art Wolfe **2, 14, 39, 56–57, 59, 71** (right), **112**